D1491733

THE RAILWAY GAME

CLIFFORD DYMENT

➤➤➤➤➤➤➤➤➤➤➤◄◄◄◄◄◄◄◄◄

The Railway Game

An Early Autobiography

A railway isn't just carriages and a locomotive
and a permanent way. It's a sort of door. At
any time you can open it and take to the road,
turning your back on a home that's dreary and
on a life that's a misery to you. Any time you
fancy you can whizz off to a new home and a
new life, in any place you choose. Whenever
you're down in the dumps—just open the door.
                                        ALBERT BELTON.

READERS UNION
J. M. DENT & SONS LTD
LONDON 1963

This RU edition was produced in 1963 for sale to its members only by Readers Union Ltd at Aldine House, 10-13 Bedford Street, London W.C.2 and at Letchworth Garden City, Herts. Full details of membership may be obtained from our London address. The book is set in 12 point Fournier type leaded, and it has been reprinted and bound at The Aldine Press, Letchworth. It was first published by J. M. Dent & Sons Ltd.

To
Peter and Martin

INTRODUCTION

→→→→→→→→→→→←←←←←←←←←←

THE TWO most vital and interesting forms of English imaginative prose literature in the mid twentieth century are the new historical novel and new poetic autobiography. Both may be regarded as part of the reaction against the naturalist 'slice of life' novel of the Zola – George Moore – Arnold Bennett school. The first great wave of reaction against 'slice of life' naturalism was the famous 'stream-of-consciousness' school of Dorothy Richardson, Virginia Woolf and James Joyce. The prodigious virtuosity of Joyce made any further advance in this direction impossible, at any rate for a long time. The new historical novel based on modern scholarly reconstruction of the remote past was another way out of the prison-house of naturalism. It started with Robert Graves's Roman novels and has been brilliantly developed by Alfred Duggan, Mary Renault and Rex Warner. The ancestry of the new poetic autobiography is not so easy to trace. I suspect that it owes something to Proust and a great deal to Joyce's *Portrait of the Artist as a Young Man* and the autobiographical parts of the writings of D. H. Lawrence, especially *Sons and Lovers*. An early example of this sort of autobiography was Dylan Thomas's *Portrait of the Artist as a Young Dog*. The form may be said to have reached its maturity in James Kirkup's *The Only Child* and *Sorrows, Passions and Alarms* and Laurie Lee's *Cider with Rosie*. These delightful works, if they are not outshone, are at least rivalled by Clifford Dyment's *The Railway Game*. Like James Kirkup and Laurie Lee, Clifford Dyment is a practising poet, and, like them, he comes from a working-class background. Like theirs his book recaptures a child's view of that background with the delicacy, precision and imaginative power of a mature artist. Yet *The Railway Game*, though belonging to what is now a well-defined class, is wholly original and wholly individual.

Dyment does not merely recall the world of his childhood; he re-creates it and makes us see, hear, smell and feel that vanished provincial England of the second and third decades of the twentieth century. It is a world full of memorable figures, which are drawn with a startling, almost Dickensian, vividness: Will, the father, that admirable carpenter and lover of rare and beautiful woods; the formidable Aunt George and her coarse husband, Uncle G.B., with his passion for Westerns; the abominable Mrs Belton and her lover Sailor Sam; Sid and Pearl, those engaging Bohemians of the Nottingham streets; Tishy, the good skivvy; and above all the noble and pathetic Mr Belton, with his poetic devotion to railways, his heroic championship of the L.N.W.R. and his hatred of the Great Western. Dyment's triumph is his power of conveying to the reader in the prose medium the child's fresh, unsophisticated vision—the vision of the innocent eye. It is the child's vision that dwelt lovingly on 'the rosy satinness of planed boards of mahogany, with white holly and lime, fawn maple, close-grained hard box, mackerel-patterned pale oak' in his father's workshop; it is the boy's delighted perception of the quality of Victoria plums: 'Oh, those Victoria plums! The skin cool as a spring in summer, the plump beauty yielding ripely to gentle pressure, the golden pulp pregnant with a Niagara of juice!' It is the power of evoking the wonderful dream of the magic train 'flashing over Persia at five hundred miles an hour', the poem of romantic travel that consoled the fatherless little boy in that strange world of unsympathetic grown-ups in the drab Nottingham suburb in the nineteen-twenties.

In this book the author has not given us 'a slice of life' but what D. H. Lawrence called 'the thick blaze of being'. To contemplate that blaze is to share in the excitement of a notable imaginative adventure.

V. DE S. PINTO.

The University, Nottingham.
 May 1961.

CONTENTS

→>→>→>→>→>→>→>←←←←←←←←←←

CONTENTS

MY FORMER SELF

I speak to him and he doesn't answer.
　　Does he hear, I wonder?
Why does he look around in the garden
　　With so much wonder?

Why should I mind that every moment
　　He wants to treasure?
He pulls up butterfly after butterfly
　　As he digs for treasure.

He reaches up into the sunlight
　　And picks flower after flower
In a broken looking-glass garden
　　Where seed runs to flower.

　　　　　　　from *Experiences and Places*, 1955.

I

My Two Birthplaces

I was born in two places. One, actual and official, is entered in a register at Newport Mon in that surprisingly unofficial handwriting that looks as though it was executed with a hairpin dipped in ink made of tears and rusty nails. The other, adoptive and private, has never been put down anywhere until now except in the Perfect Biographical Note which I used to draft in my rough book at Loughborough Grammar School and, many years later, in my head while sitting on the top of a bus queueing in Oxford Street.

DYMENT, CLIFFORD, O.M., C.H., C.B.E., F.R.S.L., M.A.(Cantab.), M.A.(Oxon.), Hon.D.Litt.(Oxon.), Hon.D. Litt.(Cantab.), Hon.D.Litt.(Harvard), Hon.D.Litt.(Yale), Hon.D.Litt.(Princeton), Hon.Ph.D.(Hawaii). Poet, playwright, novelist, critic, film scenarist, broadcaster, lecturer. Born in humble circumstances in . . .

and so on, until there came *Publications*, a list of books beginning with twenty novels including *Days of Glory* (on the title-page: 'Oh talk not to me of a name great in story, The days of our youth are the days of our glory'—Byron); *The Circle of Flesh* (on the title-page: 'There is no escape from this circle of flesh'—Sir Thomas Browne); *The Strong Tower* (on the title-page: 'The name of the Lord is a strong tower; the righteous runneth into it and is safe'—Proverbs) and ending with the titles of thirty other books—plays, collected poems, essays, biographies, short stories—with, as a climax, a very special work of literary criticism: *K = ?: A Study of the Use of Alphabetical Abbreviations in European Literature. With an Appendix on Asterisks, Dots, and Dashes* (Demy 8vo., pp. 2,000, with 5 plates, bibliography, glossary, notes, index). ('Mr Dyment has rendered a signal service to modern letters. . . . His study is a masterpiece of

1

scholarship and lucid exposition. . . . A landmark not hereafter to be removed,' *vide* Press.)

My actual and official birthplace (in spite of the confusing Newport Mon registration) was 18 Cressy Road, Alfreton, Derbyshire. As soon as I was old enough to think about the matter I began to feel that Alfreton was an unsatisfactory town to have been born in, not because it was in a colliery district—for I like industrial landscapes: I like the contrapuntalism of field and factory, the dynamic of the tree and the chimney; I enjoy wading through ponds of bluebells while a noon hooter calls like a frantic cuckoo for its lost note; I prefer a working countryside to gigolo scenery, like, that is, giving and taking country and not just taking prospects (taking from tourists, I mean)—no, it wasn't because of the waste tips, the great bicycle wheels Indian-inked on the sky at the pitheads, the buses with coal sawdust on their floors, it wasn't because of these that I was dissatisfied with Alfreton as a birthplace: it was because in Alfreton I had no ancestors.

The town you call your native town should be your *family home*. It ought to have signs of your forbears all over it, their litter scattered around: the bench near the ornamental ducks in the park should still show the dent where your grandfather sat; on the post office counter there should be your second-cousin's forgotten fountain-pen; your grandmother's great Bible, open at the catalogue of births, marriages, and deaths, should be lying casually on the churchyard grass; your aunt's laid-down knitting should add a domestic touch to the cement telephone kiosk; your father's bits and pieces of wood and tools should clutter the High Street. But there were no such commemorative plaques in Alfreton. None of my father's or mother's family had been born there. It was my native place by accident, for me as devoid of autobiography as a New Town.

The way I came to be born in Alfreton was this. My father had a sister, Georgina—my Auntie George—who had been a hospital matron specializing in obstetrics. She had left the West Country where she had been brought up (she had been born, like my father, in Glamorgan) and gone to join the staff of a hospital in Chesterfield (or perhaps it was Derby, or Matlock, or Hucknall).

While there she had fallen in love with a railway clerk named George Buller—known as Uncle G.B. because it was awkward to have two Georges in one house—who was a native of Heage (or perhaps it was Ripley, or Bolsover, or Kimberley) and on her marriage to him had given up nursing and gone to live with her husband in Alfreton, to which town he had been transferred from Heage (or perhaps it was Langley Mill, Codnor, or Clay Cross) by the Midland Railway Company. My father was very fussy about his pretty young wife and wouldn't trust anybody but his sister to bring his first-born into the world. And so it came about that I was taken to Alfreton in my mother's womb and taken from it in a rush basket.

2

'Caerleon was all romance
and Rome to me'

THE PLACE I was taken to, at one month old, was the place in which I should like to have been born: my private and adopted native town, Caerleon-upon-Usk. It is a fitting origin for a literary man, especially a poet, to see against his name in *Who's Who*—just as Cardiff is right for a sailor, Stepney for an orphan, Tunbridge Wells for a bishop, East Ham for a pop singer. It's as rich in romance as a novel by Jeffery Farnol.

Caerleon, city and village, Isca Silurum. Isca Silurum, a name honouring the Silures, the intolerant mountain men of Monmouthshire and Glamorgan, whose land the Romans seized but had to hold in a grip of iron; Isca Silurum, garrison of the Second Legion of Augustus, six thousand soldiers, where generals composed victory marches on maps stretched over desks of marble, where the proud legionaries looked down on the mere auxiliaries and where glamorous legionary and glamorous auxiliary took the local girls from the local boys with a beam of bronze, silver, and gold; Isca Silurum, eyrie of the Roman eagle, crowded and loud with men, horses, and engines of war, where arrived baskets of quail, pheasant, peacock, thrush, dormice, and snails, trays of figs and cakes sweetened with honey, jars of wine and oil, nets of mullet, bags of shellfish, wagons of corn and pork sent in by the grumbling farmers, unpaid feeders of the army of occupation; Isca Silurum, along whose famous Roman roads walked goldsmiths, tinsmiths, armourers, wheelwrights, masons, glaziers, bakers, confectioners, cooks; walked soldiers to Mithraic caves; walked sporting men to the amphitheatre to watch chariot races, wild boar hunted in real woods and naval engagements fought on real water, gladiator killing gladiator, beast killing beast,

4

gladiators and beasts killing each other. Isca Silurum, Britannia Secundus, outpost of Empire: Caesar, Consul, tribune, centurion, lictor; Julius, Claudius, Nero, Trajan, Hadrian; Suetonius, Frontinus, Agricola; aqueducts, highways, arches, villas; pottery, mosaic, enamel, fresco, bracelets, brooches.

Caerleon-upon-Usk, where King Arthur held his court and received tribute from vassal kings, earls, and barons, where mass for his household was celebrated in thirteen churches, where the courtiers slept on satin and fur, dined at silver tables inlaid with gold and pearl and ate off dishes of gold, silver, and buffalo horn, where there was roast buck and flagons of mead and minstrelsy and games; Caerleon-upon-Usk, where on festal days the flowers of the field were outmatched in colour by the striped tents and flying pennants and by the ladies' gowns and the lords' surcoats and the knights' glinting armour and jewel-hilted swords; Caerleon-upon-Usk, where you walk on grass over which the knights galloped to crash with each other in the jousts; Caerleon-upon-Usk, where the daily round was polishing of shields, sharpening of swords, washing of armour, shoeing of horses, where the ambitions were tournaments and quests, where the talk was of sieges, brachets, harts, and palfreys, of griffins, dragons, and the Sangreal, where the gossip was of chivalrous knights and false knights and virtuous women.

Caerleon-upon-Usk, home, chapel, and workshop of Cistercians, who ploughed, planted, and reaped in white habits that were streaked with loam and the grease of sheep's wool and were thin at the knees from canonical hours of kneeling; Caerleon-upon-Usk, where the years passed and the monastery bell marked time across the fields until the monks departed and the iron rusted and the tower toppled and there was no marking of time in Caerleon's fields.

3

1, Ashwell Terrace

THE HOUSE in which we lived at Caerleon was No. 1, Ashwell Terrace, one of a row of cottages that have since been condemned. My father took it because it was cheap—and because he was married, young, and a carpenter only just starting in business as a cabinet-maker. I remember that when I played on the bit of pavement outside I could look right through the cottage as though it was a telescope, through the front door seeing the back garden so close I was afraid of being stung by bees. The reason was that the cottage was only one room wide—there was one room downstairs for cooking, eating, and living in, and one room upstairs for all of us to sleep in.

There was no gas in the house: cooking was done on an open fire or in an oven at its side heated by hot embers, the embers being scraped with a steel rake from the fire to a space under the oven. For lighting we had an oil lamp which stood in the middle of a beautiful pear-wood table made by my father. That oil lamp was a beauty, too: made simply to be practical it was as graceful in profile as a piece of Samian ware. Its brass curved sides were as full of little squares and circles of reflected daylight as a polished bed-knob, and through its globe of translucent porcelain you could see shadowy images of the furniture on the other side of the room. It was my father's job to light the lamp in the evening. To me this was a ritual and a spectacle that invested him with priestly power and glory. He held a match to the wick and the wild wick snatched the flame from his hand and threw it up in the air and bounced it on the floor and hurled it up to the ceiling and flung it from wall to wall: it was a rough and playful exhibition of the eternal conflict between the forces of light and darkness. Majestically my father turned the lamp's brass wheel and the romping flame was hauled instantly back into the lamp like a tiger into

6

its cage: the ceremony, short, brilliant, and daunting, was over. Now a cone of sunshiny radiance hung placidly from the lamp to the floor, and until it was time for me to be put to bed I scrambled about in a bell-tent made of light.

In the daytime I played in the back garden, where my father grew leaves. There were millions, billions, trillions of them. Leaves were my ceilings, walls, partitions: they pressed me down and shut me in, and when I resisted they tugged at my hair, slapped my face, pushed themselves up the legs of my short trousers, sealed my nostrils, gagged my mouth, tolled at my ears, jazzed before my eyes; and sometimes my forehead smarted and ached from the brutal rebuff of wood as a branch denied my thrusting head. All the same, I liked the leaves, and spent hours in the thousands of acres where they grew, breathing foreign green air and getting tipsy on sappy, fruity smells.

After these exotic holidays in the leaves I made my way back to everyday life by staggering across our living-room to the street. It wasn't a street really—it was more of a lane. In it there was our row of cottages, whitewashed and blue-roofed, the white walls stained, broken, and mildewed, but seen by me now through a haze of years that gives them a dairy sweetness; and alongside them were the few flagstones of pavement, then a dirt roadway, then a hedge with a wicket gate, and then beyond the hedge, as far as I could see, nothing—though a grown-up could have looked over the hedge and viewed fields and beyond them Tyn Barlym mountain hunched low to let the clouds pass over.

I wasn't the only child in the lane. There was my younger sister Susie, and several other girls and boys busy with various occupations—chalking faces and 'Follow this line' on flags and bricks, gathering the dust of the road between their hands into little heaps shaped like children's drawings of mountains, chasing each other, pouring water from a tin teapot into tin teacups, closing eyes and counting ten, swopping licks of lollipops.

One of these children was a mystery to me. She was thin and white and ragged and hare-lipped, and she talked in grunts like an animal because she was deaf and dumb. She was always asking my mother, in her pig-speech, for something to eat. And my mother gave her something—slabs of yellow cake with mice droppings on it. I was fascinated by the monstrous child and amazed to see her eating her filthy food with such relish. It wasn't until many years afterwards that I discovered that the food my mother gave her wasn't something the mice had been on, but was caraway seed cake. Today I'm inclined to avoid cake and bread containing caraway seed.

This same girl sometimes earned a penny by taking Susie and me out in our pram. One day she stopped the pram in the middle of Caerleon Bridge and, lifting me out, held me as far over the side of the bridge as her arms could reach. At first I didn't mind—this unusual view of the world was interesting. Then, missing the support of the pram under my back, feeling all of me dangling from a point just under my armpits, I looked below. When I saw nothing but air, and deep at the bottom of the air the River Usk like a hurrying road, I was terrified. I screamed and struggled. The girl was taken by surprise and I began to slip. Instinctively she tightened her grip so that as I descended my arms hit her clutching hands with a jolt and were jerked upwards. I now screamed with pain as well as fear. Scared, the girl pulled me back and bundled me into the pram. I cried all the way home. When my mother asked for an explanation of my crying the girl, of course, couldn't give one; neither could Susie, for she was too young; and my power of speech was inadequate to describe what I had felt and seen. But whenever the deaf-and-dumb girl wanted to take me out again I protested with screeches, sobs, and rages: neighbours commiserated with my mother for having a difficult child.

Sometimes a few big boys came to play in Ashwell Terrace. On one occasion they appeared with a live grass snake fastened to a string. I watched them having fun with it, laughing and whooping as they took turns to whirl it around like a bullroarer, drag it at speed along the road, slap it against the trunk of a tree. At last, when it was almost dead, they tossed it high into some branches and left it dangling there, green among the green leaves, a novel twitching fruit.

I was often with the other children of Ashwell Terrace, playing, but what I liked doing most of all was standing at the door of our cottage in the hot sunshine—it was always sunny in Caerleon—watching for the two big events of the day. The first was the arrival of the baker's cart, at about eleven o'clock in the morning. This was a rakish yellow vehicle with an arched black canvas top and enormous yellow wheels with iron tyres that rolled along the road with a noise of crunching nutshells. Between the yellow shafts was a pony whose coat was the same colour as the loaves he hauled from door to door. He had a superb tail, thick, biscuit-brown, and long—so long that it trailed on the ground, leaving a wake in the dust that remained long after the baker's man had finished his rounds. If I was lucky the pony would raise his tail—the dark root jutting outwards and upwards so that the brushy hairs curved up, out, and down like a plume of water in a fountain—would raise his tail and excrete right in front of our door. I was enormously interested in the way the black rubbery anus protruded and expanded and then extruded the balls of fresh khaki dung—manure, we called it euphemistically—which fell to the road and lay there glistening and with the steam curling off them. There was something admirably frank about the baker's pony doing what he wanted to do while standing boldly up between the shafts and giving us clean scented food for the garden.

The other big moment was the passing of the cows. Every afternoon they came down Ashwell Terrace for milking, going by the cottage on their way to the farmer's white five-barred gate at the end of the lane. They knew the journey well, these cows, and needed no urging with sticks or reminding with shouts, so that the young man in charge dawdled a long way in the rear, using his switch only to swipe at the dog roses in the hedge or to bring down with a sharp report on his shapely black leather leggings. The cows approached the cottage, heads low, horns prodding the sunshine, muzzles beaded with strings of silvery mouth-wet, straight-backed, barrel-sided, mahogany-rich, their hoofs shuffling through the dust with a continual pattering rhythm like the sound of rain on trees.

I—small on our doorstep—watched them come. Suddenly—and I terrified but staying there—the herd was level with me, a high breathing wall, was passing me, so close that I felt warmer in its heat, saw the pink flesh of eyelids and the hairs inside ears; saw the veins—like rivers on maps—spreading over the bulged udders.

A cow stopped, a head turned, a cow's eye was on me. The cow bellowed, my heart capered, the cow moved on.

Every afternoon, always, there was this beautiful moment of peril. And when it had passed, what a relief to watch the cows move on to their gate, splashed hindquarters rocking, tails swinging.

Tails swinging! I concentrated all my mental and physical power upon the base of my spine, willing a tail to move as I willed my big toe to move. But the base of my spine paid no attention to me. I tried again and again in a scarlet intensity of effort, and still my spine was indifferent. Baffled, I cried.

'Whatever's the matter, lovey?' asked my grandmother. And my mother examined my knees and hands to see if there were any cuts or abrasions there, and finding none felt me over from chest to tummy to see if I would cry out loud at some internal pain. But the internal pain I felt wasn't physiological and so she remained perplexed.

I was crying because I could move my arms and legs, could wag my fingers and toes, could bend, could turn my head, could trot, walk, hop, crawl, yet felt that these were feeble attainments compared with being able to hang out a tail in an arch like the baker's pony or flick a tail up over my back like an afternoon cow. When I put my hand to my bottom and felt only space there I had a piercing sense of deprivation, but it wasn't the absence of a tail that caused this so much as the realization of my lack of control over the end of my backbone, its utter disregard of all my exhausting attempts to animate it and through it a tail. Why should a privilege granted to ducks, cows, and horses be denied to me? I felt aggrieved. And so I whimpered, moaned, wailed for hour after hour, Susie staring at me contentedly with big round dark eyes, my grandmother getting irritated at my snivelling and muttering 'Ach y fi' from her rocking-chair.

I was crying when my father came home from his work. He

took me in his arms and held me high above the limestone slabs of the floor, on a level with his face. His soft, dreamy, sad eyes looked deeply into mine. Immediately, as though by some power of paternal divination, he knew what I wanted. He put me down, went to the tool chest he kept in a black hole under the stairs, took out a coil of rope, frayed the end with his knife to make a tuft, and knotted it around my waist. And so at tea time in my private tall chair I cropped grass; next morning I stood at the front door of the cottage dozing behind blinkers; and after dinner I wobbled about the back garden on hands and knees, mooing.

4

My Father, the Carpenter

THIS fitting me up with a tail made me aware that my father was *near*. Until this moment he'd been a tall column of brownness moving on the circumference of a circle of which I was the centre. Now, suddenly, he had come close to me. From this time on I felt his warmth, breathed in his tobacco, petrol, oil, wood emanations. There had come into existence a distinctive father-smell.

The tool chest I have mentioned was kept in the space under the stairs because in 1916 my father had suspended his one-man business as a cabinet-maker in order to do essential war work on the Great Western Railway. But although busy for ten hours or more a day among the G.W. locomotives and rolling stock he still had the wish and the energy to do some woodworking of his own in the evenings and on Sundays, and so there were always planks of oak and walnut or scantlings of box and alder propped against the floral wallpaper of our cottage. My father liked to work with the woods of fruit trees, apple, pear, cherry, and he was fond of experimenting with timbers that are not much used, such as young sweet chestnut, laburnum, and holly. When he wasn't constructing some large piece of furniture he filled in his time fashioning small articles out of fragments that had taken his fancy: he made walking-sticks from buckthorn, snuff-boxes from maple, axe and hammer shafts from ash, egg-cups, napkin-rings, spoons, bowls, dolls, horses, little tables and chairs from beech, lime, horse-chestnut, and elder. He was always on the look-out for a bit of promising timber somewhere under the sky. Our downstairs and upstairs were scented with sawn-up trees.

Tools were a familiar sight also. Near the window, covered with sacking during the day, was a lathe worked by a treadle; and in a corner there was a rough table used as a bench, fitted with a vice and a sawing-board. A spirit-level was sometimes left on the mantelpiece, a mallet on a chair. I didn't think there was anything odd about having wood and wood-working implements in your house: they were among the first things I fixed my gaze on and I accepted them as natural phenomena like fire and food and furniture. I took it for granted that everybody lived in a cottage like ours and had tools and timber in their living-room.

For my father, the purpose of life was doing rather than being; for him, therefore, to be idle was to be unhappy. His fingers had eyes at their tips, ceaselessly searching the world for jobs to be done. One of his favourite jobs—when he wasn't turning or mortising—was repairing old petrol lighters. I think he felt that he had a mission to perform among the maimed, the halt, and the blind lighters of Monmouthshire, seeing his duty plain to make the broken casing whole, the dull spark wheel bright, the crooked snuffer straight. He could never resist the appeal of a disabled lighter, and in consequence collected a whole infirmary of brass invalids from his friends and workmates. On these he would operate in our beautiful lamplight, patiently dismantling, cleaning, filing, oiling, polishing, rewicking, reflinting, rewadding, reassembling. Out of five sick lighters he would make three healthy ones, and these he would sell for shillings to the friends from whom he had bought them for pence.

But although—as the above shows—my father had a business sense as pushful as a bradawl he would never do a job for the money only. He enjoyed his tools and timber too much for that. It was only when he had given to some piece of work in wood all the time, experience, and care that were necessary and added a little more of each out of sheer affection—it was only then—that he became what he was commonly called, a tradesman, and began to think of costs and profits. And although he took only a small return for himself his prices had to be high, for he refused to deliver to a customer anything but perfection. He had many temptations. Because his products were home-made people expected them to be cheaper than the shiny, swollen, knobbly factory splendours they saw in the big shop windows of Newport Mon and Cardiff and were puzzled to find they weren't. My father explained. Sometimes the inquirers were willing to pay his price; more often they weren't. He never quoted a figure lower than the one he had originally given. Occasionally there were people who, after listening to the reasons for his high charges, said to my father: Couldn't you, just for this once, use not *quite* such prime timber, and couldn't you, just for this once, put not *quite* so much labour into it, couldn't you . . .? But my father always refused. He had only one standard.

All the same, I don't think my father was an artist. He was a good plain cook rather than a chef. His care was that all his materials should be wholesome and all his uses of them honest. For this reason he took just as much trouble over backs, which nobody sees, as with fronts; for this reason he would never use plywood to fill in large surfaces, but stuck to solid wood everywhere; for this reason he preferred wax finishing to French polishing because it revealed the quality of the timber; and for this reason he hated veneers because they were deceptions and avoided carving, inlay, painting, gilding, graining, and moulding because he believed that virtue is intrinsic and not a matter of outward appearances. His aim was to maintain the tradition of the local craftsman, the man near the village green or on the market square whom you once went to when you wanted a new pair of boots, a carriage, a stool, an iron gate, or even a picture. He had no pretentious notions about this, however, and would have gone red to hear the phrase 'His aim was to maintain the tradition of . . .' used about him. He was no goody-goody, no Plymouth Brother of carpentry. He was worldly. He was ambitious. He wanted to get rich. But the object of getting rich for its own sake bored him. He thought of wealth not as gain but as reward— reward for work well done.

Naturally, my father's conception of work was costly in time as well as in materials and labour, so that nearly always in my memory of him he is handling wood and tools. I see him with the rosy satinness of planed boards of mahogany, with white holly and lime, fawn maple, close-grained hard box, mackerel-patterned pale oak, red cherry and pear and brown apple; I see loved and lovely implements taken out of their box one by one and laid on the floor in order to search for a dropped silver bit at the bottom; I see his plane skinning the plank and the plank swallowing his drill; and I see the hand-saw with its oily smile and its wolf's teeth eager to devour and I feel safer when my father puts on its leather muzzle.

My father's thoroughness wasn't confined to his work bench. All that he ever did was equally thorough. One day when he was courting my mother he called unexpectedly at her home in Bank Street, Newport Mon, in order to take her out. He discovered that she'd already gone out—with her father, into the country. My mother's father was a great walker and a great man for the countryside: my father was neither. Nevertheless, he set out after them: he'd decided to be with my mother that day and be with her he would. He followed the elderly man and the young woman with unfaltering tenacity, tracing their route by inquiries at cottages and public houses and by noting places where my grandfather had plucked wild herbs and flowers. In the late evening my mother and grandfather arrived home; there, hours afterwards, my father caught them up: he had taken exactly the same walk as they had, but had taken it many miles in their rear.

Later, when they were a young married couple, he and my mother were walking in the neighbourhood of Caerleon; as they passed an oak tree growing near a brook my father commented that it was a tree that would cut up into nice timber. My mother forgot the remark, but it wasn't an idle one on my father's part. He'd taken a liking to the tree and had decided to have it, for he was turning over in his mind the idea of making a special adjustable armchair for the fireside of 1, Ashwell Terrace. The more he thought about it and the oftener he went to look at it the more he was convinced that oak was just the timber he wanted.

One black night, working by the glow-worm light of a screened bicycle lamp, he cut the tree down and levered it over the grass into the stream, where it sank into mud and weeds and was hidden. On later nights, with the help of two G.W.R. workmates with whom he had arranged to share it, he sawed the oak trunk into planks and again hid the wood in the stream. The railway line ran through the fields not far away, and on successive evenings my father and his friends transported the planks to the track, loaded them on to a wagon, attached the wagon to a goods train, and, at a point within walking distance of Ashwell Terrace, flung them overboard, afterwards jumping off the moving train themselves.

My father got his share of the wood home single-handed, crossing several reens—Monmouthshire for ditches—by laying one of the planks across as a bridge and carrying the rest over on his shoulder. When he got the planks to the cottage he stacked them inside, telling my mother that he'd got them through a deal, because if she had known what he'd been up to she would have been scared stiff. Next day—he was so keen—he began wcrk on the chair.

The exploit shows the lengths to which my father was prepared to go in order to get what he wanted. He stole the tree, yes; but I would defend him by saying that his was a *crime passionnel*, similar to that of the hard-up scholar who steals a desired book from a library or shop. Reprehensible it may be, but an act of love rather than of larceny.

Yes, as I've said, my father was no Plymouth Brother. In his teens, wanting to see the world but having no money to pay for travel, he signed on at Newport Mon as a ship's carpenter, giving a fluent and convincing account of his experience in that line. In truth, he'd never set foot on board a ship in his life, and when, in the Bay of Biscay, he heard squall-wet sailors calling out 'Chips! Chips!' he had no idea that the shouts were for him and remained in his bunk, sea-sick. Eventually, with a one-way voyage to his credit and therefore able to claim extensive knowledge of international ships and shipping, he joined another ship at Buenos Aires and worked his passage half around the world before returning to England and resuming his trade terrestrially. A man of ruses my father was, but they were never mean ruses: he had that romantic touch of the rascal so helpful to success in this world.

One day I saw my father walking about the cottage in stiff unaccustomed clothes.

'Your daddy is a soldier now,' Grandmother said.

But weeks before this we had all—Father, Mother, Susie, and I —gone on a train ride to Cardiff. It was a holiday, but I realize now that Susie and I enjoyed the excitement and the sunshine more than our parents, because the purpose of the Cardiff visit was to be photographed as a family group before we were broken up by my father's departure for France. He had volunteered for the army under Lord Derby's scheme and was expecting his call-up papers every day.

We took it in turns, Susie and I, to be hoisted on Father's shoulder and carried along the white, packed pavements and across the wide, racing streets. I'd never heard so many people, motors, carts, horses; never seen trams hiss by on flashing rails and wires, monster fireworks with men and women sitting comfortably inside. It was thrilling; and if it hadn't been for Father and Mother, frightening.

'This is the shop,' said Father, and we entered a large hushed gloom. After the pavements, treading the carpet was like walking on cushions.

'This way, please.'

A man with a head as bare as a lemon led us to the far end of the long room, and there by a miracle I was able to stand under a blue sky and look at trees, waves, and a boat. The man raised his arms and the fresh air was wafted to the roof. Where the sky and the trees and the waves and the boat had been there was now a broad marble staircase and pillars and ferny plants. The wizard looked at the marble staircase and then at us and—hey presto!— the marble staircase and the pillars and the ferny plants vanished and there was the blue sky again.

'You just there, sir; and your good lady, I think, just here; and you little ones, up you go!' and he lifted Susie on to a table. And then me. The man switched on lamps, full moons, and I couldn't see anything—not the man, not Susie, not Mother or Father: I looked into a fiery hurting nothingness. I cried.

After the readjustment of the lights I was given a walking-stick to hold. I saw a wooden box creep towards us; it stopped creeping and from behind it a golliwog popped up suddenly. I cried again. But the golliwog got rid of his darkness and became the man with a head as bare as a lemon. He gave me a pear drop to suck.

We all stood and sat quite still, my father soaring above us, pale and grave with the ends of his moustache given a special Sunday-best waxing and a curl upwards, my mother wearing her polite public expression, Susie believing in the dicky bird and I doubting.

Susie's faith was justified: a dicky bird did appear, a yellow fluffy chick with a red paper beak. The lemon man gave it to her for being so good.

There came the morning when my father put his feet one by one on a stool and bandaged his legs with puttees. Then on went the webbed belt, the leather bandolier, the flat peaked cap. He caught me up in his arms and hugged me and my face was hurt by one of his new buttons. He put me down and took up Susie. He kissed Grandmother, Mother. Then we all went to the door.

It was early still, still smelling of night. Mistiness and coolness touched our faces; there were long lengths of sun and shadow on the road. Mother and Father, Susie and I walked along the pavement.

'Lift me up on your soldier,' I asked my father, and he smiled and hoisted me up as in Cardiff and carried me a little way so that I could see over hedges. Then, leaving him, three of us walked back to our cottage.

We stood on the pavement, Grandmother just behind us in the doorway's shade, and watched the father, husband, son going from us. He went quickly, not looking back.

He went quickly, and far, and we watched him all the way. At last we saw the small khaki figure stop and turn and wave to us. We waved back, waved, waved, waved. Susie and I called to him, but he didn't hear. Mother held Susie high, then me, and he signalled with his cane and his cap to show that he had seen. The nickel-plate on his military cane glinted in the sun, but no light shone from his cap badge because my father was 287076 Spr W. C. Dyment RE and the insignia of the Royal Engineers was a dull bronze.

We expected him to stand there for a long time, waving to us, and were surprised when he suddenly spun round and walked away. A hedge partly screened him from us. There were trees now and the hedge got higher and soon there was nothing of him but his cap above the hedge bobbing with his stride as a rider goes up and down with his horse. The cap receded, getting smaller and more indistinct, until we didn't know whether we were seeing his cap or the leaves of trees. Susie and I continued to stare, hoping it was his cap. Mother continued to stare, too, at the empty hedge and fields. And neither Susie nor I noticed her go in again, she went so quietly.

5

Army Post Office

CHURCH ARMY RECREATION HUT OR TENT
OPEN TO ALL

On Active Service with the
British Expeditionary Force

My own dearest wife and children and Mother,

Thank you so much, my dear, for your two letters. I have not had time to answer them till now, though I wanted to badly, thinking of you all day as I do. Your letters are very welcome to me. They make this life out here a little more endurable. Please write as often as you can.

I was sorry to hear that the children have not been well. You did quite right in telling me. Please do not keep anything back from me because you think it would hurt me to know. If you do not tell me of these unhappy things, I shall only suspect them, imagine terrible illnesses and difficulties about which you keep silent for my sake. I shall worry like that. So please tell me all.

I am glad both the children are better now. It must be awfully trying for you having to deal all by yourself with the children. I wish Clifford did not cry so much—I do not know what on earth to suggest to keep him quiet. I fear he looks like developing into a troublesome child. And then on top of all this there is the house-work and the shopping. That must be difficult with rationing, I know. You mention being short of sweet things for the kiddies. You will remember we used to find Lyle's Golden Syrup good, but I suppose it is as hard to obtain now as sugar. I shall be glad of the day when I am back in Caerleon to help you. But there does not seem much chance of that at present. The leave I mentioned in my earlier letters as being likely has been cancelled.

Twice that has happened already. Truly, my luck seems at the bottom of the sea.

I must stop now. Forgive the gloomy tone of the last sentence —life is as pleasant as it can be here on the whole, but I was so looking forward to leave. Write to me soon, dear. How is Grandmother? I hope her heart is not giving her too much trouble? Perhaps you might be able to get in a bottle of brandy? It would do her the world of good, I think, when she is not feeling well. Tell her to write to me. I want to hear from her. My love to Clifford and Susie, and many, many kisses for you, my darling wife.

Your affectionate

WILL

PS. It was good of you to send the photo as I asked—it helps me so much to see you, if only on a picture. God bless you.

ON ACTIVE SERVICE

My dearest wife and children,

Your parcel came this morning. Thank you for putting so many good things in it. It was well packed. Only the rather crumbly shortbread was broken. The ointment I find good, but the powder is useless—the lice gobble it up. They grow fat on it. You can almost see the loathsome creatures squatting back on their heels and laughing. But the ointment *kills* them. Lice here are as big as rabbits. I've heard that Boots the chemists sell some good stuff that you put in the seams of your clothes and it keeps the vermin away. It's about 1/– a tube. Perhaps you could inquire about it some time?

Well dear, this isn't a very beautiful letter, I am afraid—but out here sordid facts cannot be avoided. But this is really only a note to tell you I had the parcel and to thank you for it, and to send my love to you and mother and the kiddies.

Good night, my dear. Kiss the children good night for me.

Your affectionate

WILL

PS. George sent me a parcel a little time ago. Some cake she had made, and a dozen of her lemon curd tarts—she knows how I like them. She makes them like nobody else in the world. I am writing to thank her this afternoon.

My own dearest wife and children,

I am scribbling this in a few moments I have after breakfast, sitting in the sunshine on some sandbags. I just wanted to let you know, my dear, that I have heard there is a good chance of leave soon—any time now. Do you know, we have 14 days leave now from leaving London till the day we report back there—that is, 13 clear days. I hope they will not alter this arrangement by the time I get my leave! Real Dyment luck that would be!

I want to come dearly to see you, darling, and yet I feel I shall be unhappy when I do because I shall be thinking all the time of going back. Going back is a bitter thought in the heaven of being with you, my dear one. Sometimes I feel I would rather stay out here with no leaves at all until the whole terrible business is over —and then come home to stay for good. What a wonderful day that will be!

Will you tell me what the children would like for presents when I come? If this leave materializes, I mean. You see, I may be able to come home suddenly, and I would like to know of something they would be fond of that I could bring them. I should not like to bring presents that would be a disappointment to them. I could buy their presents—and one for you, my darling!—while I am waiting at Paddington for the train.

Excuse this bad writing—I'm writing on my knee with a bit of blue lead that needs sharpening. Looking forward to your letters.

Your affectionate

WILL

NOTHING   IS   TO   BE   WRITTEN   ON   THIS   SIDE
EXCEPT   THE   DATE   AND   THE   SIGNATURE   OF
THE   SENDER.   SENTENCES   NOT   REQUIRED   MAY

BE ERASED. IF ANYTHING ELSE IS ADDED THE
POSTCARD WILL BE DESTROYED. POSTAGE MUST
BE PREPAID ON ANY LETTER OR POSTCARD
ADDRESSED TO THE SENDER OF THIS CARD.

I AM QUITE WELL

~~I HAVE BEEN ADMITTED INTO HOSPITAL~~

~~SICK~~   ~~AND AM GOING ON WELL~~

~~WOUNDED~~ ~~AND HOPE TO BE DISCHARGED~~

~~SOON~~

~~I AM BEING SENT DOWN TO THE BASE~~

                              LETTER DATED *Sept. 27th*

I HAVE RECEIVED YOUR   ~~TELEGRAM DATED~~

                       ~~PARCEL DATED~~

LETTER FOLLOWS AT FIRST OPPORTUNITY

I HAVE RECEIVED NO LETTER FROM YOU

~~LATELY~~

FOR A LONG TIME

SIGNATURE ONLY   *W. Dyment*

DATE: *12.10.17.*

My dearest wife and children,

A short letter this, my dearest, dashed off in an odd spare
moment, written on my knee out of doors. I have had nothing
from you for days—I am a bit worried—I feel I must write to
you—I am longing to be with you tonight. The sun has gone
down, and I can smell apples. It reminds me of the evening we
talked so long in your father's garden, among the fruit trees. So
many things like this remind me of you. A thousand times a day.

                         Your affectionate

                              WILL

*B

My dearest wife,

Still no news! I hope you are not ill, or the children. I am very anxious. Because I have no new letters from you, I have been reading your old ones. I am worried about your generosity. I am proud that I have a wife of your beautiful nature, so kind to others, so thoughtful always, but really my dear you must not go on giving things away as you do. It was because you have the fine qualities of a true lady that I fell in love with you, my dearest, but *only a rich woman* can be a Lady Bountiful. You will be starving yourself soon if you are so free with your food. Do not have pity for tramps—they are nearly always scoundrels. They do not become tramps out of poverty—plenty of poor people are not tramps—but because they refuse to do any work. They come so often to you because each tramp chalks a mark on the gate of a house where he has been treated well, as a sign to other rogues of his sort that this is a good place. They must *all* put their marks on *your* door. Fancy giving away the last bit of your sugar ration like that! To a jail bird, probably. I do not want to seem annoyed, but my dear do not do that again please. You and the children need all the good food you can get. It is your duty to look after yourself—and the duty of others to look after themselves. Like so many good people you suffer because of your goodness. You are so unsuspecting, so naturally trusting and generous, that more cunning people take advantage of you. You are so delicate I do not want you to be knocked about by the world. It is all right for me—I can stand it and give as good (or as bad) as I get. But you need someone to protect you, as you protect the children. That reminds me, dear—*do not* put the children outside in the sun. It is the worst thing you can do. Not even a sun bonnet will prevent them getting sunstroke. And be careful of yourself. Always carry a sunshade in hot weather, won't you, dear?

Thank Grandmother for her letter. I will reply soon. Tell her I send 69 kisses for her birthday! My dear mother! And for you, my darling, kisses too—not 69, but more, as many as you will let me give you. And for Clifford and Susie. Remember about the sun.

Your affectionate

WILL

PS. Just had two letters from you. It was such a pleasure to see your writing on them as they were handed to me.

My own dearest wife and children,

I was relieved to receive your two letters. It seemed such a long time since I had heard from you, my dear. Grandmother, as often, said nothing about you in her letter. No, I have not had the three letters you say you sent some time ago. I do not think it likely I shall get them now. Must give them up for lost.

The reason they never reached me is probably because I am now in a new address. I have a new job, too—an excellent one. I am with the officers and do mending jobs for them. I get on with them very well indeed. They want to recommend me for a commission. They press me, say I am just the right sort of chap, but I keep on saying No. I prefer to be just what I am—not what is called a temporary gentleman. Of course, if anything should happen to me out here you would get an officer's pension. That would be good for you and the kiddies. But there is no need to think of such unpleasant things at the moment—I am away from the fighting at present.

My address is:

104 Infantry Brigade H.Q.,

B.E.F.

France.

Write there next time, my dear.

I was amused to hear that you had been studying the war in the newspapers. Some of the details you mention are not quite correct, and I hope, my dearest, that you will not think I am preaching to you if I explain a little, so that when you read the newspapers you will know what these things are.

Well, to begin: a Division is a very large organization of men.

Three Brigades make a Division. Up till December 17th there were 4 Battalions in a Brigade, but since the New Year one Battalion has been taken away from each Brigade throughout the army. The 104th Brigade—which as you will see from my new address is mine—consists (in addition to the R.E.'s Coy.) of the 17th and 18th Lancashire Fusiliers and the Durham Light Infantry Battalion. The 20th Lancashire Fusiliers have suffered some heavy losses and are split up therefore between the 17th and 18th Battalions. The 105th Brigade consists of the 15th Notts. and Derbys., the 15th Cheshires, and the 4th North Staffords. The 106th Brigade consists of the 17th Royal Scots, the 12th Highland Light Infantry, and the 18th Highland Light Infantry. In all, that comprises 9 Battalions of fighting men—and that makes up the 35th Division. With the Division there is a Company of Field R.E. and a Company of Signal R.E., and an Ambulance Coy. You will be wondering now what a Company is! Well, each Battalion is split up into four, each one of which is called a Company. In a Company there are any number of men from 150 to 200. So now you can have a sort of arithmetical table of army organization:

$$200 \text{ men} = 1 \text{ Company}$$
$$4 \text{ Companys} = 1 \text{ Battalion}$$
$$3 \text{ Battalions} = 1 \text{ Brigade}$$
$$3 \text{ Brigades} = 1 \text{ Division}$$

from which table you can calculate, if you wish, the number of men approximately in a Division.

This 35th Division, to which my Company of R.E.'s is attached, is a noted fighting Division. We are what is called a Flying Column, that is, we are sent quickly to any part of the line where the fighting is heaviest and good help is needed. We were fortunately the only Division that Jerry could not break through on 21st March of this year. Our reputation is now linked with the Guards', which is considered the best in France.

But no more war! I have enough of that out here, and when I write to you I like to put it out of my mind. I live for the time when I shall be able to dismiss it from my mind for good. That will be when I shall come home to my darling wife for ever and for ever. I want her to take care of herself and not to worry about money and business: I want to see her looking well and beautiful when I come home. That will not be long now, I hope.

I have just been sent for, so shall have to end this now. Good-bye for the present then, my dearest, and write to me soon. Give my love to Grandmother.

Your affectionate

WILL

PS. We are well behind the lines here. It is really so difficult to believe in the war just now, with the trees just come into leaf and the birds singing. I like to sit out in the sunshine and read your letters. Perhaps before the summer is over the whole wretched business will have ended. Write soon, dearest.

My dearest wife,

Thank you for your long letter. I was very amused at what you wrote about the children's prayers, how when you were teaching them to say 'Feed the young and tender plant' Clifford shouted 'That's me!' and when you came to 'Give us this day our daily bread' Susie chimed in with '*And* treacle'. That will make me chuckle for days. You are able to get Lyle's G.S. then. Good.

I am sorry about you not having letters from me. Perhaps by now you will have heard, because I *have* written. Remember, when the postwoman walks straight by our door, as you say she has done lately, it doesn't mean I have not written. It is simply that sometimes my letters to you are held up as yours are to me sometimes. So there is no need for your heart to sink when you see the postwoman pass our house, my dear. I hope you get this letter soon. You will probably get it with several of my earlier letters at the same time—just as I received *two* letters of yours. Write soon, dearest.

Your affectionate

WILL

PS. There is no need to be anxious about me, dear. Really, I am very comfortable in this new job, which is just right for me. It is so much better than where I was before, in the support lines. It is very quiet here.

Dear Mrs Dyment,

It is my unpleasant duty to have to write and tell you that your husband has been killed in action. The only consolation was that he died instantly and without any pain. We were being shelled at H.Q. and he was mending my table when a piece of shell hit him on the head and killed him instantly. We all feel his loss tremendously, from the General downwards we thought the world of him, he was such a splendid fellow, always cheerful, a lion for work and a good friend to everyone he came in contact with. I feel his loss as keenly as I would that of a brother officer. If everyone would carry on as he did we should feel the world was a better place to live in. I know how you and his kiddies will feel it but you will I know be a little consoled to know that we all thought him just as fine a fellow as you did.

Needless to say his funeral was as solemn as it could be out here. His grave is well behind the line and a cross will be erected.

If there is anything I can do or tell you please don't hesitate to write to me. My address is the same as your late husband's.

Yours sincerely,

W. O. Rushton
Captain.

6

Journey to Nottingham

FOR SOME time my mother was too stunned by my father's death to think or do anything about our future. She didn't express her sorrow openly, but Grandmother did. Grandmother, in her black hissing skirt, her black shining brooch, her black fringed shawl— her black beaded bonnet hanging on a hook behind the door— Grandmother in her rocking-chair wept and wailed all day, the rockers pounding the stone floor in a monotonous bass accompaniment to the elegiac mumble given out by her mouth.

A Mrs Pryse called to see my mother the day after Captain Rushton's letter arrived. Mrs Pryse told my mother that she would gladly give half her life to be in my mother's place. 'Oh, how I envy you!' she said. 'If it were only my husband who had been killed instead of yours!' Every morning, Mrs Pryse said, she looked for the welcome telegram of bad news, every night prayed that her husband would be killed next day.

My mother was ill after this visit. She was shocked to know that bereavement was something that could be coveted. She was bewildered at the senselessness of an unwanted man surviving and a loved man dying. She was grieved at the cruelty that kept a hated man alive to be hated even more.

One morning a parcel of my father's 'effects' arrived from the War Office. Day after day the parcel lay on the pear-wood table, untouched. But at last my mother nerved herself to open it. As she undid the string she smelled a familiar tobacco in the air and she turned round quickly in surprise and smiled. 'Will!' she exclaimed. But Will wasn't standing behind her, the smoke coming greyly from his lips—only, in the parcel when she turned to it again, his pipe, still half full of the Wood's Hand Cut Virginia he was smoking when the shrapnel hit him. It was the briar with the hexagonal amber stem and silver band that his mother had given him on his twenty-first birthday, and my mother put it away hurriedly so that Grandmother wouldn't see it. If she did she'd get her bad heart and demand the brandy bottle. But Grandmother swishingly shuffled over to the table and rummaged in the parcel wrappings and among packets of letters tied with an army bootlace, wool mittens and socks, handkerchiefs with W.C.D. in the corner, tins of insecticide, a booklet of souvenir photographs entitled *Après le Bombardement*, large flat carpenters' pencils and a brass spirit-level, his wallet, watch, and petrol lighters, and some French and Belgian coins, she found his red identity disk, cased in flaking mud. That started Grandmother off. How, she cried, stumbling back to her chair, how did his identity disk come to have mud on it if he spent all his time in the officers' headquarters mending for them? No, no—she'd been told lies, she complained, looking accusingly at my mother, her dear son hadn't been safe and clean but had been out shivering amongst bomb craters full of dirty water, corpses, barbed wire entanglements, old shell-cases, rusty tins. She'd seen it all in the pictures in the *Daily Mail*. On and on she went, swaying and whining, clattering and nattering.

Mother gave her the brandy bottle.

The day after the opening of the parcel there arrived a postcard from Auntie George. It was for me. It was a picture postcard showing a small boy looking up admiringly at a soldier in full fighting kit: under the picture was the caption ' AND REMEMBER, LADDIE, THAT YOUR DADDY IS A MAN '. The irony of this message spurred my mother to write to Auntie George in West Bridgford—Uncle G.B. had by now had another move, from Alfreton to the Midland Railway's Carrington Street Station in Nottingham—to tell her the sad news. A reply from Auntie George came by return of post. My mother must realize her position, Auntie George wrote; she was now a war widow (as if mother needed to be told that!); she would receive a pension; it would be a private soldier's pension; a private's pension wouldn't be enough on which to keep a family of three —four including Grandmother; my mother must therefore be prepared to go out to work; Auntie George was perfectly aware that she had very few qualifications and very little experience but she wasn't to worry about that—Auntie George would find a job for her; all that Mother had to do was to sell up the home in Caerleon and come to live in Nottingham.

So my mother set about selling up the first and last home of her married life. Callers became frequent at the cottage—Great Western men my father had worked with, their wives, strangers who had heard of the sale and hoped to pick up something cheap. People tapped on the front door, or thumped it, stood on the step talking, came doubtingly inside and opened cupboard doors, raised flaps of tables, measured heights and widths, examined themselves in the dressing-table mirror, spread tools and wood and the pieces of the unfinished adjustable armchair on the stones, made offers, shrugged their shoulders, walked out. The men wore blue or brown suits with brown or black boots—when they sat down Susie and I could see loops sticking out from the backs of these boots like little cotton handles—and they all had gold or silver watch-chains winking on their bellying waistcoats. Some wore caps, which they carried in their hand, and others deposited hard smooth black hats or soft furry brown hats on the pear-wood table. The women moved about like upright cloth tubes, the skirts of their costumes touching the floor, the hems of their coats reaching to their knees. Some carried baskets of celluloid fruit on their heads, others arsenals of long sharp pins. The cottage smelled of serge and moth-balls.

Not a lot of the furniture was sold, even at my mother's naïve prices, so the bulk had to be stored at a weekly rental in the spare bedroom of a house in the village. Then, our clothes packed in a brown-bread coloured tin trunk and several butter coloured rush baskets bound with straps, Mother, Grandmother, Susie, and I walked out of 1, Ashwell Terrace for the last time.

The train journey to Nottingham lasted days, weeks, months. It was hot scratchy seats, tepid milk in old medicine bottles, sandwiches, buns, bananas, a cakewalk through the corridor to a pitching and tossing W.C., wheels hitting rails in an ever-lasting postman's knock, backyards of washing, eternal clanking tunnels that smelled of grey blankets rolled in damp coal dust, eye-hammering powerful daylight, hotter and ticklier seats, warmer milk, another ride on the bucking broncho W.C., engine shrieks and fleeting platforms, hairy blue ticket examiners with Monmouthshire, then Gloucestershire, then Oxfordshire, then Warwickshire, then Leicestershire, then Nottinghamshire voices.

When our carriage had finished funeral marching past Stephen's Ink and Virol and had stopped and the door had been yanked open by a porter and Mother, Grandmother, Susie, and I stood on the platform with our luggage and paper bags and bottles, we saw Auntie George and Uncle G.B. come pushing through the crush to meet us. Auntie George stooped to kiss me. The disk of her huge hat descended upon me like a lid and the frills, ribbons, and laces flapping from the bosom and sleeves of her frock tumbled about me like paper streamers. Uncle G.B. didn't kiss, but raised his light grey homburg.

'Pleased to meet yuh, ma'am,' he greeted my mother. 'And yuh, too, Missie,' he said, smiling down at Susie. 'And I reckon that goes fer yuh, too, son,' he grinned at me, ruffling my hair.

Uncle G.B. was dressed immaculately for summer in a suit that was light grey like his hat; he wore a silk shirt with a bow tie; and instead of a waistcoat a band of pale alpaca swathed his globe-shaped stomach, fitted with pockets for carrying a watch and chain.

When the welcomes were over Uncle raised his hat again and addressed us all.

'Waal, I guess yore thoughts is on the cook-house after yore long trail. What about some pork'n beans, huh? Or a choice dish uv spare ribs?'

'Well, I'm sure either would be very nice, G.B.,' Mother was saying politely, when Auntie George chimed in.

'I've got a lovely pork pie for you,' she said, 'two-and-six from Parr's. And some pressed beef I made last night. And some of Parr's best York ham. And a raspberry jelly and a chocolate blancmange specially for you,' she added, beaming down at Susie and me. 'I knew you'd like that. You do, don't you?'

'Yes, please, Auntie,' Susie and I replied together.

'Let's git along to the stage, then,' suggested Uncle G.B.

'No, not a bus,' Auntie George smiled. 'A taxi.'

'Shore,' Uncle G.B. answered. 'Shore. If yuh'll excuse me, ladies'—he lifted his homburg to Mother and Grandmother— 'if yuh'll excuse me, reckon I'd better git goin' to see where they keep the hired automobiles on this here outfit.'

When he had gone, his cream-and-tan shoes picking a path through churns and mailbags and his Malacca cane gleaming, Mother asked very quietly:

'George, why does G.B. talk in that queer way?'

'Queer?'

'Well, yes . . .'

Auntie George looked at my mother blankly. Then she laughed.

'Oh, I know what you mean—I'm so used to it I don't even notice it any more! It's the cowboy stories he reads, that's all. He started to talk like that as a joke, and now he doesn't realize he's doing it. Don't take any notice.'

Auntie and Uncle lived in Rectory Road. We travelled there in a taxi as tall as a top-hat and with daisy-white tyres. As soon as we drew up outside the front garden gate a girl—dark, pretty, and young—ran out to greet us. She helped to unload our luggage from the taxi roof, took Grandmother's arm and led her tenderly along the asphalt path all the way from the gate to the front door, took her black coat and bonnet, took Mother's coat and hat and Susie's, made tea in a brown pot and carried it into the front dining-room where she had already laid our places and brought up the chairs ready for us, fetched extra hot water in jugs—and found time to sit down with us at the table and have tea herself. Her name was Tishy, and she was Auntie's maid.

Our tea was a real Midland tea, a sit-down, knife-and-fork, meat-sweets-and-cake tea. When it was over Uncle G.B. walked with Mother, Susie, and me to the new home that he and Auntie George had found for us in West Bridgford, Grandmother not coming with us because from now on she was going to live with Auntie George and Uncle G.B. in Rectory Road. We didn't have to walk far—to the house of Mr and Mrs Belton in Carlyle Road. The houses in Carlyle Road weren't so good-looking as those in

Rectory Road—they were set nearer to the pavement, were smaller, had bay windows downstairs but not upstairs, were less like villas and more like boxes. But they had front gardens, which showed that they weren't common. You couldn't see the gardens from the pavement, however: not because they were too small to be visible to the naked eye (which was almost true) but because they were hidden behind walls built of solid slabs of marzipan.

I got to know these walls of sandstone very well in the course of the next few years, for when I wasn't at school I saw more of the outside of our house than the inside. Mrs Belton liked Susie and me to play in the street all day, for then, she said, she could get on with what she wanted to do in the house without our bothering her.

7

Children's Games

IT WAS very soon after we had gone to live with the Beltons that I first came under the influence of Byron. Byron—his first name was Sid—was the son of a traction-engine driver. He lived midway between Carlyle Road and Rectory Road in a house that *was* common: it had no front garden at all, not even a mingy one, and when you were inside and wanted to leave you opened a door and found yourself stepping right off on to the pavement.

Sid Byron's face was round and creamy, with freckles, and his hair was black, curly, and unbrushed. He was always dressed in a sailor suit of long bell-bottomed trousers and tight-fitting tunic, with a real sailor's square striped collar spread across his back. Inconsistently, he wore a naval officer's cap that was lavishly braided with gold and had a crescent peak as smooth and lustrous as glass. There was a jagged tear in the seat of his trousers, but he didn't seem to mind.

He was a big bold boy, adept at boys' skills. He could wrap a length of cord or a leather thong around a mushroom top and jerk it through the air so that it landed on the road erect and spinning. He could throw a stone so that it became a bird, soaring over houses or dipping to the ground, skimming along, and rising again like a swallow over water. He could shoot a marble like an expert, nipping it within his bent-round forefinger and propelling it with a galvanic thrust of his thumb. He could kick a cocoa-tin with force and accuracy. He could play exhilarating rattling rhythms on two flat meat bones gripped between his fingers. He could whistle by putting two fingers in his mouth. I found him a learned and exciting companion.

There were other thrills in Carlyle Road besides Sid. Three times a week the ice-cream man drove through, calling out 'Oke! Oke!' as he passed from one end of the street to the other.

He wore a coat as white as Monday's washing and sat behind a bony horse in a fun-fair booth on wheels. His seat was in the rear part of the booth and his weight caused his end of the cart to sink and the shafts to point to the sky—with the result that the horse was at any moment liable to be transformed into a flying horse. When a customer came the man rose and stepped to a place between two enormous brass bins, this causing the forward end of the cart to descend suddenly, the shafts dropping in the harness with a violent rattle and thud. The horse was accustomed to the continual seesawing of his burden and accepted it with the bored resignation exhibited by all experienced draught animals. Eating ice-cream from the gay cart was nice, but it was almost as nice watching the man sell it. He lifted a great cymbal of a lid and lowered his right sleeve up to the elbow in a plunging bin, bringing out a trowel laden with summer snow. This he transferred to cornets, a penny, and to sandwiches, twopence. The cornets were as richly filled as cornucopias, while the sandwiches were made in an instrument like a large safety-razor which ingeniously delivered the sandwich when completed into the hokey-pokey man's hand.

Another pony-and-trap traveller along Carlyle Road was the rag-and-bone man. His cart went round in circles—celluloid windmills whirled, balloons spun on their strings, goldfish homelessly circumnavigated their homes. In a stiff breeze the windmills revolved so rapidly that they seemed not to move: they drew light to themselves as an electric fan draws air and with so much of the day packed in so small a space they became incandescent. The individual colours, red, green, blue, yellow, were obliterated in the heat and each windmill became a white lamp burning on the top of a firewood pole. One windmill consumed a whole granary of rags—so I don't know what you had to give for a goldfish. Perhaps all the skeletons in all the cupboards of West Bridgford.

Saturdays were great days. On Saturdays my mother, instead of returning from work in the evening, came home at dinner time—so at ten o'clock in the morning every Saturday Susie and I would be at our stations watching for the hatted, veiled, and long-skirted figure of Mother to appear at the end of the road. Usually she brought us presents. I remember a line of coloured paper flags and a silver trumpet decorated with cords and tassels. Susie once had a Nigger Minstrel with a white mouth.

One of Sid's pleasures was to charge at the girls playing hop-scotch on the pavement and kick away the stone that they pushed seriously one-legged from hell to heaven. When they saw him coming the girls ran away shrieking and from a safe distance called him nasty names and poked their tongues out at him. One afternoon a tall fair girl didn't run away, but waited for him truculently. They met in the middle of the chalked oblong and there was a tussle. Sid got the stone and, wide trouser-legs flapping, started to dribble it along the road. The girl ran after him, furiously scooping up dirt and pebbles from the gutter and hurling them at his back. Sid could run and dribble well, but he wasn't a bully, so he stopped to let the girl catch up with him.

'Say you're sorry,' the girl demanded.

'You're sorry,' Sid said.

'*Say you're sorry.*'

'You're sorry.'

The girl stamped her foot.

'Say . . . you're . . . sorry!'

'I *have* said it,' Sid spluttered.

'No you haven't.'

'Yes I have.'

'No you haven't!'

'You said say you're sorry and I said you're sorry. Didn't I?' Sid turned to me with an aggrieved expression.

'Didn't I?' he repeated appealingly.

'Yes', I said, 'you did.'

'There!' Sid exclaimed, nodding his head in virtuous endorse-ment.

The girl looked at me.

'What's your name?'

'Clifford.'

'Cliff,' Sid corrected. 'What's yours?'

'Pearl. What's yours?'

'Sid. My dad drives a traction-engine.'

'My dad's a fitter's mate,' Pearl rejoined proudly.

Sid sat down on the kerb and cleaned his nose with his finger. He put the debris in his mouth.

'Everybody's doing it, doing it, doing it,' Pearl sang. 'Picking their nose and chewing it, chewing it, chewing it. . . .'

Sid pointed at me with his snotty finger.

'He don't have a dad.'

Pearl gave me a look of considerable interest.

'Honest?' she asked.

'Honest.'

'Where is he, then?'

'He's dead.'

'Oh.'

'He was Killed In Action,' I said very slowly and impressively, repeating the phrase as I had heard it used by Mother and Grandmother and Auntie George.

Pearl joined Sid on the kerb and I sat down beside them. I lowered my face to my shorts and stared at my Roman sandals. My knees felt cool on my cheek-bones.

'Did your dad win any medals?' Sid inquired.

'Yes. Lots.'

'I bet he didn't win the V.C.'

'He could if he'd wanted to.'

Sid held his hand high in the air and brought it down with a sudden swoop.

'Captain Albert Ball, V.C.!' he shouted exultingly.

'My dad's a soldier, too,' Pearl said.

Sid snorted.

'You said he was a fitter's mate!'

Pearl coloured.

'I meant my old dad,' she defended herself. 'It's my new dad who's a fitter's mate.'

'I've only got an old dad,' Sid said sadly.

'I've got a stepdad!' Pearl boasted.

'We've got a door-step at home,' Sid laughed. 'Door-step dad! Door-step dad! I'm glad I haven't got a door-step dad!'

Pearl narrowed her eyes and grabbed at Sid's sailor collar, pulling it until she almost tore it off. Sid fought her good-naturedly. Then he said:

'Come on, let's play.'

And so we played, that afternoon, and many other afternoons, mornings, and evenings. One end of Carlyle Road was rooted in the shopping and residential area of West Bridgford like a finger in its palm, but it then stretched out until its tip touched the countryside. Sometimes we walked to its end and strayed off its finger-nail into lanes and pastures. There we cut and peeled pliant sticks, stuck acorn cups on to twigs and called them pipes, listened at telegraph poles for secret messages, jumped ditches, put horses' tails up our sleeves and wriggled our arms until they emerged from our collars, trapped butterflies in our caps (Sid's, being stiffened, was very good for this and mine, being floppy, very bad), made tin whistles out of elderberry stems, and poked bunches of stinking nannies into each other's nostrils.

In autumn and winter afternoons, when the sun rolled red behind the trees and roofs were plum-blue mountains in the sky, we made lamps out of clay scooped from a brook in one of the fields. Sid was the expert in this craft, our teacher and chief technician, and it was pleasurable to be playing with fire when the warmth was vanishing as quickly as the light and chilly breezes were spraying the backs of your knees and the tender thighs inside your shorts. The clay lamps were oblong—hollow bricks—and we filled them with touchwood which we broke in lumps off the inside of a rotten tree. The touchwood was extremely brittle: a slight pressure of our fingers and it crumpled into a slithery brown powder to which Pearl or Sid put a match. When lit and blown on the touchwood shone like charcoal. The blowing was a matter of life or death for the fire, so we sucked in cold twilight and spewed out hot breath—in, out, in, out—until we were quite light-headed. Four human bellows, on our bit of waste ground, we crouched protectively around our puny brazier, holding out our hands to cherish its feeble radiance and moving in close to hug its pygmy heat.

A variation on the clay lamp was the vegetable lantern. For

this you needed a large turnip. When the flesh was scraped out and ventilation holes made in the sides a candle-end could be put in and a patchy unreliable illumination given out. In the turnip lantern the candle smoked and smelled and hissed and sizzled in raw culinary juices and when we put our faces near to look we all got jaundiced complexions. Moths and sparkling night insects sometimes hovered around the lamp and the lantern. In the lamp they were quickly incinerated; and they often succeeded in getting into the bubbling port-holes of the turnip—they broiled there for a second and remained as crumbs of greying ash.

Often, when it began to get really dark, we played nocturnal hide-and-seek. For this we searched for a short stick and inserted it in the flaring turnip. Carrying the turnip by this stick, one of us streaked off into the blue-black mists while the remaining three turned our backs and counted. When we reached ten we swung round and ran after the blob of light that dipped and wobbled in the distance like a drunken man's cigar. When we got close the hunted player spitefully covered the lantern with a coat or cap, blindfolding us with night. 'Where are you? Where are you?' we called, groping with senseless eyes, and after a few moments the mocking flame bobbed up in a quite different place and with feeling eyes again we raced after it as it bounded along until once more it vanished and once more we were fumbling and stumbling in black blinkers.

8

The Beltons

OUR LANDLORD and landlady were not a happy couple. Perhaps this was because Mr Belton was ill.

You could see that Mr Belton had once been a fine strong man because of his large frame, height, and long feet, but the padding of muscle that should have given a welter-weight's wideness to his back was gone and his jacket now hung from his bony shoulders in empty-looking folds, like a garment draped over a chair. His cheeks were drawn in as though he was permanently sucking something, and his skin had the yellowish brittle appearance of a cold roast chicken's, except where tracings of scarlet and purple veins ran as delicately as lines drawn with a mapping pen. He was going bald, but he grew his hair long on one side of his head and brushed it across the desert skin, sticking it down with brilliantine: it looked like a band of satin gummed on his skull. He looked so melancholy so much of the time that it was a surprise to see him smile—but the surprise vanished almost at once because the smile fitted so naturally on his face that you realized it had been there all the time hidden under the sick man's mask.

Mr Belton didn't go out to work like other men, though Susie and I knew that he'd once been on the railway like Uncle G.B. Because he was an invalid he stayed at home and spent most of his time in the best room, which meant the front room. What he did in there Susie and I didn't know, for we were forbidden to go in. We often heard strange noises coming from inside—hammerings, screeches, scrapings, squeaks. Did he torture cats and dogs? we wondered. *Did he kill people?* We hurried past the door, frightened at its mystery.

41

Unlike her husband, Mrs Belton was healthy, and looked it. It wasn't only her cheeks that were healthy: her hair was healthy, too, for it was a bright carrot. The dyeing had been done some time ago, however, and the carrot was now a little mixed with parsnip. She was a short, soft, rounded woman who wore woollen dresses that clung to her body and revealed its curvilinear construction. While at work in the house her hair was covered by a mob-cap and her stomach by a hessian apron, but she took both of these off for the evening.

On three evenings a week she really dressed up. These were her Sisterhood evenings, and for them she wore a smart navy-blue costume with a fur—mandibles, tail, paws, and all—curled around her neck.

Mrs Belton's Sisterhood was a secret society. Her husband was always trying to wheedle a description of it out of her, but in this he wasn't very successful. It is true that on one occasion he coaxed her into a careless remark about Light Refreshments and that on another he contrived to make her go so far as to admit to Friendly Chats—but really neither of these clues provided much enlightenment. Reluctantly—for Mrs Belton was in herself a piece of evidence to the contrary—Mr Belton came to the conclusion that the Sisterhood had something to do with church or chapel.

He was confirmed in this opinion by an item in the local newspaper. It was one of the evenings when Mrs Belton had disappeared through the scullery door, the tail and hind feet of her fur frisking on her back, leaving the rest of us in the kitchen as usual.

'Dorcas!' said Mr Belton.

Mother, surprised, looked up from her sewing.

'Dorcas!' Mr Belton repeated. 'That's it.'

Mother gave him a questioning glance.

'It's something it says here, Mrs Dyment,' Mr Belton explained, pointing to the paper. 'It's about the church. It says they've got a Dorcas Society there, and it meets three times a week. There's a meeting on tonight. So that *must* be where the missus goes.'

'Yes, it does seem like it,' Mother agreed.

'I wonder what sort of Society it is?'

'Yes, I wonder . . .?' mused Mother.

'Do you know what Dorcas means, Mrs Dyment?'

Mother thought.

'Perhaps it's the name of the person who founded the Society,' she suggested.

'It might be. It can't be the vicar, though, because his name's Hargreaves. Perhaps it's the name of the sort of M.C. who runs it?'

'Yes.'

'I've never heard of a Mr Dorcas, though. Or a Mrs come to that. I wonder if it's the name of a street. . . .'

'Mr Belton.'

'Yes, Mrs Dyment?'

'Do you think it's any good seeing if it's in *Inquire Within About Everything*?'

'That's a topping idea, Mrs Dyment!' Mr Belton said delightedly. 'I'll go and see about it this minute.'

He hurried slowly out of the room. Susie and I looked at each other, each with the same serious thought. Mr Belton had gone to his awful sanctum.

A few moments later he came back, pleased, with a book in his hand.

'You were right, Mrs Dyment,' he said. 'It's in the book. And you were right about it being a name and all. It says Dorcas was a lady in the Bible who made garments for the poor.'

'Mrs Belton must go to a kind of Ladies' Sewing Meeting, then,' Mother said.

'That's about it,' Mr Belton agreed. 'It's funny, though. It doesn't seem like her, does it?'

Mother didn't answer, but concentrated on her work.

'Getting her to sew a button on my shirt is like asking a miser for the price of a cup of tea,' Mr Belton continued. 'I can't see her making pinafores and suchlike, somehow. She's not like you, Mrs Dyment.'

'I'm only doing mending,' my mother answered. 'I don't do it because I like it. It *has* to be done, that's all—the children wear their things out so quickly. I don't think the quality's as good as it was pre-war.'

This reference to children's clothes gave me the opportunity I'd been waiting for.

'Mother, will you buy me a sailor suit?'

Mother turned and looked at me.

'Why, don't you like the new jersey I brought you last week from Dixon and Parker's?'

'Yes, it's all right,' I answered. 'But I want a sailor suit like Sid Byron's. With long bell-bottom trousers.'

'Long trousers?'

'Yes. Like Mr Belton's—but ever so much wider at the bottom.'

'But Mr Belton's a grown-up man. You're only a little boy.'

'Sid Byron is a boy, but he's got long trousers.'

'Well, I don't think it's right for little boys to look like little men.'

I was stubborn.

'I want to be an officer in the Navy, like Sid.'

Mother stitched in silence for a while. I looked round for Mr Belton, thinking that he would be pleased that I wanted to wear long trousers like his and would therefore support my point of view. But Mr Belton had gone to his room. At last Mother said seriously:

'I want you to listen to me carefully, Clifford. Will you do that?'

'Yes, Mother,' I answered. Mother had brought up Susie and me always to call her Mother—never Mummie or Mam. She liked people and things to be referred to in their proper terms and hated baby talk, pet names, fashionable affectations, and superficial endearments as much as my father had hated stuck-on ornamentation.

'Well, then. Sailors in the Navy aren't proper sailors. They don't sail in the kind of ships that you like, ships that carry passengers and all kinds of wonderful cargoes. Their ships only carry shells.'

'Shells that come out of guns?'

'Yes.'

This was important. A shell had killed my father.

'Do the Navy sailors have to fire the guns?'

'Yes. Navy sailors aren't really sailors at all. They're soldiers who fight on the sea instead of on the land.'

'Wasn't Uncle Hobart in the Navy?'

'No, dear. Uncle Hobart was in the Merchant Service. He began as a sailor before the mast, then he became a bosun, and after that a chief mate. Once, in a storm, he took command of the schooner *Larry Russell* and brought her safely to port. Wasn't that a clever thing to do?'

'Yes. Where was the captain?'

'He was in his cabin.'

'Why was he in his cabin? Captains ought to be on the bridge.'

'He'd been taken ill, dear.'

'Was he seasick?'

'No. He wasn't seasick.' Mother smiled. 'Don't you think your Uncle Hobart was a brave man to take over the ship and command it during the storm?'

'Yes he was. Would he tell me about it himself if I asked him?'

'I expect so.'

'Why don't we go to see him, then?'

'He lives a long way from Nottingham, dear, in Newport Mon. But we *will* go soon. We'll go to Newport Mon for a holiday and see Uncle Hobart and Auntie Matti and Hugh and David and Olwen . . .'

'. . . and Grandmother and Grandfather,' Susie interrupted.

'And Auntie Myfanwy and Uncle Glyn and your cousins Dilys and Rae,' Mother continued. Then she laughed. 'We won't have much time to feel lonely, will we?' she said.

All our conversations at the Beltons had to be in the communal kitchen and were usually listened to by Mrs Belton or Mr Belton or both, for we had no room of our own, except at night. We all slept in one bedroom, Mother and Susie in a double bed of black iron garnished with corner knobs like great brass onions and I in a sort of cot pushed into a shadowy nook. There was lino on the floor, very cold; a mahogany wash-stand with a marble-slab top, very cold; and on the marble slab a pink-flowered basin with a jug full of water, very cold.

We had all our meals with the Beltons, at the table spread with oil-cloth in the kitchen where we all lived. Regularly at tea time Mr Belton made his joke, because he liked to see Susie and me laugh. He picked up the jar of bramble jam and solemnly read aloud the words on the label.

'Home and Colonial,' he pronounced slowly, turning the jar before his eyes as though deciphering an ancient inscription. 'Branches Everywhere. Now'—winking at Susie and me—'I don't mind them putting branches in the jam so long as they don't leave the prickles on!'

The crockery, the knives, forks, and spoons, and the remains of food had to be cleared quickly if the table was needed for writing on, or making pastry on, or ironing on. There was ironing to be done nearly every day at Carlyle Road, for there was always underwear—the Beltons' or ours—drying or airing on a string in the scullery. When my mother ironed she hummed tunes wordlessly, shut in a private parlour of concentration on her work; but almost as often she sang the words of the song, too, very quietly, not singing to anyone, not even herself. She had been brought up with song. At home, in Monmouthshire and Glamorganshire, all her relations sang, either as soloists or as members of choirs.

Sometimes, as she ironed, she sang her father's favourites, Welsh folk-songs and others: 'The Ash Grove', 'All Through the Night', 'Annie Laurie', 'Mary of Argyle':

> I have heard the mavis singing
>   His love-song to the morn.
> I have seen the dew drop clinging
>   To the rose just newly born;
> But a sweeter song has cheered me
>   At the ev'ning's gentle close
> And I've seen an eye still brighter
>   Than the dew drop on the rose;
> 'Twas thy voice, my gentle Mary,
>   And thine artless winning smile
> That made this world an Eden,
>   Bonnie Mary of Argyle.

Sometimes she sang ballads like 'The Rosary', 'A Perfect Day', and 'I'll Sing Thee Songs of Araby'. Sometimes she sang hits from musical shows, such as 'If You Were the Only Girl in the World', 'Chin Chin Chinaman', 'My Hero'. And sometimes she sang the hymns that she had learned as a little girl after she had signed the pledge and joined the Band of Hope.

Swish-s-s-s-s—the flat-iron snowshoed over my shirts and Susie's liberty bodices; bump, thump—it pressed seams; clatter, click—it was put to rest on the ironing-stand; plap, plip, plop—drops of water were spattered on parched cotton. And through, over, under the duet of steel and textile there sounded a third voice—my mother's clear steady soprano:

> Merry Dick you soon would know
> If you lived in Jackson's Row;
> Each day with a smiling face
> He is ready in his place;
> Should you ever with him meet,
> In the shop or in the street,
> You will hear him blithe and gay
> Singing out this merry lay:

> My drink is water bright,
>   Water bright, water bright;
> My drink is water bright
>   From the crystal spring.

'Mother.'

'Yes, Clifford?'

'Can I have an apple?'

'Of course you can, dear. You know you can take one any time, without asking.'

'Can I, Mother?' Susie asked.

'Of course. You both can.'

I took an apple. Susie took an apple. Mother said:

'That's why I bought them and put them in that big bowl. So that you can have one whenever you feel like it.'

I bit into the polished red fruit. Juice spurted into my mouth like tart lemonade. There was a tingling and stiffening sensation in the linings of my cheeks and under my tongue, and suddenly

C

gushing saliva forced me to swallow hard. In the snowy sparkle of the apple my teeth had left three small spade marks.

'Mrs Belton said we couldn't,' I retorted, chewing. 'She smacked Susie.'

'*Smacked* her?' Mother repeated sharply. 'Did Mrs Belton smack you, Susie?'

As she said this, Mother, out of habit, lowered her voice so that the Beltons wouldn't hear, though we were alone. Susie nodded.

'Mrs Belton smacked Susie because she took an apple without asking,' I spoke up. 'She said she did it to learn us manners.'

'When did she say that?'

'Yesterday.'

'And did you ask Mrs Belton nicely today if you could have an apple?'

'Yes.'

'Did she give you one?'

'No.'

'Did Mrs Belton give you an apple, Susie?'

'No.'

'Perhaps Mrs Belton gave you a bar of chocolate instead?'

'No, she didn't.'

An unhappy look came into Mother's face. She resumed her ironing, but she didn't sing.

Mr and Mrs Belton were important people to Susie and me at this time, even more important than Mother. We saw Mr and Mrs Belton throughout the days of the week, but we saw Mother only for a little while in the evenings and on Saturday afternoon and Sunday. We knew that when we weren't seeing Mother she was in the Record Office.

The Record Office was a huge block of wall and window in Nottingham near the Midland Station. It had been meant for a departmental store, but owing to the war had never become one and was now utilized as a temporary government building. Its proper name was the Army Records Office. It contained hundreds of desks—boards laid on trestles—which were smartly formed up in line as though for parade or inspection; and in fact the men and women who sat at them were on parade and were drawn up for inspection because throughout the working day officers paced the wooden ranks to see that every man and woman was busy transferring demobilized soldiers' letters and numbers from one brownish-yellow form to another. If an officer spotted a man or woman who appeared to be idle—even for a moment—he would have a dismissal notice put in his or her pay envelope at the end of the week. Every clerk worked in fear of redundancy and as a result was careful to maintain a permanent hunch over the desk and to keep the steel pen moving continually over a piece of paper—it didn't matter what marks the pen made on the paper so long as it could be seen to be in ceaseless motion, from left to right. Sometimes there was a shortage in the supply of documents to be copied: then one precious paper was retranscribed a dozen times and begging letters slunk from desk to desk offering bribes —five Woodbines, a rock cake at tea time—for a spare sheet of work.

In that great room the clock was a round-faced Buddha, worshipped from nine till six. A dozen times an hour were the eyes of the faithful lifted to him, a dozen times an hour their prayers for deliverance were silently offered to him, a dozen times an hour they scanned his face for a sign of mercy in him. But the clock wasn't a smiling Buddha and was on the side of the authorities.

Mother was very miserable in the Record Office—it was the post that Auntie George had found for her—but as she had no idea of how and where to look for other work she went there dutifully year after year. The wages were low, but they were enough to enable her to buy extras for us—apples, oranges, pears, bananas, nuts, cream, butter, eggs. It distressed her to find that Mrs Belton wasn't giving us these things, and, shy and peaceful woman that she was, it must have been very painful and taken a great deal of courage for her to raise the matter with Mrs Belton.

But she did. It was one evening when both Mr and Mrs Belton were in the kitchen. There was quite a scene. Mrs Belton took the inquiry very badly, declaring herself to be highly offended, wounded to the quick, grossly insulted, completely misunderstood. She was shocked that my mother could ever for one moment . . . why, she'd been a second mother to us . . . never before in her whole life had such a thing . . . She was upset, she was reproachful, she was abusive; she was piteous, she was threatening. Mother had the misfortune to be the parent of two very mischievous children. We were ungrateful. We were hypocrites. We were tale-bearers. We were liars. However, she didn't blame Susie so much as me. I needed a good hiding. It was bad for a boy to be deprived of a father's stern hand. Perhaps I ought to be put into some kind of home. . . .

Mother looked pale and serious. She made no answer to Mrs Belton's tirade. Susie and I, frightened, guilty because the quarrel was about us, cowered in a corner.

Perhaps it would be better for everybody, Mrs Belton said with a self-righteous sniff, if she gave Mother a week's notice. . . .

Here Mr Belton, who had been reading a paper all through his wife's harangue, stood up. Now, now, now, he said. When the fire's hot the saucepan boils over. And that makes a mess. Let the matter drop for the present, he said, and then, when tempers have cooled down . . . His wife glared at him. Then, giving another sniff, she strode into the scullery.

'You come with me, lad,' he concluded, stooping and putting his hand on my head.

Mother looked alarmed.

'Mr Belton!' she exclaimed.

'It's all right, Mrs Dyment,' he reassured her.

And moving his hand to my shoulder he guided me out of the kitchen and into the hall.

He was taking me to his own dreadful room. I felt terrified. What was going to happen to me?

I waited, heart pounding, while he unlocked the mysterious door.

'Come on in, lad,' he said.

I took two or three trembling steps forward into darkness. I heard a match strike and the gas pop, felt a lot of light, shut my eyes, quickly, and then opened them to see Mr Belton standing under the gas-lamp reducing its ferocity by pulling down one of its twin chains.

In the creamy light I gazed in astonishment round the room.

'Oh, look!' I cried in admiration.

'Yes, lad,' smiled Mr Belton. 'Yes. I thought you'd be interested.'

9

The Trip to the North

THE ROOM was full of model railway engines!

There were engines on the mantelpiece, where people usually had a clock and two rearing bronze horses; there were engines on wooden stands, where they usually had aspidistras; there were engines on wall brackets, tables, window ledges, shelves—everywhere I looked I saw small locomotives and carriages. If it hadn't been for the work-bench, and the scattered tools, and the treadle fretsaw, and the stacks of old magazines and books pushed against the walls I would have thought I'd walked into a toyshop.

I was standing close to a funny locomotive with a chimney like a factory's and a tangle of girders and rods surmounting its boiler: it looked like one of the machines used by road-menders for spreading tar, except that this engine was clean and decorated with stars at the points where its polished brass fittings reflected the gaslight.

'You've never seen an engine like that one, have you, Cliff?'

'No, Mr Belton.'

'No, I was pretty sure that you wouldn't have.'

'Why were you pretty sure, Mr Belton?'

'Because it was built a long time ago. Before you were born.'

'How long ago, Mr Belton?'

'More than a hundred years ago. It was one of the first railway engines in the whole world. It was called the "Puffing Billy".'

'Puff, puff, puff, puff,' I imitated, moving my arms like coupling rods.

'That's it, lad,' said Mr Belton. 'That's why it was called the Puffing Billy—not many people had seen a steam-engine then, you see.'

'Was the Puffing Billy the first steam-engine in the whole world?'

'No, it wasn't that. You see——' Mr Belton paused, gazing at me earnestly. 'Would you like me to tell you about these old engines, lad?' He swept his arm around his room, taking in all the engines at one go.

'Yes I would, please, Mr Belton.'

'You're sure? You wouldn't rather go back in the kitchen and read your comics?'

'No, Mr Belton.'

'That's all right, then.' A happy, relieved smile came into his face. 'Well, there *had* been steam-engines before this Puffing Billy, but they'd been used for working the pumps that sucked water out of coal-mines, do you see? Here'—Mr Belton pointed an almost fleshless finger at a horizontal cross-arm above the network of steel over Puffing Billy's boiler—'this thing here is called a beam and that's why the olden-time engines were called beam-engines. One end of the beam was moved up and down by a piston in a cylinder and the other end also moved up and down and operated the colliery pump. Do you understand?'

I nodded.

'They were stationary engines—they stayed where they were built. Now the Puffing Billy—this one here—was one of these stationary engines fixed on wheels. The beam worked wheels instead of a pump. See?'

I nodded again.

'And so it ran along the rails. It was a stationary engine that got a move on, like.' Mr Belton laughed. 'Come here, son.'

He tugged excitedly at my sleeve and pulled me a foot or two towards another old high-chimneyed engine with a string of wagons behind it. He pointed at some lettering on the boiler.

'Can you read that?'

I stared at the name, feeling my face go red. It was a long, hard word.

'Come on, lad!' Mr Belton encouraged, nudging me. 'Show me what they learn you in school.'

'Lo—co——' I spelled out. 'Loco——'

'Right first time!' exclaimed Mr Belton delightedly, patting me on the back. 'Locomotion! That's an old-fashioned word that means moving from place to place. A locomotive is a steam-engine that can travel from Nottingham to London. See?'

'Yes, Mr Belton.'

There was a fluttering thrill in my inside because an old man like Mr Belton considered me grown up enough to talk with him about grown-up things.

'That was the first train in the whole world,' Mr Belton said, laying his hand affectionately on *Locomotion* and the carriages behind it. 'The very first train in the whole world! What do you think of that now?'

'The very first train in the *whole* world!'

'It was. It ran on the Stockton and Darlington Railway, in 1825. There was no Flying Scotsman then. No big stations like Crewe or Euston. Just fields and roads. If you wanted to go from one town to another you had to ride on a stagecoach.'

'Stagecoaches were robbed by highwaymen,' I said.

'They were, lad. And then this little train came along and changed everything, running from Stockton to Darlington and from Darlington to Stockton—the first public railway in the whole world.'

His finger rested on the last of the carriages.

'But I haven't finished this model yet,' he said with a sad fall in his voice. 'There ought to be thirty-three wagons coupled up and I've only built twenty-nine so far. It's a lot of work, you know.'

I nodded sympathetically.

'Come on here, son. Here's a train I *have* finished.'

I followed him to a part of the room where one of his many models had a table all to itself. It stood on a proper permanent way, with a ballast of tiny stone chips between the rails, and the lovingly painted and burnished locomotive headed a procession of carriages got up as merry as roundabouts.

'There!' said Mr Belton with great pride. 'The first passenger train in the whole world!'

'The first in the whole world?'

'Yes, boy. The Liverpool and Manchester Railway, 1830. That was the first *passenger* train, understand, because the Stockton and Darlington, although it carried passengers sometimes, was really a goods line. It was a proper Goose Fair when the Liverpool and Manchester ran for the first time, I can tell you. You can see how the carriages are all rigged out to look bright and gay. There were thousands of people present. There were flags. There was music. Why, even the Duke of Wellington was there!'

Mr Belton had described the occasion in such detail that I felt half sure he must have been present himself. If not, how could he have known what it was like?

'Were—were you there, too, Mr Belton?'

Mr Belton let out what was, for a sick man, a great guffaw.

'No, Cliff, I wasn't there. It was a bit before my time, you know.'

He sat on a stool.

'I know I'm a crock, but I didn't know I looked such an *old* crock as that,' he said.

He looked glum, and I wondered if I had offended him.

'Shall I go now, Mr Belton?'

'No, no, you needn't go, lad—unless you want to. Do you want to?'

'No, Mr Belton.'

'Then you can stay a bit longer. Shall I go on talking to you about trains?'

'Yes, please, Mr Belton.'

I waited for him to speak, but he remained silent, sitting bent on the stool and staring for a long time at the Liverpool and Manchester Railway's carnival of coaches. Then he said:

'Trains are wonderful things, lad. I'm glad they interest you. Some folk think I'm cracked, playing with trains at my age, but they don't understand. A railway isn't just carriages and a loco- motive and a permanent way. It's a sort of door. At any time you can open it and take to the road, turning your back on a home that's dreary and on a life that's a misery to you. Any time you fancy you can whizz off to a new home and a new life, in any place you choose. Whenever you're down in the dumps—just open the door.'

Mr Belton seemed almost to have forgotten me, so I said:

'Yes, Mr Belton.'

*c

At the sound of my voice he turned his face to me and gave a laugh.

'Young lads like you are never in the dumps, are they?'

'I used to be once,' I said. 'My mother says that when I was a baby I was always crying and my father thought I might turn out to be a troublesome child. But I'm not, am I?'

'I don't think so.'

'Mrs Belton thinks I am.'

'Yes.'

'I only *asked* for an apple. I didn't take one *before* I asked.'

Mr Belton caught my hand, pulled me to him, and ran his fingers through my hair.

'Don't you worry about that, son. From now on, whenever you or Susie want an apple—just you take one and say Mr Belton said so.'

'Is that good manners?'

'It wouldn't be, if the apples weren't yours. But these are. Your ma buys them for you.'

'And doesn't Mrs Belton know that?'

'She doesn't properly understand. But she will when I explain it to her.'

'Oh.'

'Now,' said Mr Belton, getting up from the stool. 'Tell me what you like doing most.'

I thought, frowning. Was it eating apples? Or ice-cream? Or was it meeting Mother on Saturdays?

'Is it,' asked Mr Belton coaxingly, 'is it riding on trains?'

'I haven't been on many train rides,' I answered truthfully. 'The longest was when we came from Caerleon.'

'Ah, that was the Great Western. It's not so bad, the Great Western, not so bad. But it's been up to some funny things in its time, has the G.W.'

He pointed.

'That's a G.W. engine over there. See it?'

I walked to the spot he had indicated and saw a green engine with gold letters and lining on it.

'Not so dusty, eh?' Mr Belton said, joining me.

'It's topping, Mr Belton.'

'Yes, it's not so dusty—for the G.W.R. In its day I suppose it was just about the most powerful express engine running.'

'Was it really, Mr Belton?'

'Well, about. And the biggest.'

'What, that little engine?'

'Yes, I suppose it was. The most powerful and the biggest.'

'In the whole world?'

'Yes, in the whole world.'

We were silent, occupied with thoughts of the small engine's greatness. Then Mr Belton said:

'In the Albert Hall, in London—you've never been to London, have you, Cliff?'

'No, Mr Belton.'

'Well, I dare say you will, one day . . .'

'Is London very big?'

'Yes.'

'How big?'

'Very big.'

'Bigger than Nottingham?'

'Oh, yes. Much bigger.'

'How much bigger?'

'Well, let me think . . .'

Mr Belton stroked his chin, ruminatively.

'A hundred times bigger?' I asked eagerly.

'Well . . .'

'A thousand times bigger?'

'Well . . .'

'A million times bigger?'

'No,' Mr Belton answered decidedly. 'It's not a million times bigger. But it's bigger than Nottingham. And it's bigger than Derby. And it's bigger than Crewe. And what's more—it's bigger than Caerleon.'

'I know that,' I said. 'Is it a city?'

'Yes, it's a city.'

'Are the shops open all night?'

'Well, I dare say some of them are. Chemists, and so on.'

'Not sweet shops?'

'No, I don't *think* sweet shops are.'

'And not toy shops, either?'

'No, I don't think toy shops are, either, somehow.'

'Can you walk into a shop and buy *anything* you want?'

'Well,' said Mr Belton. 'I dare say you can buy most things, but I'm not so sure you can buy *anything*.' Then, seeing my disappointment, he added: 'But there are some marvellous sights in London—like the Albert Hall I was telling you about. That's a famous building where they have prize-fights and bands and suchlike. A great round place it is. Now'—there was a subdued but firmly resonating note of pride in his voice—'let into the stonework of the Albert Hall there's a likeness of that engine.'

I gazed at the tiny green and gilt locomotive in wonder.

'Mr Belton.'

'Yes, lad?'

'Why is it called *The Lord of the Izzles*?'

'You mean *The Lord of the Iles*,' smiled Mr Belton.

He bent his long and narrow body in the middle as though he was a folding rule and peered closely at the name emblazoned on the engine's side.

'*The Lord of the Isles*,' he read aloud thoughtfully. 'That's funny, now you've made me think of it. There weren't any islands where that engine ran. Unless—unless it was the *British* Isles they meant. Yes, that must be it, Cliff—the British Isles. They meant to say that the engine was the Lord of the British Isles.'

'The Lord of the British Isles!' I repeated, enjoying the march of sound and the pomp of meaning in the name.

'Just the sort of thing the Great Western would say!' snorted Mr Belton. 'It was always a conceited line.'

Now I knew what conceited meant, because I had heard Mrs Belton say sometimes that Mrs So-and-so was conceited and had heard her say at other times that Mrs So-and-so was stuck up, so I knew that the two terms were the same. But I was puzzled.

'Mr Belton, how can a railway be conceited?'

Mr Belton laughed.

'You're right to pull me up over that, Cliff! Grown-ups often say things they don't mean, just because they're used to saying them. Of course, I meant to say it was the men who built and worked the Great Western who were conceited, not the railway.'

He began to pace the room slowly, glancing affectionately at his models as he passed them.

'That's a nice engine—the old *Copper Nob* of the Furness Railway. *The Lion*, of the Liverpool and Manchester—it took me days, lagging that boiler with wood strips. There's Stephenson's *Rocket*, the most famous locomotive . . .'

'. . . in the whole world,' I joined in, boldly walking beside him.

He put his hand on my shoulder and grinned at me.

'And there's another old G.W.R. engine—the *North Star*, which hauled the first passenger train out of Paddington in 1854. Yes, as I was saying, G.W.R. men have always been an amazingly conceited lot. And the most conceited of them all was a man named Brunel. Isambard Kingdom Brunel! What a name to go to bed with, eh? He was an engineer and laid out the Great Western line from London to Bristol. He had a lot of fancy notions and was sure they were *all* right. They were all pretty daft notions, really. But the daftest notion of the lot was—well, what do you think it was?'

Of course, I hadn't any idea.

'What, Mr Belton?'

'Making trains go without engines!'

'But nobody could do that, could they, Mr Belton?'

'That's what everybody said—that nobody could do it. But Brunel—trust him—was cocksure about it. He said *he* could and *he* would make trains go without using any engines.'

'How, Mr Belton?'

'He said he'd make them go by suction.'

'Suction?'

'Yes, suction. The trains were to be *sucked* along—like you suck up lemonade through a straw.'

'Did he do it, Mr Belton?'

'Of course he didn't!' said Mr Belton joyfully. 'It was impossible. But a failure like that—which would have finished most men—didn't worry Brunel. He went on, sure of himself as ever. He was typical of the Great Western. Typical.'

'It wasn't the Great Western that was conceited, was it? It was Brunel.'

'That's right. Brunel. And after him the others. All giving themselves high and mighty airs. Do you know what they said when somebody asked if the G.W.R. was ever going to carry third-class passengers?'

'No, Mr Belton, I don't.'

'Well, what they said was that they would no doubt *eventually* carry the very lowest order of passengers—that means people like *us*, Cliff, your ma and Mrs Belton, and Susie and me and you— *the very lowest order of passengers*, but they'd have to travel in very slow trains, once a day, in inferior accommodation, and probably at night. What a prospect!' Mr Belton blew his nose angrily. 'And what do you think all that meant, Cliff, when it came down to brass tacks?'

'I don't know, Mr Belton.'

'It meant that what the G.W.R. did, when they eventually condescended to consider third-class passengers, was to send them by *goods train*. Yes, my lad—goods train! Just as though we were sacks of barley. What do you think of that for over-bearing, high-handed, arrogant haughtiness, eh?'

Mr Belton sat on his stool again, overcome by indignation that was one-third play and two-thirds genuine.

I didn't know what to answer. As Mr Belton described it, the Great Western seemed an awful railway. But I was a little mystified.

'Mr Belton.'

'Yes, lad?'

'When we came from Caerleon the Great Western didn't send us by goods train.'

Mr Belton let out another of his incongruous guffaws.

'Of course they didn't!' he laughed. 'By the time you travelled the Great Western had been forced to improve its service. They'd been *shamed* into giving third-class passengers decent treatment by the example of other companies—such as the one I worked for, for instance.'

'What company did you work for, Mr Belton?'

'I worked for the London and North Western, which is known as the Premier Line because it was the first main line railway ...'

Mr Belton looked at me expectantly, a gleam in his eye.

'... in the whole world!' I concluded, prompt on my cue.

'That's right, lad. At any rate, part of it was—the old London and Birmingham Railway from Euston to Curzon Street.'

'But you don't work on it now, do you, Mr Belton?'

'No, lad, I don't.'

'Didn't you like it?'

'Like it?'

Mr Belton stared at me incredulously.

'Did I like it? I loved it—every minute of it. But I had to give it up because I was taken poorly. That's why I came here to Nottingham, you see, lad — to take a less tiring job on the Midland.'

'Uncle G.B. is on the Midland.'

'He is that. It was him who told me all about you.'

'All about me?'

'Yes, about you and Susie and your ma. One day he came to see me when I was at home on the sick list and said he had relations coming from South Wales and wanted to find digs for them. He knew we had a spare room, and a bit extra coming in might help, like—and so, here you are! Do you like being here?'

'I like being here with you, Mr Belton.'

'And I like being here with you, Cliff. If you come often you could soon know as much about railways as me.'

'I'd like to come often, Mr Belton.'

'That's the spirit! How would you like to lend me a hand sometimes, eh?'

'You mean—help you when you're making engines and carriages?'

'That's right.'

'Oh, yes, Mr Belton!'

'That's settled, then. We'll say you're Assistant Mechanical Engineer, shall we?'

I nodded, thrilled.

'Now, before you take over your new duties', said Mr Belton, 'I think you ought to inspect the motive power and rolling stock in our possession, don't you?'

'Yes, Mr Belton.'

'Come on, then.'

He caught me by the sleeve of my jersey and took me on a conducted tour of his collection.

'Most of what we've got is L.N.W.R. stock,' he said, 'because that's my favourite railway.'

'Is that because it's the best railway?'

'Yes. Didn't I tell you it was the Premier Line? That means the first. Here's an early model—Allan and Trevithick's *Columbine* of 1845, the first of what was called the Crewe type of locomotive—here's *Jennie Deans*, one of F. W. Webb's engines—they were called Cauliflowers: yes, I thought that would make you laugh—Ramsbottom's *Lady of the Lake*, a pretty engine, that one—two more of Webb's: a Jumbo 2-4-0 and a Greater Britain compound 2-2-2-2—and here's'—there was a grin in Mr Belton's voice—'and here's a nice pair of Bloomers.'

I stared hard at the two engines he pointed out to me, red with bright brass domes and both exactly alike except that one had slightly larger wheels than the other. Why were they called Bloomers? There were two kinds of bloomers: one kind was often joked about by Mrs Belton—and these engines certainly bore no resemblance to them; it must be the other kind that was meant. . . .

'Do you mean they were mistakes, Mr Belton?'

'No, they weren't mistakes, Cliff. They were very good engines, very good engines indeed—worked the crack expresses. They were called Bloomers because, well, look at the wheels, son.'

I looked.

'They're all exposed,' continued Mr Belton. 'Like the ladies' legs were when they wore trousers.'

I thought how funny a lady would look wearing Sid Byron's bell-bottomed trousers, dribbling a tin down Carlyle Road.

'I didn't know ladies wore trousers,' I said.

'They don't now,' Mr Belton said. 'They did once, though, in the olden days. I never saw them—it was long before my time. Still,' he continued reflectively, 'it's getting on for quite a while since I first joined the L.N.W.R. I was a proper nipper when I did that.'

'Were you as old as me?'

'Just a wee bit older. I'd always wanted to be on the L.N.W.R. and as soon as I left school I went to Crewe station and got a job. I had my first long trousers on—talking of trousers—and a stiff celluloid collar and a trilby hat. I felt like a real toff. But all I was wanted for was making tea and running errands. But I moved up.'

'Where to, Mr Belton?'

'The Corridor.'

'The Corridor?' I repeated, puzzled.

'Yes. That was our name for the West Coast Express from London to Scotland—because in those days, you see, when I was a young man, corridors all the way through a train from beginning to end were a bit of a novelty. That was a fine train, I can tell you.'

'Did it go at sixty miles an hour?'

'Sixty miles an hour? Faster—much faster! I say, lad—how would you like to come up on to the footplate with me—for a trip to the North? Eh?'

'On the Corridor?'

'Yes, on the Corridor.'

'I'd love it, Mr Belton! I'd love it!'

'Up you come, then.'

Mr Belton placed his hand under my elbow and eased me closer to him.

'Let's say our engine's one of Webb's 2-2-0's, a hundred and eighty pounds boiler pressure. See, the needle's showing a hundred and eighty pounds now and steam's blowing off at the safety valves. The platform inspector has blown his whistle and all we're waiting for is the guard's green flag. Are you looking out, fireman?'

'Yes, Mr Belton.'

'Don't say "Yes, Mr Belton". Say "Yes, driver".'

'Yes, driver.'

'Did you say "Right away, mate"?'

'No, Mr Belton.'

'Fireman, you must say "Right away, mate. . . ."'

'Right away, mate,' I sang out.

'Right away it is! Regulator handle across the quadrant plate —just a few notches at first—cut-off at eighty per cent—we're moving!—four hundred tons of us are on the move out of Euston—gradually I open up a few more notches—easy does it— too much at one go causes wheel-slip—now it's full regulator and full cut-off for the Camden Bank!—up we go—fireman, look after that sanding gear—this is where we need it . . .'

'Right you are, driver,' I called out.

'Incline here is one in seventy for almost a mile—up we tramp—engine panting, blowing out black smoke, spitting red cinders—up we plod, foot by foot—it's a stiff climb, is the Camden Bank—has to be, to clear the Regent's Canal—but here we are going through Camden Town and once past Camden Town the line's as level as a saucer of tea—Willesden Junction—now I can bring the cut-off back a few notches and we go lolloping along a treat—we're touching sixty as we go through the fields at Harrow—over sixty now—I can ease back the regulator—it's a picnic for footplate men, this line of Robert Stephenson's from London to Brum—fine grading, easy curves—he had to dig through millions of yards of rock and earth to make it so flat and good, though—passing Hemel Hempstead—now the engine's got hold of 'em — we're doing well over sixty, fireman — approaching Tring Cutting—rattling over the viaduct—Leighton Buzzard, Bletchley, Wolverton—now Roade Cutting—fireman, look out for Kilsby Tunnel . . .'

'Kilsby Tunnel ahead, driver . . .'

'Right you are, fireman—now we roar into Kilsby Tunnel— it took two and a half years to build this tunnel, fireman—it's as black as the inside of a Kodak—the smoke and the steam make you choke—see it swirling in the light from the fire-hole door—there's such a din I can't hear myself speak—screw up your eyes, fireman, and watch out for a pin-point of light in front—see it?—it grows bigger—soon we'll be out in the sunlight again—and here we are! rubbing our eyes—now it's as quiet as if a door had been shut to keep out the noise—and on we go, racing along the straight, leaning round curves, comfy as a car ride—Rugby, Birmingham—keep your eyes on the signals, fireman . . .'

'Right you are, driver . . .'

'. . . and now we're running over the old Grand Junction section—all's fine until Madeley Bank—that's a three-mile pull at 1 in 77—a longer cut-off and open regulator gets us up Madeley—and now a nice fall from the summit as we go coasting down to Crewe—good old Crewe!—and from Crewe there's the little hump of 1 in 135 to Acton Grange Junction and down to Warrington—nearly full cut-off up to Boar's Head now—Preston, Lancaster—and now we're on the stiffest section of the trip—the old Lancaster and Carlisle Railway's line up the Lune Valley, the Pennines to the east of us and the Lake District to the west—thirteen miles of steady climbing from Milnethorpe through Kendal to Grayrigg, then only a couple of level stretches near Low Gill and Tebay before we're on a gradient of 1 in 75 over Shap Fell—fireman, it's grunting and pounding and gasping higher and higher until our engine's up in the sky and we're dizzy and *praying* for the long float down to Penrith and Carlisle—we can't hold on a minute longer!—and we top the hill—just in time!—and we drift down, thanking God, towards Penrith, our fire low, pressure falling, regulator at the first port, cut-off back, until I put on the brakes outside Carlisle and here we are, fireman, tired and dirty, but almost in Scotland—open your nostrils wide, Cliff, draw in the bracing air and put your head back—can't you feel the brogue of the Highlands blowing into your face, eh?'

10

The Wonderful Tin Fish

HAVING, with such delightful consequences, solved the mystery of the Beltons' front parlour I became a regular visitor to it, being taken on by Mr Belton, according to his promise, as Assistant Mechanical Engineer. I guarded the glue pot, to watch out for the moment when the slabs of inedible toffee turned to brown malodorous fluid; I held strips of metal in place while Mr Belton soldered them; I fetched templates and micrometers and files and screwdrivers; I handed him dies and taps, reamers and punches; I collected up and put away nuts and bolts and brass rodding and rivets; I cleaned paint brushes.

I enjoyed the responsibility of handling these tools and materials, but I enjoyed even more watching Mr Belton's hands and listening to his talk. Although poor health had made Mr Belton's fingers as knobby as a cane they possessed a workman's matter-of-fact competence; as grimy as a grate at their tips, their long nails were indispensable for levering up tongues of steel and copper and poking escaped components out of inaccessible hiding-places; and they made excellent tweezers for holding the heads of mettlesome bolts while the nuts were being screwed on and for nipping the ends of wires and pulling them through their appropriate holes. To manicure an artisan is to disable him.

As for talk, Mr Belton was my Homer. For hour after hour, sometimes in the day and sometimes in the evening, we sat in a front room that shone with the glamour of the golden age and shook with the triumphal march of legendary heroes. Enchanted and entranced, I heard tales of feats, endurances, and giants: of the crossing of Chat Moss, the conquest of Kilsby Tunnel, the Rainhill Trials, the Battle of the Gauges, the Railway Races; I heard of Richard Trevithick who built the first practical railway

66

locomotive, of the primitives John Blenkinsop and Timothy Hackforth, of George Stephenson the pioneer and Robert Stephenson the successful engineer, of John Ramsbottom the genius of Crewe, of Thomas Russell Crampton who was not without honour save in his own country. Except in moments of exaltation —and they were not few—Mr Belton's narrative style was that of a Midland plainsman, slow, honest, utilitarian. He spoke veritable prose, but I heard veritable poetry—epics and sagas, fables and fantasies that made me quake with the dark roll of drums and shiver with the sensuous excitement of strings and flutes. My mind became a roundhouse of knowledge. I learned what call-boys were, and fire-droppers, and boiler-washers. I learned that at one time the Midland Railway's trains used to arrive paradoxically at the Great Northern's King's Cross Station. I learned why booking offices were named booking offices, what Müller's Lights were, what Castleman's Snake was. I learned that plate-layers were called plate-layers because in the early days of colliery lines rails were made of wood and men were employed to lay metal plates on them to give them greater durability; I learned that permanent way is called permanent way to distinguish it from the impermanent way laid during the construction of a new railroad. My mind became a bazaar of splendid technical arcana: flying junctions, ruling gradients, four-foots and six-foots, cross-heads and shoes, blast pipes, superheater headers, soot blowers, gudgeon pins, eccentrics, cranks. And as I went about the house and the streets I recited the lovely lyrical lines that I knew by heart: the Vale of Rheidol Railway, the Great North of England Railway, the Swindon, Marlborough, and Andover, the Newport, Abergavenny and Hereford, the London, Chatham and Dover, the Kendal and Windermere, the Preston and Wyre, the Burry Port and Gwendreath Valley, the Highland, the Cornwall, the Taff Vale, the Wirral, the Barry, the Birkenhead.

As I remember, we did an astonishing amount of work in that best parlour in Carlyle Road, even though Mr Belton was a very sick man and had to visit the doctor every other day. On these doctor's days he and I set out from the house together in the early morning, in clear sunlight or chilling mists, keeping each other company and discussing our Enormous Project. This was the construction of a complete railway—not simply a series of immobile scale models such as we were building at present, but a *working* railway with locomotives operated by steam power, extensive rolling stock for passengers and goods, sidings, marshalling yards, tunnels, embankments, viaducts, bridges, and stations, with a practical signalling system and—as a romantic extravagance—equipment for the automatic collection and delivery of mailbags while the trains were in motion. We walked and talked, gazing at visions, until it was time for us to part, he to the surgery, I to school.

I had been going to school for some time. The school I attended was an elementary school, a box of pink bricks and green-framed windows that stood near Rectory Road where Uncle G.B. and Auntie George lived. I was called 'a scholar' and the class of which I was a member was 'a standard'. We learned to read *The Water Babies* and *The King of the Golden River*, practised copper-plate handwriting with malicious steel nibs, made pastel drawings of houses and flowers on brown paper, worried at mental arithmetic, and were taught to sing from a couple of yards of printed oil-cloth unrolled and slung humpily over the blackboard and called, mysteriously, *The Modulator*.

Before I had been promoted to a standard I had been in the Infants' School. Here, under our headmistress, a matronly martinet called Miss Kirshop, we five-year-olds were trained in a stern regard for the responsibilities of life. In the big hall we sat cross-legged on the floor like pious little tailors and were talked at by Miss Kirshop; and when she stopped talking at us we got to our feet and sang national songs and hymns:

> What can I do for Eng-land
> Who has do-one so much for me?

we asked anxiously; and with fervent conviction piped our respective answers:

> One of her faithful child-ren
> I can a-and I will be!

I love her dunes and head-lands,
Her vill-a-ges so fair;
Her cott-a-ges and cast-les,
Her gree-een fields ev'rywhere.

Sometimes the patriotic theme was expounded in a variant song:

Above the throne of England
May fortune's star long shine!
And round the sacred bulwarks
The olive branches twine.
Among our ancient mountains,
And from our lovely vales—
Oh, let the prayer re-echo:
God bless the Prince of Wales!

But patriotism, as we all know, is not enough: it must pass away with all earthly things. And what then? In this extremity Miss Kirshop did not fail us: mortality, she instructed her congregation, has its hopeful sequel. And so, with an emotion of overwhelming relief and gratitude, we sang out in soprano and treble:

There's a home for little children
Above the bright blue sky. . . .

and hoped that some foretaste of our reprieve would be immediately enjoyable. But no, Miss Kirshop hadn't finished with us yet. Before she allowed us to escape to our lessons we had to sing a song that recommended the prudent use of time-tables:

So here hath been dawning
Another blue day:
Think wilt thou let it
Slip useless away?

and when we had finished thankfully we went off to be educated until our dutiful day was done and we piled our little yellow chairs on our little yellow desks and with our eyes closed and our palms pressed together stood before the chairs and the desks as though they were deities and prayed, while the late afternoon sun sloped through the chalk-sprinkled and plasticine-scented air in beams that alighted on the parquet flooring in oval brightnesses and lay strewn upon it like glowing raffia mats.

One lovely summer morning, just as we were getting ready to go to school, a most extraordinary thing happened—Susie and I were given grown-up permission to play truant! It happened in this way. For some time Mr Belton had been getting worse instead of better and spent hours shut in his room, too miserable to see even me. For days together I had no contact with him except through his coughing, which I heard coming through the wall that divided his front room from our kitchen. On this particular morning I had seen him briefly before he had gone off to catch an early train to Birmingham where he had an appointment with a specialist. He had been gone an hour, and now Susie and I were waiting for our lunches to be packed up—lunch at the elementary school was a break of ten minutes at eleven—when into the kitchen walked a man! He was a stranger! He was a sailor! He said he'd come to take us all out for the day! He'd brought presents for Susie and me!

Susie's present was a cardboard shop with miniature bottles of real suckable sweets. Mine was a fishing-rod, almost a real man's rod, made of sections of cane that you fitted together: it had a cork handle, a length of gut loaded with shot just above the hook, a quill float, and a silk line that wasn't knotted to the end of the rod but was threaded through a series of brass rings to a big reel that could be rotated with a proper ratchety noise.

'Hurry up! Let's go! Get ready!' the sailor shouted to us as we gloated over our gifts. 'I'm your Uncle Sam!'

He was a tall, broad man, with a red neck and black greased hair that gleamed like a polished boot.

'But we've got to go to school,' I protested reluctantly.

'If we're not there soon the School Board Man will come after us,' Susie whispered fearfully.

The School Board Man was the Schools Attendance Officer, whose job was to investigate absences and round up truants: he was the terror of all the boys and girls in the neighbourhood.

Uncle Sam got into a crouching posture, like a boxer's, and put up his fists. He shot out his left and then followed it with a right hook to the side of an invisible head.

'That's what I'll do to the School Board Man if he comes

here,' he shouted angrily to Susie, winking at Mrs Belton. 'I'll give him what for, all right. I'm not the skittles champion of the Nottingham Navy for nothing.'

Mrs Belton was partly cross and partly uneasy.

'You can't encourage them to stay away from school, Sam,' she remonstrated.

'Why not? It won't do them any harm. In fact, it will do them a lot of good. On a day like this it's much better to be out of doors than cooped up in a stuffy classroom. You'd like to come out for the day, wouldn't you, petty officer?' he asked me.

'Yes,' I nodded eagerly. I was keen to try out my fishing-rod.

'There you are!' Uncle Sam said. 'That decides the matter.'

'Their mother won't like it,' Mrs Belton complained.

'I'll explain to her,' Uncle Sam said authoritatively. 'I'll take full responsibility.'

Mrs Belton still looked unconvinced. Uncle Sam laughed and put an arm around her waist and with his free hand smacked her behind.

'Come on, old girl,' he cajoled. 'Don't be a wet blanket on a nice sunny day like this!'

A tiny smile crept out from under the wet blanket and ran across Mrs Belton's face.

'Sam,' she said confidentially, 'I'm thinking of us. Those two will be on our hands, you know. We won't have much freedom.'

'There'll be plenty more days,' Uncle Sam said. 'And nights, old girl,' he added, hugging her close and kissing her neck.

'Oh, do give over, Sam!' Mrs Belton pleaded, now laughing. 'You're tickling my fanny.'

Uncle Sam released Mrs Belton with a final kiss on the ear and turned to Susie and me.

'Shake a leg there! Get into your Sunday slops! Hurry up!' he bellowed to us genially.

Curiously enough, Mrs Belton was already dressed for going out—that is, she was in her Sisterhood clothes—just as though she'd been expecting the sailor to call this morning: but Susie and I had to hurry upstairs to make ourselves suitable for a holiday. That meant that Susie put on a clean frock decorated with French knots and a yellow straw hat with a chaplet of pink-and-blue flowers encircling the crown; and I exchanged my school jersey for a grey flannel shirt that was almost new and was still pleasingly fragrant with shop-dressing.

'We're going to Colwick, where the cheeses come from!' Uncle Sam beamed when we got downstairs. 'Ready?'

'Oh, yes!' we answered jubilantly.

Colwick! Colwick, where the cheeses came from! I was truly thrilled, because Colwick cheeses, with their sour and dewy compact coolness that cut and bit clean and didn't leave a glutinous coating on the knife and the palate like ordinary cream cheeses but sped down your throat like a custard on a slide, why, they and Scott's Emulsion were the gastronomic joys of my life!

I have never since tasted such fabulous cheeses as those dazzling white castles that we fetched from the milkman's house in the darkening summer evenings, bearing them in front of us like crowns on cushions, cheeses as large and round as dinner plates, their surfaces wrinkled and chequered all over with the imprint of muslin cloth, oozing and glistening in the late slanting sun and imprisoning in their squat towers the piquant essence of all the dairies in Nottingham.

'If everybody's ready', urged Uncle Sam cheerily, 'let's go.'

We were all marching out of the front door when I remembered something:

'I want a jam jar to put the fishes in!'

Uncle Sam looked apologetically at Mrs Belton.

'He's right, you know.'

'Aren't we optimistic!' sniffed Mrs Belton. But, making an irritable clack-clack with her tongue, she went back to the scullery to fetch a clean jam jar.

While we were waiting by the front door Uncle Sam, rearing above Susie and me like a mainmast, felt that he had to make small talk and, looking down from one of us to the other, asked:

'And how old are we, eh?'

I was occupied with my fishing tackle, trying to unwind the gut and shot from off a shuttle-shaped bobbin, so Susie answered for us both:

'I'm five and a half. He's six and seven months. We're twins.'
Uncle Sam roared with laughter.

'You *are* a comical thing!' he said. 'You deserve a present for that. Let's see if I can find a new penny in my pocket.'

In a moment his massive hand was full of riches, which he turned over with an equally massive blunt-ended thumb and forefinger.

'Not a this year's,' he informed us, searching the coins. 'But here's a last year's—it'll buy just as many goodies as a this year's. See how it shines.'

He threw it up into the air, caught it, squatted on his heels, and pressed the penny into Susie's palm. Susie smiled, pleased to have the bright coin; but she hadn't laughed when Uncle Sam had laughed, obviously unable to see anything funny in what she had said. I was puzzled by Uncle Sam's laughter, too. I was also puzzled by Uncle Sam himself. Was he really our Uncle Sam? If so, why hadn't Mother ever told us about him? And why had he never come to see us when Mother was at home? Still, I decided after fairly lengthy reflection, if unexpected uncles arrived so efficiently equipped with presents they ought to be welcomed uncritically—the more the merrier, in fact.

'Well, here's the jam jar, *at last*,' Mrs Belton announced, returning from the scullery. 'Had to wash it and dry it and all.' She held the jar out to Uncle Sam. 'Here, do a sailor's knot, Sam.'

Uncle Sam took the jar and the piece of string that Mrs Belton had been fiddling with and, lassooing the jar under its rim, deftly attached a carrying loop to it.

'Here you are, Lord Nelson,' he said, giving the jar to me.

I took the jar from him and as we walked down the path swung it hopefully by its string handle.

'Do you know what this funny little girl told me just now?' Uncle Sam asked Mrs Belton, tilting his head at Susie. 'She said she's five and a half and Cliff's six and seven months and they're twins.' He started to laugh again, very loudly, and Mrs Belton joined in.

As we were going out of the gate I thought of something else that was very important. Quickly, before we left the garden behind us!

'Worms!' I cried in a desperate voice. 'We've forgotten the worms!'

'Worms?' repeated Mrs Belton, horrified. She spoke as though I had suggested taking worms to eat for our lunch. 'Do you mean to say we're going to have *worms* crawling all over us on this outing?'

'We won't be wanting anything to do with worms,' Uncle Sam assured her quickly.

'But, Uncle Sam——' I began in bitter disappointment.

Uncle Sam cut me short.

'Look!' he said.

He rummaged in the pocket of his blue flannel blouse and brought out a fish.

'I'm going to buy the bosun here some maggots and the lady in the shop is going to put them in here,' he said, flourishing the fish under Mrs Belton's nose.

This was too much for Mrs Belton.

'Maggots!' she screamed. 'Maggots! Do you mean to stand there and tell me that we've got to carry a lot of stinking maggots about with us?'

'You've got to have maggots for coarse fishing,' Uncle Sam explained patiently.

'Coarse fishing!' shrilled Mrs Belton. 'Coarse is hardly the word for it, if you ask me. I should say it's downright disgusting!'

'It's only this once, Myrtle,' Uncle Sam said in a soothing tone. 'Just for the nipper to try out his new fishing-rod. Just this once, Myrtle dear.'

A little mollified, but determined not to give in immediately, Mrs Belton stalked ahead of us towards the front garden gate. Uncle Sam held out the fish for me to see it, prising off a lid and flashing before me the fish's silver inside.

'Pop it into your jar, admiral,' he said, giving me a wink.

So I popped it into my jar—a tin shaped and coloured like a glowing goldfish.

We travelled to Trent Bridge in one of the West Bridgford

Urban District Council buses. These buses of the twenties weren't as dignified as mahogany sideboards, like modern buses, not shock-absorbed, streamlined, silenced, insulated, air-conditioned: they shook and rumbled and rattled in the way that really co-operative machinery should. When you set your foot on one of these vehicles and felt your body vibrating as the bus's body vibrated you knew that you had entered into a partnership of power, and that knowledge gave you pleasure.

When we reached Trent Bridge and I saw the river running lush and wide between its scrubbed doorsteps I thought of fishing and of my maggots.

'All right, all right,' sang Uncle Sam, and made us walk a long way until at last he led us into a workman of a street—a footway of leaden stone setts flanked by smoky brick walls from which came whirring and stamping noises. Half way up this street there was a shop, its front hung with stained metal and paper advertising signs which were bent and peeling as though the building was suffering from some sort of scaly skin disease. In the window—which wasn't a shop window but an ordinary house window—there was a piece of cardboard on which was written in modest pencil: 'MAGGOTS'.

Uncle Sam and I went into the shop, leaving Susie and Mrs Belton to wait outside. It was what was known as a general shop, dealing in soap powder and salt, loaves and firewood, sausages and paraffin, starch and prunes, corned beef, margarine, sago, mouse-traps, bath-bricks, candles, mops, pails, and clothes-pegs, with cricket bats and fishing tackle as sidelines. I watched with great interest as the lady behind the counter removed a cloth from a bin that stood on two barrels and shovelled up maggots with the sort of scoop that I had seen grocers use for sugar. The maggots had been dwelling in easy circumstances and were fat, waxy white bloated bodies tapering to shining specks of faces, as sleek and soft as big-business men. They squirmed, lashed their tails, writhed, and frenziedly knotted themselves up in alarm as they were rammed into the scoop and measured carefully into my tin; there, they waved startled heads above the rim and peered with bewildered terror into the smelly air. Then the lid was snapped down on them, and with the living fish in my jar we went out of the shop.

Back at Trent Bridge we joined a midsummer queue on the landing stage to wait for the steamer that would take us to Colwick. The railed landing stage, with its wooden floor and its prow lapped by the wavelets of the River Trent, was a boat in itself, especially as it rose and sank gently on the swell. We all began to feel very gay—even Mrs Belton smiled at Susie and me and seemed to have forgotten about the maggots—because the sun was shining and we were on the water and everybody was wearing carefree clothes. Among the straw boaters and waspish blazers and white flannels and the flowery frocks and hats Uncle Sam stood out conspicuously, a colourful foreigner in his navy blue uniform. I studied him carefully, from the saucy round hat to the protuberant buttocks and the trousers terminating in cones that completely hid his boots. He was Sid Byron enlarged, and I felt once again—how keenly I felt it!—that it must be a fine thing to be able to wear a sailor's suit with long trousers that flapped. But Mother had said that Royal Navy sailors like Uncle Sam weren't real sailors—and perhaps she was right. If Uncle Sam *was* a real sailor why wasn't he on a vessel trading in copra among the South Sea islands? Or rounding the Cape of Good Hope with a cargo of ivory? Why wasn't he with a ship bringing spices from the Caribbean? *If* he was a real sailor why was he in Nottingham, which was a funny place to be in, for a sailor, seeing that it wasn't a port? Yes, perhaps Mother was right.

So I turned from Uncle Sam to look at the other people surrounding us. I wasn't the only boy with a fishing-rod. Several of the other rods, I observed, were grander than mine—longer, with burly cork handles and reels the size of saucers. I felt the corrosive spirit of jealousy poisoning my bloodstream and I conceived the ambition to catch such a vast quantity of fish that every possessor of lordly equipment would smash it across his knee in despairing envy of my skill.

What surprised me most about the steamer, once we got on it, was its immaculacy. Its wooden cambered deck was as smartly ruled with planks as the painted tin boards of a toy boat; the lifebelts and lifeboats were as dazzling as new sheets; the bridge was a scoured chalk cliff; the brass rims of the port-holes blazed like haloes. When we went below everywhere smelled of Ronuk and Brasso, and the engine-room, where I had expected to see men slaving among cranks and flywheels in oil and coal and hair-reddening light, was as clean and commodious as a butcher's shop on early closing day. Two men in unblemished blue uniforms walked about on stainless steel and attended to gauges, dials, and levers; and the nearest approximation to the inferno I had expected was a ferric monster that, caged within brass rails on which you could lean and look, toiled incessantly with silvery Brobdingnagian limbs in a pit below the floor.

After a time of gazing at this mesmeric monotonous motion I decided that it was more invigorating above among the crowds. There, in the breeze, kneeling on a kind of park bench that ran continuously along the ship's bulwarks, I looked overboard. The Trent wasn't a townee now, forced to trot, curbed by straight stone embankments, but was running wild through fields and under trees. I leaned out and listened to the paddle-wheels slapping the water and turning it to milk, then watched, farther off, the blue-and-green layers of the waves meeting and inter-folding with the smoothness of oiled sheets of silk.

Sometimes we met other steamers and communicated on watery wavelengths that made both boats rock, and sometimes at five knots we raced past stationary houseboats. Once we passed a bathing-station where boys at varying heights stood on diving-platforms and spring-boards like thin china figures in a cabinet; the majority of them wore abridged bathing-trunks—mere strings—and some wore no trunks at all: a few of these stood with their legs apart and exhibited themselves impudently at our steamer as it paddled by. Most of the people on our boat pointed at them (they were probably one of the best-known sights on the river) and laughed, but a few ladies blushed.

When we arrived at Colwick we went straight to a beach of shelving clay soil to fish. It was a lovely day. The warm air smelled like new bread. Above our heads a dozen swallows walked the high wire on outstretched wings. Uncle Sam showed me how to get my rod ready, how to pierce a squirming, reluctant maggot with my hook, how to cast. We were getting along famously, I thought, when Mrs Belton muttered something and Uncle Sam nodded and then said to me:

'Fill up your jar with river water, skipper, and then you'll be all shipshape.'

I did as he instructed, and then, with the jar of khaki water beside me waiting to receive my catch, and with Susie as a bored spectator, I began to angle. It was interesting at first, watching the red-and-white quill float downstream, keeping a vigilant eye on it for the moment when a giant cod or halibut would drag it under the water; but after a time the protracted staring made my vision blur and I began to feel weary through standing so long. Besides, I had several disappointments. Twice the float went under and I pulled in hopefully to find that it had merely been submerged by wavelets; and once it went joyfully down for about a foot but when I lifted my rod and reeled in I found a bicycle inner tube on my hook. Other anglers were about, mostly boys, and every now and then a rod would be raised smartly and a bit of flashing air speed in an arc to the bank. I saw my hope of fame vanish and began to feel desperate.

I looked round for Uncle Sam, to seek advice. He wasn't there.

'Uncle Sam!' I called.

'Uncle Sam!' Susie cried in her little voice.

'Uncle Sam!'

'Uncle Sam! Uncle Sam!'

'Mrs Belton.'

The fishing boys looked at us and grinned, but no Uncle Sam or Mrs Belton appeared. Susie began to cry. I took her by the hand and we wandered off. We walked quite a long way from the river, up a path and along a road, keeping a look-out for naval blue and carrot hair. I began to feel miserable and frightened. Suppose we were really lost? Would I be able to find my way, with Susie, back to Carlyle Road? It was a long way. Would I be able to manage the steamer and the bus? And I hadn't got any money, so how would I be able to pay for our tickets? Should we have to go and give ourselves up to the police?

At last, as we were walking past a kind-looking lady sitting on a bench, the lady stopped us and inquired what was the matter.

'Have you seen Uncle Sam?'

'Perhaps I have, dear,' the lady smiled, stroking Susie's hair, 'but I wouldn't have known him if I had. You'd better tell me what he looks like.'

'Have you seen Mrs Belton, then?'

'What does Mrs Belton look like?'

'Uncle Sam is a sailor,' I explained.

'A sailor? Well, it shouldn't be difficult to find *him*, if he's a sailor. Let's all go and look, shall we?'

'Uncle Sam's not a proper sailor,' I said.

'Not a proper sailor? Do you mean he isn't wearing his uniform?'

'Oh, no, I don't mean that. He's got sailor's clothes on.'

'Then what do you mean? Do you mean he's wearing fancy dress?'

I shook my head.

'No. I mean he's in the Royal Navy.'

The lady looked mystified.

'But if he's in the Royal Navy he's a proper sailor, isn't he?'

'No.'

The lady seemed to be at a loss for a moment. Then she said:

'Never mind. We'll go and look for a man wearing sailor's clothes, whether he's a proper sailor or not. Is that all right?'

'Yes,' I answered, feeling that this was a very satisfactory solution.

The lady took each of us by the hand and led us away on our search. But first she took us to a kiosk and bought us two glasses of lemonade and two twopenny bars of Cadbury's nut milk chocolate and that made us both happier.

'Where did you last see your Uncle Sam and Mrs Belton?' the lady inquired.

'When I was fishing,' I answered.

'In the river,' Susie amplified.

'That means you last saw them when you were fishing in the

D

river, I suppose,' the lady said. 'But it could mean', she went on, smiling down at Susie, 'that when you last saw them Uncle Sam and Mrs Belton were *in* the river. Bathing, I hope,' she added with a laugh.

Susie and I looked at her blankly.

'Never mind. I was only teasing. Now, let's go, shall we?'

We nodded our agreement. All the time as we walked the lady talked to us.

'I think the best thing is to make our way back to the river. You see, while you two have been wandering about looking for your uncle and Mrs Belton they've probably been wandering about looking for you. In that way, people can go on missing each other for hours. Much better for one of the parties to stay still in one place, preferably somewhere well known to both. That increases the chance of discovery by fifty per cent.'

What was she talking about? Still, if she could help us to get joined to Uncle Sam and Mrs Belton again I didn't much mind whether I could understand her or not. And she did. Quite suddenly, as we were passing a house printed all over with words—TEAS WITH HOVIS THE RULE OF THE ROAD, CYCLISTS' TOURING CLUB, ROSS'S BELFAST GINGER ALE, MAZZAWATTEE TEA, NEEDLER'S CHOCOLATES, SUNRIPE CIGARETTES—we saw Uncle Sam come running towards us from the front door.

'We thought they'd stay by the river until we went to fetch them,' he explained to the lady. 'Where's your rod, Admiral Benbow?' he asked me.

'I left it,' I answered guiltily, having forgotten all about it in my worry at being lost.

'On the bank? We'll have to go and fetch it, then, by and by —*if* it's still there.'

Uncle Sam thanked the lady for taking charge of us and then led us into the house. It was full of tables and chairs and people and dishes, and at one of the tables, with a cruet and a teapot and lots of cups and saucers and plates in front of her, sat Mrs Belton. Her face was flushed and she glared at us as we reached her table.

'What have you two been up to?' she snapped.

'We got lost,' I mumbled.

'You wouldn't have got lost if you'd done what you were told. Why didn't you do what you were told?'

'I don't know.'

'Well, I think it's a good spanking that you need, my lad. Your mother gives in to you too much. The end of a belt now and then would do you the world of good.'

Susie started to whimper. Mrs Belton was about to abuse her, too, when Uncle Sam interrupted.

'That'll do, Myrtle,' he said. 'They've had enough. We'll get 'em something to eat.'

He tickled Susie under the chin, and that made her smile and her large dark eyes opened wide.

'You'd like some lemonade, wouldn't you, duckie?' he asked her.

She nodded.

'And what about you, commander? Tea or lemonade?'

'Lemonade,' I said.

'Lemonade what?' snarled Mrs Belton.

'Lemonade, please,' I answered.

'That's better,' she grunted.

While we were waiting for the waitress to call at our table— the room was crowded and she was terribly busy—I looked around. Just as the outside of the house looked like the advertising section of a magazine, so did the inside. There were messages everywhere:

THIS IS THE

PLAICE

FOR FISH AND CHIPS

FLOATING KIDNEYS ANCHORED
IN OUR HOME-MADE MEAT PIES

YOUR PLEASURE IS OUR BUSINESS

The waitress side-stepped the importunate tables, carrying plates of sausages and chips, fish and chips, egg and chips,

tomatoes and chips, bacon and chips, rissoles and chips. I stared
hard at the plates.

'Uncle Sam. Do they make Colwick cheese here?'

'Shouldn't think so, commodore.'

'But this is Colwick, isn't it?'

'That's right.'

'Then why don't they make Colwick cheese here?'

'This is just a café. I don't reckon they make anything here—
except brass.'

'But you said just now this was Colwick.'

'Yes, this is Colwick. And this is where they make Colwick
cheese. But it doesn't follow from that that *everybody* in Colwick
makes Colwick cheese. Savvy?'

I said that I did.

'All the same,' he went on, 'though I don't suppose they make
Colwick cheese here, they might *sell* it. Sweetheart!'

He leaned forward to touch the waitress, who was just there
hurrying past our table, on the arm. She was a very pretty girl.

'Like to do me a favour, sweetheart?' he asked, holding her by
the wrist.

The girl rested her other hand—this happened to be one of the
rare moments when both hands were empty of dishes—on her
hip and looked Uncle Sam up and down, grinning.

'I might think it over, sailor.'

Uncle Sam shot a cautious glance at Mrs Belton, but she, having
drunk another cup of tea, had got over her bad temper and was
now beaming indulgently.

'Go on with you!' she laughed, wagging her finger at the
waitress in mock reprimand. 'How dare you give the glad eye to
my husband!'

The waitress smiled.

'Can I bring you anything, madam?'

'Well, yes. It's the boy. He wants some Colwick cheese.'

'Oh, dear!' The girl gave me a sympathetic glance. 'That's
just what we haven't got! Jelly, blancmange, jam tarts, chocolate
cake, ice-cream—but no Colwick cheese. Where do you come
from, sonny?'

'West Bridgford.'

'Well, you wait till you get back to West Bridgford. That's where you'll get Colwick cheese. Not here. We send every bit away as soon as it's made—there's such a big demand for it, you see.'

So Susie and I had lemon blancmange, damson jelly, and raspberry jam, with bread and butter.

'Eat up!' Uncle Sam soon called out. 'Time to go!'

Uncle Sam paid the bill at the

PAY HERE
PLEASE COUNT YOUR CHANGE BEFORE
YOU LEAVE THE PREMISES, OTHERWISE
THE MANAGEMENT CANNOT BE HELD
RESPONSIBLE FOR MISTAKES

desk and then, leaving Mrs Belton, Susie, and me standing in the doorway, went back into the café to tip the waitress. He was absent for quite a long time. Mrs Belton got impatient. When he eventually returned she asked crossly:

'Been helping with the washing up?'

'I had to go where you couldn't follow me,' he countered artfully. 'Now let's go and look for Cliff's fishing-rod.'

'What! Do you mean to say we've got to go trapesing back to the river bank again?'

'It's all right, old girl—it'll only take a few minutes.'

'What's the use, I'd like to know? It'll be gone by now.'

'Well, just let's go and make sure.'

'He would have to go and lose the blooming thing,' grumbled Mrs Belton, giving me a cuff as a kind of exclamation mark. 'Why can't you be well behaved like your sister?' she asked me. 'Nobody would think you'd had the same upbringing, you two.'

'Come on, Myrtle, old girl,' Uncle Sam coaxed, putting an arm around her and jollying her up. 'What's the time, eh?'

Mrs Belton gave a little smile and looked at the gold watch she wore suspended from a chain round her neck.

'Half past four.'

'Fine. That means they'll be open soon after we get back and we can go and have a couple before the old man gets in. How about it, love?'

'I'd like that, dear. You know I would.'

'Fine.'

They walked along arm in arm.

When we got back to the river bank we found that the fishing boys had vanished. But, miraculously, the rod was still there. The boys had been tampering with it, however, and the line was gone and the reel was broken. Still, I had recovered the rod and I was pleased. And Uncle Sam assured me that a new line would cost only a few pence and that he could mend the reel easily. So everything was all right.

The tin fish was there, too, hidden in the grass. I picked it up and dropped it with a splash into my jar of River Trent.

'You'll drown the maggots, midshipman!' warned Uncle Sam.

'And a good job, too!' declared Mrs Belton.

I left the tin in my jar of Trent water. The glass and the water combined to act as a magnifying lens, enlarging the tin fish until it was the size of a salmon. My salmon reminded me, painfully, of my ambition of a few hours ago—the desire to catch such a lot of fine fish that the boys with arrogant rods would be put to shame. The salmon in my jar—my plump, coruscating, prismatic, crimson salmon—did a great deal to compensate me for my failure to catch thousands of fishes and I stole proud glances at it as we walked along. I noticed that other people were glancing at it, too. As we made our way to the landing-stage, people continued to look, raising their eyes from the jar to me with astonishment. On the landing-stage, while waiting for the boat, the boys with the expensive rods looked most of all, staring at my enormous, wonderful fish with puzzled envy. But it was on the boat itself that I had my greatest triumph. I traversed the decks from stem to stern, holding up my jar and its catch as conspicuously as possible. I exulted. I was the prince of anglers, the champion of champions, bearing home the rarest fish ever to be taken in the River Trent! No, no! My fish was more than rare—it was unique!

I became aware that my cap was extremely tight, so I took it off and stuffed it into the pocket of my shorts.

The wonderful tin fish attracted attention all the way home to West Bridgford. We were half down Carlyle Road when I spotted Mrs Grudgings, the Beltons' next-door neighbour, appear at her front gate and come running—in her indoors apron —along the road to meet us. One or two other Carlyle Road residents, men and women, were also at their front gates showing an interest in us.

'What's up now?' muttered Uncle Sam.

Mrs Belton murmured an uneasy reply and hurried forward.

'I've been looking out for you, my duck,' Mrs Grudgings called when the two had drawn near enough for talk. 'Something's happened and I wanted to tell you so you wouldn't get a——' She paused mysteriously.

Uncle Sam and Susie and I now joined Mrs Belton and Mrs Grudgings in the middle of the road.

'What's up?' Uncle Sam repeated.

'It's Mr Belton. He's been taken badly.'

'What's he doing home at this time of day?' asked Mrs Belton. 'I thought——'

'I don't know anything about that,' Mrs Grudgings answered rather sharply. 'All I know is that Mr Belton came home and couldn't get in and so I asked him into my place for a cup of tea. I'd just turned my back to put the kettle on when he fell off his chair. It was such a shock!'

'Where is he now?' asked Mrs Belton.

'He's still in my house. I had to get the doctor. I didn't know what to do.'

'Did the doctor say what's wrong with him?' Uncle Sam put in.

'A stroke, he said.'

Mrs Belton shook her head and shrugged her shoulders.

'You'd better be getting along, Sam,' she advised.

'I'd like to come in and help, Myrtle. I wonder if——'

'No, I think it would be better if you didn't, somehow.'

'Perhaps you're right, under the circumstances.'

'Yes. You'd better get along.'

'Yes, I think I'd better, as things have turned out.'

So Uncle Sam went back the way he had come, while Mrs Belton, Susie, and I, accompanied by Mrs Grudgings, continued what had become for me a sad walk home.

I I

The Trip to the West

FOR ME, now, the house in Carlyle Road was a place of dreadful awe—I was daunted and yet impressed by Mr Belton's sudden, solemn illness and by the whispering drama of the brisk visiting doctors and the many tense conversations. The upshot of all the conferences and comings and goings was that Mr Belton's bed was brought down in pieces—he was too ill to be moved upstairs—and re-erected in the front room. So there he lay from this time onward, and to us in the kitchen he became an invisible throat-clearer on the other side of a wall. And quite soon the shock of his collapse wore off and the repetitious rasp of his gullet diminished into its place as one of the ignored sounds, sights, scents, of home.

The only person in the house who hadn't been greatly upset by Mr Belton's breakdown was Mrs Belton. She had done all that was required of her in the way of nursing and so on, but had never once stepped so much as one foot off the straight line of duty and at no time had she shown any of the concern that you would expect a loving wife to feel. The truth was, of course, that she wasn't a loving wife. Her affair with Uncle Sam had been going on for many months, the times of her meetings with him being, by a remarkable coincidence, identical with those of her visits to the Sisterhood. But the only sisterhood which Mrs Belton ever knew in her life was the sisterhood—and brotherhood—of the bars where she caroused with her friendly sailor.

All this I came to know later. I also learned later what had actually happened on the day of our trip to Colwick, where the cheeses came from. It seems that in Birmingham Mr Belton had run into an old colleague of his L.N.W.R. days who had found him a place on some sort of express freight train that had got him back into Nottingham a lot earlier than he had expected. Finding his house locked up he had accepted Mrs Grudgings's invitation into her kitchen, as she had truly informed us, but had there received information which had not been as restricted as Mrs Grudgings had made out. On the contrary, Mrs Grudgings told him everything she knew—she was an accomplished neighbour —maliciously, in detail, and with relish. The gossip disabled the weak Mr Belton like a blow.

After a few weeks he had recovered enough strength to make it possible for me to resume my visits to him. However, the prospect of seeing him again wasn't altogether welcome to me. In the six or seven weeks that had gone by since his collapse he had receded in my mind, becoming a person to be identified rather than recognized. His remote, reduced figure was masked in my thoughts by nearer, larger figures. Besides, his illness had removed him from the realm of everyday, setting him apart as abnormal, an elect, almost freakish being about whom I felt curious and at the same time fearful.

So, on the first of the new series of visits, I tiptoed into his room with trepidation. I'd been warned not to talk much or to stay long. The first thing I was aware of, after I had carefully closed the door behind me, was that the Venetian blinds were down, with the slats partly opened, so that the room seemed to be dozing with its eyes half shut. It was very quiet, very still. I stood near the door for a few moments to get used to the greenish dimness, then turned to the long, white shape that I knew to be the bed. Reverently, I stepped noiselessly forward to look at Mr Belton.

It was he himself who had asked for my visit, and he had therefore been prepared for my arrival, propped up on pillows. He was thinner and yellower than ever and his fingers were sticks. He smiled, and said in a voice like a wisp of smoke:

'Hallo, lad. Sit you down.'

'I'd rather stand up, thank you, Mr Belton.'

'That's all right.' He smiled again. 'Wish I could say that.'

There was silence. Then he said:

'But I'm on the mend.'

There was silence again. The bedclothes were tucked up underneath the mattress, giving me a clear view of under-the-bed secrets. There was dust felted into rolls like small fur tippets, a sock, a forgotten stiff collar, a sheet of newspaper, a chamber-pot. The chamber-pot had a rose on its side and was full to the brim.

'Yes, I'm picking up nicely,' Mr Belton said. 'Soon you and me'll be able to start work again.'

I nodded.

'Bet you're looking forward to that, eh, lad?'

I nodded.

'You've missed me and the engines, no doubt.'

I nodded.

'I dare say you'd like to take a look at the models again after all this time.'

I nodded.

'Go on, then, lad.'

I crept round the room—ill at ease, feeling somehow that I had to move in whispers—looking at the locomotives and coaches on their short lengths of track and gravel. Many were in shadow and difficult to see; all those not under glass wore jackets of dust; brass was brown. They looked strange. It was hard to believe that only a few weeks ago these engines were as personal and exciting to me as my birthday. What could I say?

I was wondering, staring at a Cauliflower—again, as I remembered it, the name seemed funny—when the door opened noisily and Mrs Belton came in.

'Time's up!' she said to me. 'You mustn't tire Mr Belton out any more with talking.'

She came and stood by the bed, with her hand resting heavily on my shoulder, and looked down upon her husband.

'He's sinking fast, the doctor says'—she spoke as if her husband were stone deaf—'so you mustn't tax what bit of energy he's got left. What we must try and do for him now, poor love, is to keep him quiet and comfy until the end comes. So out you go, nipper!'

'Come again soon, Cliff,' Mr Belton called feebly.

Mrs Belton bundled me before her into the dark passage.

I went in to see Mr Belton frequently after this. He enjoyed my visits, and they did him good. Every new day—probably to his wife's disappointment—found him a little stronger, with his eyes brighter and his lips regaining colour. His hands moved on the counterpane like a man's and not a patient's. He talked a lot and, as before, his technical and historical knowledge impressed and thrilled me. I became interested again in the neglected models and, under Mr Belton's direction, with brush, duster, wash-leather, and metal polish, I spick-and-spanned them so that the boilers and cabs of the engines and the sides and roofs of the carriages were as clean as scrubbed knee-caps and the brass fittings flared like lighthouses.

In Mr Belton's state of increasing health and optimism there was only one thing that depressed him and that was Railway Amalgamation. This, now due in a few months' time, was the consequence of the Railways Act of 1921, which provided that the hundred-odd separate railway systems of Great Britain were to be re-formed into four big combines—the L.M.S.R., the L.N.E.R., the G.W.R., and the S.R. Each combine, as Mr Belton explained to me, was to consist of Constituent Companies, that is, the larger lines in its territory, and Subsidiary Companies, the smaller lines. All these Companies, Constituent as well as Subsidiary, were to lose their identities in the digestive processes of four monster corporations. Mr Belton's pride and joy, the L.N.W.R., was to be swallowed by the L.M.S. This was a great grief to him, but what made it worse was the knowledge that while the name of the London and North Western was to disappear for ever, rubbed off the map overnight, that of the Great Western was to be perpetuated. Why, Mr Belton wanted to know, was the G.W.R. the only Constituent or Subsidiary Company— yes, the *only* one!—whose name had been chosen as that of one of the new groups? Why was the G.W.R. alone selected for immortality? If the *Great* Western, he asked indignantly—what was so great about it, eh?—why not the *London and North Western*? He was convinced that the villain was the G.W.R. itself, which, cocky and pushful as ever, had succeeded once again in shouting its name so loud that everybody had been forced to listen to it.

I tried—with fair success—to switch him from the gloomy line of L.N.W.R. humiliation to the sunny one of L.N.W.R. glory. With blunt, artful questions I encouraged him to reminisce, instruct, describe. And so he would speak to me of the magnificence of Euston Station which was, he said, like a Grecian temple in its beauty, with noble fluted columns and a name written up in letters of real gold; in the old days, he told me, it had the lovely title of Euston Grove and after that was Euston Square, but now everybody called it just Euston; and he would then describe to me the splendours of Euston Great Hall with its ceremonial staircase and its marble pillars, its statue of the great George Stephenson and its lofty panelled ceiling, the largest of its kind in the whole world; and he would recount to me L.N.W.R. exploits such as its news service during the American Civil War, when it kept a team of impatient trains flashing from Holyhead to London with the latest dispatches; and he would always find new tales to be told of the surprising history of Crewe, which one quiet day alighted like an iron raven on a farmer's fields and grew as the railway grew until it was a blackening, straddling, clamouring giant incubating the mightiest railway engineering works in the whole world.

Sometimes he asked me to read to him from his *History of the London and North Western Railway* or his *Railways of England* or sometimes out of a curious work called *Catechism of the Steam Engine*; at other times I read to him from one of his many bound volumes of *The Engineer* and *Railway Magazine*. I didn't understand all that I read, but I liked the pictures. Nor did I understand all that Mr Belton told me, but I was again elated by his words and again intoxicated by the names of men and engines that had for me the renown of artists and their master works. The impression went deep. Many years later I thought of Ramsbottom's *Lady of the Lake* and Leonardo's *Virgin of the Rocks* with equal respect, Allan and Trevithick's *Columbine* seemed more attractive to me than Beaumont and Fletcher's *Philaster*, and the fame of Webb's *Jupiter* was as stirring to me as Mozart's. The names of Matthew Kirtley, William Wordsworth, Thomas Gainsborough, Dugald Drummond, John Constable, Patrick Stirling, Joseph Beattie, Robert Burns, and William Stroudley all had an equal romantic chime for me because they all rang with the same syllabic music.

Autumn and winter came. Mrs Belton still insisted on Susie and me spending a lot of time out of doors.

'You mope in the sick-room too much, my lad,' she used to say to me. 'Get into the fresh air. Out you go!'

This was all right when the weather was fine, but when the pavements were wet and couldn't be chalked on or sat on, and even the birds stood motionless in the trees with their hands in their pockets and their shoulders hunched up, the winds made your skin goose-pimply and gave you a headache. In order to keep warm I sometimes persuaded Susie to run races with me up and down Carlyle Road, impersonating the trains on the rival West Coast and East Coast routes to Aberdeen in 1895. Sometimes we joined Pearl and Sid in sports such as jumping on to a small hill or heap of rubble and shouting:

> I'm the king of the castle
> And you're a dirty rascal,

fighting anyone who tried to pull us down. Another of these romps was 'What's the time, Mr Wolf?' in which we taunted Mr Wolf to leap out and catch us with the words:

> Mardy, mardy mustard
> Can't eat his custard,

'mardy' being an invaluable Midland dialect word comprising a variety of useful meanings—cowardly, goody-goody, maudlin, petulant, vain, spoiled.

As a rule, however, Sid and Pearl disdained such diversions. Sid preferred football played with a tennis-ball, and Pearl, who was now quite old, nine or even ten, considered them juvenile. She had her own sources of entertainment: stories about Englishmen, Irishmen, and Scotsmen, which she told us with giggles, and rhymes such as:

> The wind is on the rippy side
> So I am on the nippy side;
> The roads aren't on the grippy side
> But on the very slippy side
> This night in February:

> A wind that's on the lofty side,
> Or even on the wafty side,
> Puts you off the coughty side
> And keeps roads on the softy side
> And makes you feel all merry,

which she bawled into the polar blasts.

One day, shivering in my paper overcoat, I defeated my depression by inventing a wonderful game for myself. I remembered what Mr Belton had said : 'A railway isn't just carriages and a locomotive and a permanent way. It's a sort of door.' And so when I found Mrs Belton's door closed against me I opened Mr Belton's. As quick as thought there arrived in Carlyle Road a magnificent Corridor, of which I was the driver. I climbed on to the footplate of its engine, the latest and fastest express locomotive in the whole world. We were flashing across Turkestan at five hundred miles an hour. I moved the regulator handle several notches across the quadrant plate and we increased speed to one thousand miles an hour. We darted across the Tyrrhenian Sea, leapt the Appalachian Mountains, pounded the Argentinian pampas, hovered above Everest, crossed the Great Bear Lake, crossed the Sahara Desert, sped with cut-off down to ten per cent through Alexandria, Strasbourg, Rio de Janeiro, Rouen, Havana, Peshawar, Foochow, Wagga Wagga, Suva, Pago Pago and soared, soared, high, higher, accelerating, climbing, higher, highest, until it was impossible to tell whether the enormous flashes in the sky were sparks from our chimney or were the Pleiades.

Mr Belton continued to lie in bed in the front room. Mrs Belton's visits to the Sisterhood ceased. Now, she and Sailor Sam —Mother had explained to Susie and me that Sam wasn't a relation, so after the day at Colwick we didn't call him uncle any more—met and went about together quite openly. Sailor Sam had bought a motor-cycle, a twin-cylinder Douglas, and with his square collar fluttering behind him like a flag and his trouser-legs rippling he came regularly to the house on it, riding up to the front gate with a stupendous roaring and spitting of the engine. On these visits he never forgot to bring Susie or me a present—

a knife, a doll, a slave bangle, a pencil-box, a hair ribbon. But he never took me out fishing again. The wonderful tin fish he had given me got rusty and the colours peeled off: I longed to prise it open and peep inside to see what had happened to the maggots, but I daren't, for fear of meeting one insane survivor that would rear up from a stinking mass grave and glare at me with resentful, reproachful eyes. So, guiltily, I carried the noisome tin to a far field and buried it deep.

The battledore-and-shuttlecock, pancakes-tops-and-marbles season came round again. Mother announced that we were going to Newport Mon for Whitsun. From the time of this pronouncement to the day of departure I was so excited that I could hardly eat or sit still. But there was one thing that worried me. I knew that to get to Newport Mon we would travel by the Great Western—and how was I going to break this distressing news to Mr Belton? I felt that, coming on top of Railway Amalgamation, the information would be too much for him. And yet I was so eager to see Newport Mon that I would have travelled a million miles on the infamous G.W.R. if necessary. Besides, I was curious to inspect personally a line that had managed to inspire such a controversial reputation. I felt that I was a bounder, an ingrate, a traitor, a cad. I postponed and postponed my declaration.

I delayed so long that eventually Mr Belton mentioned the matter himself.

'Your mum says you're going away for a bit of a holiday,' he said to me one evening.

I felt my chest tighten and a pounding behind my ears. I was relieved at finding that the responsibility of broaching the subject had been suddenly taken from me; but I also felt ashamed of my lack of candour. I was afraid that Mr Belton would think me 'close'.

'Not like you to say nothing about it,' he went on. He cleared his throat. 'You've always been so open. Don't you want to go?'

Here was another dilemma! If I answered no I was being disloyal to my mother; if I answered yes I was being disloyal to Mr Belton. Oh, dear—and all because I didn't want to hurt people's feelings!

'I hear it's not a bad place where you're going. There's the castle, and the Transporter Bridge—that must be worth seeing, Cliff—and there's the mountains and the sea and the ships. You'll have a good time there, I reckon.'

'Yes, I reckon I will, Mr Belton.'

'Your mum says there isn't any beach there. Pity. You'd like to muck about on the sands, wouldn't you?'

'Yes I would, really,' I said.

'You'd like Morecambe.'

'That's on the L.N.W.R., isn't it?'

'It is, Cliff. Mrs Belton and I went there on our honeymoon. We used it as a jumping-off point for seeing the Lake District. We went to Ennerdale Water on the Cleator Joint Lines, we had a trip on the Ravenglass and Eskdale narrow-gauge railway, we went to Lake Windermere on the L.N.W.R. branch line from Oxenholme, and we travelled on the Furness Railway to Coniston and Ulverston. Those Furness trains were a treat—red engines and blue-and-white carriages. They were as gay as a rainbow after they'd been in the rain and the sun was shining on them.' He looked happy at the memory. 'Yes, we had a nice honeymoon. In those days, Cliff, I used to collect train rides same as you collect marbles.'

'Did Mrs Belton collect train rides, too?'

Mr Belton didn't answer for a while, then he shook his head and said:

'No, son. She was more interested in collecting inn signs.' He smiled at me. 'But to get back to Newport. Sands or not, you'll have all your folks to see there. Your auntie and uncle——'

'My Uncle Hobart Harry's got an arm he can screw off,' I interrupted.

'Unscrew,' Mr Belton remonstrated gently. 'You screw *on*.'

'And there's Grandma and Grandad. And', I continued eagerly, for surely Mr Belton would be very interested to know this, 'there's Uncle Glyn who's a signalman on the . . .'

I pulled myself up sharply, my blood surging again. How was I to tell him? And yet I would have to, sooner or later. I decided to be bold.

'. . . who's a signalman on the G.W.R.,' I said brazenly.

'Is he?' Mr Belton said, impressed. 'Then you're going to have a really good time, I can see.'

He had taken the hurtful information beautifully. In fact, in his unwell way he was looking very well indeed. I thought I could now reasonably take the risk of telling him everything.

'Mother and Susie and me are going to Newport Mon by the G.W.R.,' I said in a loud firm voice.

As I spoke I kept my eyes fixed on Mr Belton, half afraid that he would have an immediate relapse—or even die. But all that happened was that he laughed.

'Of course you are!' he chuckled. 'It's the chief line in that part of the country.'

I felt enormous relief. Why hadn't I told him before? Obviously, I'd given myself a lot of anxiety for nothing. He wasn't a bit upset.

'I've never been to Newport, though, myself,' he continued, 'nor Plymouth, or Torquay, or Bournemouth. It's ridiculous, I dare say, but I somehow found the stations on the L.N.W.R. were the ones I liked best. And now the L.N.W.R.'s gone and the G.W.R.'s still with us'—there was a long pause—'but I don't suppose I'll ever travel on it now.'

He turned his head on the dingy pillow and looked at me with a smile.

'So you see, Cliff, that's something you can do for me—you can take a trip on the Great Western and then come back and tell me all about it.'

'Yes I will, Mr Belton. Do you think I'll see Brunel?'

The name of Isambard Kingdom Brunel occurred so often in the books and magazines that I read aloud to Mr Belton that I never thought of him as a defunct historical figure like Julius Caesar or Simple Simon. In my mind's eye I saw him fiercely alive, a dynamic little man with a big hat and a big cigar, hammering away at one of his ample G.W.R. tracks, stopping every now and then to make hasty sketches in a notebook, suddenly hopping on to a passing G.W.R. engine and driving it tremendously fast for several miles, and then just as suddenly leaping off on to a

G.W.R. station and striding up and down the platform bellowing orders to the station-master and passengers.

'No,' said Mr Belton. 'He's dead and gone. Like most of what he did for the G.W.R.'

'Won't I be able to see any of his inventions?'

'No. They were all too daft to last. Like that cock-eyed idea of making trains go without engines.'

'What other cock-eyed things did he do?'

'There were so many of them. I don't rightly know where to begin.'

'Tell me the daftest, then.'

'The daftest? Well, I suppose the daftest was Broad Gauge.'

'You mean seven-foot track instead of four-foot?'

'That's right. That was really barmy, that was.'

'Why was it the daftest, Mr Belton?'

'Well, it meant that Great Western trains couldn't run on other company's lines. If you wanted to go on a long journey in Brunel's day you had to keep getting in and out of carriages all the time, changing from a broad train to a narrow train and then back to a broad one again. Break of gauge they called it.'

'Brunel must have been a blithering idiot.'

'That's about it, Cliff. He couldn't see farther than the end of his cigar. Not like George Stephenson—*he* was a man of vision. When he built the Stockton and Darlington—and that was the only railway in the whole world then, mind—he knew that one day England would be covered by railways and therefore advised the new companies to make all their tracks the same width so that later on they would be interconnected. It took real imagination to see into the future like that, eh?'

'Yes, Mr Belton. Can't you remember any other cock-eyed things that Brunel did?'

'Well, he didn't believe in sleepers, so laid his track without them. Result: he had to pull the track up and start all over again, *with* sleepers. And he had rum ideas about engines, too. Result: the early Great Western engines were so unpunctual that the company had to scrap all its time-tables. But the worst thing was Broad Gauge—that did the most harm to the railways.'

'Will we travel on Broad Gauge to Newport Mon?'

'No, lad—the G.W. was converted to Standard Gauge a long time ago. And converted is the right word, too—it saw the light at last and undid Brunel's mischief. So nowadays it isn't such a bad railway as all that.' He grinned. 'Mind you, I'm not saying it's a patch on the L.N.W.R.' He listened. 'Isn't that your mum?'

'Yes, Mr Belton. I've got to go to bed.'

'See that cash-box?'

He pointed to a black metal box on a shelf under his books.

'Yes,' I said.

'Fetch it here, then, lad.'

I took the box to him, depositing it on the bedclothes covering his chest. It rose and fell with his heavy breathing. He unlocked it and took out sixpence.

'Here, Cliff. Take this and buy yourself a nice big copybook and a sharp blacklead. When you go to Newport I want you to keep a watch-out for anything interesting you see on the Great Western and write it down in the book. Then you can show it to me when you get back.'

I put the sixpence in my pocket, safely under my handkerchief.

'That's a ripping idea, Mr Belton!'

'Then we'll both be able to enjoy your trip to the west, won't we?'

'Yes!'

'Good night, lad.'

'Good night, Mr Belton.'

'Don't forget about the book, mind!'

'I won't, Mr Belton. I'll buy it tomorrow and I'll watch out all through the journey and I'll put down *everything*.'

'Everything that's *interesting*. Good night.'

'Good night, Mr Belton.'

I 2

The Shell

THROUGHOUT that wonderful journey from the Midlands to Monmouthshire I kept my copybook open and my pencil going. But, with his parting remark, Mr Belton presented me with a recurring problem—how to choose between what was interesting and what wasn't. What standards was I to apply? Everything was interesting—to me. I didn't come to a decision until we reached Rugby: there I made up my mind to write down only strictly railway observations. So I omitted Rugby schoolboys, about whom I had a great curiosity, thinking of them as inmates of a superior Dr Barnardo's Home; I omitted, reluctantly, the cakes at Banbury; and I omitted the first sight of the sea—a sheet of shine like the sky laid flat on the ground. But I made notes of the G.W.R. green engines with bright copper chimney caps; the coffee-and-cream carriages with clerestory roofs (though I didn't know that word then and wrote down 'rows of funny little windows on top'); the distant signals painted yellow instead of red; the slip coaches of which the G.W.R. was so fond; the numerous and unfamiliar 2-8-0 tank locomotives.

My pencil was kept busy all the way to Newport Mon.

Uncle Hobart Harry and Auntie Matti lived in Caerleon Road. Their house was similar to the Beltons' house—little front garden, front bay windows—but it was built with grey bricks instead of reddish-brown. It was old, and looked as battered and blackened as a thrown-out aluminium kettle, for many of its grey bricks were rotten and had crumbled away and the gaps become patched with soot. There was a narrow back garden, green with vegetables, which had a high wooden door at the extreme end of it. If you went through this door you found yourself in a cindery lane, and whichever way you looked, backwards or forwards, you saw only a perspective of all the other wooden doors of all the other back gardens of all the other houses in Caerleon Road. Once a week all these wooden doors had dustbins standing beside them, and the tall doors and the short dustbins looked like fathers and sons marching towards a smudgy horizon. Where were they marching to? I wondered, as I stood in the lane on the afternoon of our arrival. Where are they marching from? I wondered, as I did a right-about turn. The long lane with no visible terminations evoked guesses, fancies; stirred the itch for exploration. If I went this way would I reach the sea and the ships? If I went that way would I reach the mountains?

My Uncle Hobart had a big body that made his cropped head seem small. He looked like a champion wrestler or a celebrated convict. His right arm, hairy and walnut-skinned, was a model for an anatomical drawing: when he bent it at right angles and closed his fist his biceps appeared in a great hard dome like a rising gun turret; and from just below the elbow the thick shaft of his forearm, ribbed with sinew, tapered to a leather-bound wrist that was slim, strong, and flexible.

Uncle Hobart couldn't close the fist of his left arm because it was made of steel. It was a hook. He was so accustomed to the use of his false hand that you were never aware that he had only half the number of fingers possessed by a normal person, and unless you made a special point of looking you didn't notice the hook. I did make a special point of looking, for I thought it was a waste of one of the wonders of the world for the steel hand to push, pull, guide, and grip without being looked at. I envied my uncle's dexterity, and broke several plates in an attempt to make flesh and blood behave as efficiently as metal.

It wasn't only his artificial hand and arm that made my Uncle Hobart unique: he had another artificial feature—an eye. The eye, like the hand, was his left one, and if you sat on the left of him the glass eye's unremitting glare was unnerving: like the eye of a god it searched out your buried sins and illegitimate thoughts and made you squirm in your chair.

But even if you sat on his right side, Uncle Hobart had still a stern appearance. He was a man who inspired admiration rather than affection. Years ago, when young, he had been a sailor noted for daring, skill, and resource, bosun of a schooner owned and captained by Auntie Matti's uncle. The schooner's home port was Connah's Quay, in Flintshire, and she sailed, with any cargo she could pick up, to and fro along the coast of Wales. Once, when the *Larry Russell* was berthed at Newport Mon, Auntie Matti had met the young bosun and fallen in love with him; on the schooner's next visit to Newport Mon they had got engaged; and on the visit after that they had got married.

The marriage was a promotion for the bosun, for it made him a relation of the schooner's captain. The captain was glad to have a member of the family on board because, in order to obtain orders, he was obliged to do a lot of social drinking in the ports where he loaded and unloaded his cargoes and as a result, when the ship sailed, often found great difficulty in comporting himself with the authority and dignity proper to a captain: in these trying situations he relied on the discreet able seamanship of the sober and manly Hobart Harry. There was one occasion, illustrious in the family annals and often recalled by my mother, when, during a terrible storm, the captain lay senseless in his cabin and the bosun instantly elevated himself to the rank of master, saving *Larry Russell*'s life and getting her safely into harbour. But Hobart Harry, in spite of his ability, never became a captain: nevertheless, he hated the sea and one day suddenly announced that he would never set foot in a ship again. So the next time out the *Larry Russell* sailed without him, ran into some rocks, and went down with all hands. Hobart Harry never forgave himself for not being at the captain's side on that tragic voyage, and from this time on gradually developed into the morose man whom I met in his middle age as my uncle.

When he left the sea Uncle Hobart got a job as a labourer in a local steel works, and it was in an accident there that he had lost his arm and eye. I was greatly disappointed to hear this and preferred to think that he had been wounded in a fierce encounter with pirates on the Yangtze, a traveller's hazard I had heard about from Pearl, who had a book describing it. At the time of our visit he was still employed at the steel works, but owing to his disability he was now a storekeeper and not a labourer.

Auntie Matti was afraid of Uncle Hobart and through long years of care not to provoke or offend him had been made to look older than her actual age. To add to this strain on her frail physique she had borne, brought up, and kept house for a large family. She was thin and pale and quiet and very sweet.

Portraits of the family, framed tinted photographs, were ranged on top of the upright piano in the front room. Eight sons and daughters were pictured there, and five of them were dead, having succumbed to tuberculosis on reaching manhood or womanhood. Of the three living, Hugh was twenty and consumptive; Olwen eighteen and consumptive; and David five and not consumptive yet.

Hugh was tall and looked even taller because of his slender body and narrow sloping shoulders. He had fine thick wavy hair which he brushed fondly to improve its natural gloss. He did, in fact, look very like his tinted photograph, with his delicately pink cheeks and lips and neat brown suit. Olwen was a strapping wench, a beauty, all cream skin and dimples and auburn hair down to her waist. She was famous among a few for her soprano voice, and was popular with the boys in spite of being engaged to a young man called Ivor. David was as noisy and busy as a clockwork mouse.

Uncle Hobart was very affectionate towards Olwen and was always asking her to sing for him: when she consented he sat respectfully, bolt upright, on one of the velvet chairs in the front room and then, putting on his glasses, closed his eyes and listened with a proprietorial smile on his face. Hugh he disliked, thinking him a softy.

But on the evening of our arrival Uncle Hobart gave the genial side of his nature an airing. After supper he asked me, with a broad smile:

'Do you know what a ship is, mun?'

'Yes, of course,' I answered. 'Everybody does.'

'Tell me, then.'

'It's a vessel that travels on water. Like that.' I pointed to a picture on the wall, showing a liner with smoke pouring from its funnels.

Uncle Hobart shook his head.

'That isn't a ship, mun.'

'It is!' I said indignantly. 'It's like the one I went on the River Trent in last year, only it's bigger.'

'You didn't go on the River Trent in a ship.'

'I did, Uncle Hobart! Really I did!'

'Oh, no,' Uncle Hobart declared firmly, with the pleased expression of a man sure of his advantage. 'It wasn't a ship you went in. It was a steamer.'

'Well, a steamer's a ship.'

'It isn't, mun. A ship is a vessel with three or more masts, square rigged on all.'

And he then explained to me the difference in rigging that distinguishes a ship, a barque, a brig, a schooner, a yawl, a cutter, a sloop.

He gave me a piece of string.

'Put a knot in that,' he said.

I did so.

'Oh, no,' he said. 'That isn't a knot.'

This time I didn't protest, knowing better than to argue with Uncle Hobart. He took the string from me, undid what I had described as a knot, and with a fork from the table unravelled the strands at one end. He tied these together and held the result out for me to see.

'That's what a sailor calls a knot,' he said. 'What you call a knot a sailor calls a bend or a hitch.'

Feeling, no doubt, that he had teased me enough he brought out his treasure chest and showed Susie and me some souvenirs of his voyages. He had foreign coins, many with holes in the middle through which you could peep; postage stamps (he gave me some of these, pouring them like sweets into my cupped hands); postcards depicting a whole bullfight from beginning to end; a miniature mandoline made of tortoise-shell and mother of pearl; sea shells; some bright alien match-boxes; a lump of tobacco bound with string; and several relics of his Boer War service—a huge, heavy revolver, a pair of massive binoculars, and a length of rich purple velvet embroidered with gold and silver wire that had come, he told us, from a witch doctor's temple. Finally, chuckling, he produced a photograph of some Zulu girls, quite naked except for broad leather soldiers' belts around their waists.

'Go on, you!' Auntie Matti tut-tutted. 'You shouldn't show that to them.'

'Why not?' Uncle Hobart asked, chuckling louder. 'It's all right. Those girls are heathens.'

He began putting his collection back in the box. He was replacing the shells when he suddenly put one into my hand.

'Hold that to your ear, mun, and you'll hear the sea.'

I put the shell to my ear, pressing it close. I shut my eyes in order to listen better and—yes, I *could* hear something, a faint roaring like the sea far off, a swelling and fading boom as the breakers mounted towards the coast and fell there in a wrestle of weed and water and then rushed back hissing to the ocean.

'Hear it, mun?'

'Yes, uncle.'

Was it the sea? Uncle Hobart had said it was and he seemed to be right about everything.

'Fastened up inside that shell', Uncle Hobart said, 'is the whole Indian Ocean.'

I looked at the shell in my hand. It was shaped like a bird's egg, smooth and lustrous and cold, sprinkled with dark spots almost lost in blueish grey mist. On its flat under side there was a long narrow slit with crinkled edges. It was certainly a fascinating object, this shell, at once beautiful and weird, but I didn't believe that it could contain the Indian Ocean. Yet I had heard something.

'On the mantelpiece I'll put it now,' Auntie Matti said, nodding towards the table. 'All those stamps you have to carry up to your room and if you try to take the shell, too, you might drop it and the sea will come pouring out into the kitchen and there's drowned we'll all be!'

So the shell was put alongside the tea-caddy and the clock and the pincushion and I went up to bed.

Next day we were awakened early—by the sun's spotlight on

the wall behind our beds and by the trams clattering along Caerleon Road. Getting out of bed I raised a corner of the roller-blind and looked out at the strangeness of the morning. New room, new view, new sounds. Utterly different from Carlyle Road. There, no trams pitching and tossing in haste right under my bedroom window, no faint far mountains, no Welsh voices, no cousins.

Cousins—Hugh, Olwen, David: these I had met. But there were two more: Dilys and Rae. They lived with Uncle Glyn and Auntie Myfanwy in the same Bank Street house as Grandfather and Grandmother, and after breakfast Mother, Susie, and I set out to visit them.

I had a shock when we reached Bank Street, for Bank Street turned out to be two parallel blocks of red brick stamped at regular intervals with doors and windows. Where there should have been front gardens there was only pavement, and that, surely, meant that Uncle Glyn was common.

'Is Uncle Glyn very poor, Mother?' I asked, wording the question, I thought, with admirable tact.

'Shush,' Mother answered.

We walked a short way between the two blocks until Mother stopped at one of the sets of doors and windows. She knocked. The door was immediately opened, as though somebody had been standing behind it ready, and there was Auntie Myfanwy, dumpy as a robin, beaming welcome.

'So it's here you are at last!' she exclaimed excitedly. 'Delighted I am! Come in! Coffee's all waiting. Been on the table an hour it has!'

And, sure enough, as soon as we stepped inside we saw a bottle of Camp coffee on the table, with cups and saucers, and a girl hurrying in with jugs of hot water and milk. Auntie Myfanwy poured a teaspoonful of the coffee into each cup.

'Quick now, Dilys!' she urged. 'It's dying they all are for a hot drink.'

Dilys filled up our cups from the contents of her jugs and soon we were scalding our lips on the boiled liquid.

'There's nice, a cup of good coffee!' Auntie Myfanwy said.

The front parlour was crammed with furniture and people. Wedged between a sideboard and a glass cabinet of china was Uncle Glyn, a fine high man with blond hair trained back like Georges Carpentier's. He had been on night duty, but instead of going straight to bed when he got home had stayed awake to greet us. He was still in his uniform—flannely blue trousers with a scarlet stripe down each leg and a jacket of the same material with a scarlet monogram embroidered on the lapels: G.W.R. G.W.R.! I experienced a stab of guilty joy as I saw those letters so close, so intimately related to me. Perhaps Uncle Glyn would take me into his signal-box? That would be even more thrilling than going into an ordinary signal-box, because it would be like feeling at home in an enemy's house.

On a low chair sat Grandmother, in black and a white fringed shawl, looking like Henrik Ibsen, and near her, fitted into a space between the black marble mantelpiece and a mahogany coal scuttle, stood Grandfather, whose white stubble, when he kissed me, pricked my face like a field of hedgehogs. Dilys, sitting at the walnut table in charge of the jugs, was a slender child with black hair and eyes like her mother's, but whereas her mother's skin was ruddy Dilys's was brown, like a gipsy's, or an Italian's. Rae, leaning on the window sill behind the sofa, was a stoutish boy with freckles and ginger hair and long curling ginger eyelashes.

While the grown-ups provided a background noise of grown-up talk we children made friends. Dilys told us that she was at Durham Road Board School, but Rae informed us hurriedly that he had won a scholarship to Brynglas and he was obviously very pleased with himself.

I showed Dilys and Rae my shell.

'Just a cowrie shell it is,' Rae said. 'A gastropod. The gastropods we did two terms ago. A common one that is—*Cypraea turdus.*'

'All the same, you can hear the sea in it.'

'Tommy rot that is.'

'But you can,' I repeated. 'Uncle Hobart said you can.'

'A baby you are to believe such fibs.'

'You *can* hear the sea,' I insisted. '*I* can.'

'Rot!'

'You listen, then.'

Rae shook his head in contemptuous refusal, but I thrust the shell into his hand. He listened to it for a second, then, with a shrug of his shoulders, gave the shell back to me.

'Well, I can hear the sea all right,' I said defiantly.

'My turn now it is to listen!' Dilys declared.

'Yes . . . something . . . I can hear,' she admitted rather doubtfully after cocking her head on one side and wrinkling her face. 'The sea it *could* be, couldn't it?' she inquired hopefully, turning to me.

'It *is* the sea!' I informed her firmly. 'Of course it is! You can hear it. Susie can hear it. I can hear it. Only Rae can't.'

'Because there's no sea in the shell to hear,' Rae asserted.

'Well, what can we hear, then, if it isn't the sea?'

'It's the noises in the room that you hear.'

'What noises?'

'People talking.'

'I can't hear anybody talking,' I said, with my ear to the shell.

'Of course not.'

'Why can't I?'

'Because the separate sounds in the room are collected by the shell and amalgamated into one. Then as a resonating chamber the shell acts and amplifies that one sound until you can hear it quite loud.'

I wasn't sure what all those long words meant. Rae knew that —that's why he used them—and condescended at once to put his learning into such terms as a boy who hadn't won a scholarship to a secondary school could understand.

'It magnifies, see,' he explained.

'But it doesn't!' I retorted triumphantly. 'Mother and Uncle Glyn and Auntie Myfanwy and Grandmother are all talking loudly now and in the shell it sounds miles off—like a whisper.'

'There's right he is,' Dilys agreed. 'So faint it was that to hear anything at all quite a job I had.'

Rae scowled.

'Into the next room I'm going to put the gramophone on,' he announced grumpily.

'To your dad it belonged,' Dilys informed Susie and me as we stood around the gramophone. 'From Caerleon Grandad brought it when you left.'

The gramophone looked top-heavy, a tiny wooden box with a gigantic pink convolvulus growing out of it.

'A resonating chamber this horn is,' Rae said, pointing to the metal flower. 'It makes the music louder. That's what amplifying means.'

The records were in a cardboard box. We fished them out and spread them on the table—old and new, pitted and chipped, Edison Bell, Velvet Face, Winner, Gramophone and Typewriter Company, Columbia, Zonophone, some of the single-sided ones as cumbersome as manhole covers. There were lots of laughing songs and comic songs and one that I thought very gay called 'The Whistling Coon'. Rae's favourite records were 'Gas Shells Bombardment' and 'Departure of the Troopship'. In the first you heard the shuddering of heavy artillery and shells shrieked like scratches past your ears; in the second there were emotional bugle calls and screamed commands and marches performed by bands and boots, then women shouting 'Goodbye', 'I'll always be thinking of you, dear', 'Don't forget to write', then a ship's siren as sudden as a blast of explosive, repeated hoarsely right next to you but getting fainter and fainter as the ship sailed away to France and a male voice choir sang 'Home Sweet Home' very softly. Rae loved this and said it was because the record caught the scene so cleverly. Susie and Dilys liked the songs of Edna May and Evie Greene. We were listening to a record called 'The Absent Minded Beggar' when Uncle Glyn's voice called from the front room:

'That's the Iron Voiced Baritone you're listening to.'

'He can't really be named that, Glyn!' Mother's voice protested with a laugh.

'I'm not having you on I'm not,' Uncle Glyn answered. 'Honest. Ian Colquhoun, the Iron Voiced Baritone.'

All the grown-ups now came into our room and stood or sat

around gravely listening to Mr Colquhoun. He truly lived up to his title, Mr Colquhoun, a singer mined rather than born. But perhaps the instrument which my father had so proudly carried home on his eighteenth birthday was largely responsible for this effect, making the voice sound more like something rolling out of a foundry than out of a throat. It was truly a talking *machine*, that old gramophone. It had the properties of a workshop rather than a concert hall. The winding handle whirred, the motor rumbled, the needle shrilled, the turntable gathered speed like a flywheel. The voices had a case-hardened, nickel-plated brilliance which, added to the audible mechanics of the gramophone itself, gave you the impression that the singers were standing at the far end of a railway station making themselves heard through a din of escaping steam, bumping trucks, and massed conversation. How-ever, if you put your head inside the horn the singing men and women jumped immediately towards you and sounded so loud that you seemed to be perched on a tooth in the singer's mouth.

'Where's Charlie Appin to?' Uncle Glyn suddenly demanded. looking round as though we ought to know the answer. 'Auntie Bessie must hear Charlie Appin.'

'Charlie Appin *you* must hear, you mean,' Dilys demurred. 'Ellaline Terris Auntie would rather hear, I bet. Wouldn't you, Auntie?'

Mother hesitated.

'There, what did I tell you?' Uncle Glyn asked. 'It's Charlie Appin she wants.'

He turned over the pile of records, rapidly, impatiently, found the one he wanted, and placed it on the turntable. He wound the machine up, smiling at Mother over his shoulder. The gramo-phone played a few introductory bars of crackle and whistle, then a voice like the bark of a bloodhound made the pink horn tremble. Rae stuffed a cushion into its mouth and the great voice was almost asphyxiated. Uncle Glyn was indignant.

'Leave the instrument alone, can't you, mun?' he thundered.

Rae removed the cushion. 'The volume I tried to lower, that's all,' he said defensively.

'Who asked for the volume to be lowered now? Nobody. It's the *power* that makes a voice first-class!'

Subdued, Rae sat down and Charlie Appin hooted and grunted unhindered. Uncle Glyn, listening, looked as pleased as if the performance was a relation's.

'There's magnificent!' he commented at intervals. 'There's personality! There's a sense of drama!'

'I don't know,' Auntie Myfanwy remarked when the record came to an end. 'As good as Charlie Appin I think you are, Glyn.'

'There's rubbish you're talking,' Uncle Glyn contradicted, grinning with gratification.

'Too reserved you are,' Auntie Myfanwy continued. 'You wait for them to ask you to take a solo in the Glee Club. But Will Griffiths didn't wait. He spoke to Mr Hopkins. Make your voice heard you should.'

'That he shouldn't find difficult,' Rae muttered.

Auntie Myfanwy glared at Rae. Then she turned again to her husband.

'You can go lower than that old Charlie Appin, anyway.'

'He can get down as far as a bass trombone,' Grandfather said.

'Do you know, Bess,' Auntie Myfanwy went on, speaking to Mother, 'when Glyn sings "In Cellar Cool" so deep he goes I really feel worried his voice will get all dirty from the coal we keep down there!'

'I think Dad's as good as that old Charlie Appin, too,' Dilys put in. And then, liberal as well as loyal, 'and I think you're as good as Dame Clara Butt, Mam,' she added.

Auntie Myfanwy's cheeks became extra red.

'Some more coffee let us have now,' she said. 'Dilys, run into the parlour and fetch the bottle, will you?'

The room in which we were now all gathered was called the kitchen and was nominally Grandfather's and Grandmother's room. Signs of Grandmother's occupation were scattered about in the form of balls of wool and knitting-needles, a work-basket and bits of coloured material (she could never resist hoarding scraps that might come in useful), and a big reading-glass lying on top of the *South Wales Argus*. Grandfather's personality was

concentrated in Grandfather's Corner, a part of the room he had
chosen near the window so that plenty of light would come in for
reading. For Grandfather was a great reader of serious literature,
and shelves of books occupied most of his corner, together with
an armchair to read them in. Above the books, suspended from
brackets, was a trombone.

Just before our departure, when Grandfather was in the garden
picking flowers for Mother to take back to Caerleon Road, I sat
in his chair and looked up at his trombone. I would have liked to
have tried blowing it, but thought it safer to inspect his books
instead. They were old-fashioned volumes, bound in brown
leather with brown marbled-paper sides or in heavy bevelled
boards covered with brown cloth. The books had a brown smell,
too. Some of them had enormously long titles, such as *Epitome of
the Whole Art of Navigation: or, a Short and Methodical Way to
become an Astronomer and a Complete Navigator* and *The Use of
Globes: or, the General Doctrine of the Sphere with a Synopsis of the
Doctrine of Eclipses.* One in particular attracted me: Cats' and
Farlie's *Moral Emblems: Aphorisms, Adages, and Proverbs of all
Nations. With 121 Illustrations on Wood by J. Leighton, F.S.A.*
I went through the pages eagerly and was bitterly disappointed
not to find a single illustration on wood, as I had expected. Then I
had a bright idea: perhaps the pictures on oak and mahogany had
been sawn out? So I searched the shelves again, hoping I should
be lucky enough to find a book that hadn't been burgled. And I
was lucky, luckier than I had thought, for I discovered a work on
Lathes and Turning that not only had illustrations on wood but on
steel as well. I foresaw drawings in delicate line on metal plates that
were wonderfully thin, bright, and flexible—but again my
experience was disheartening. There they were once more, the
pictures on mere paper, exactly the same as those in hundreds of
other illustrated books. Why books should claim to have pages of
wood and steel when all their pages were made of ordinary paper
was a mystery to me.

Just as we were leaving Bank Street Rae ran after me.

'Your shell you left behind,' he said. 'You and your silly old
sea!'

E

That night I had a horrible dream. Uncle Hobart Harry told me to hold out my hand: into it he dropped his left eye.

'Hold it to your ear, mun, and you'll hear the sea.'

I held it to my ear, but I didn't hear the sea.

'Of course not,' clanked the voice of Ian Colquhoun, echoing as through a ship's funnel. 'It's the noises in the room that you hear. There is no sea, there is no sea . . .'

I was on the sea, the shell my ship. I was using Uncle Hobart's left arm as an oar, paddling the shell like a canoe.

From the sky fell Ian Colquhoun's words, 'There is no sea, there is no sea . . .' and their weight was so tremendous that as they clinked massively into the shell they sank it. We fell, the ship and I, deep into the cold sea, deep as a bass trombone. I woke up.

The bedclothes were on the floor and the legs of my pyjama trousers were screwed up above my knees. There was a clammy sweat on my forehead. Beating inside my head was Ian Colquhoun's phrase, 'There is no sea, there is no sea . . .' and then there came Rae's assertion, 'It's the noises in the room that you hear, the noises in the room.'

I got out of bed to lift up the tumbled bedclothes. The smallest sound I made stood out against the silence like a white pillar in the dark. I stood still, listening if Mother and Susie were stirring, and there was no noise at all. No noise at all. If there were no noises at all in the room . . . and I listened to the shell . . . and I heard something . . . it would be the sea, wouldn't it? Wouldn't it? I asked myself and yes! I answered, already tiptoeing across the bedroom. I took a long time to open the door—it seemed like an hour—turning the knob back to withdraw the bolt millimetre by millimetre and then, with the door ajar, turning it forward to return the bolt millimetre by millimetre and not taking my hand off it finally until I had steadied it with the other to prevent it rattling. I crossed the landing and went down the stairs by touch, carefully, very carefully. But it was astonishing how much creaking there was—the silence seemed to amplify sounds that weren't even there!

But was I sure the sounds weren't there? Wasn't it a clock?

Of course! the clock in the kitchen, where the shell was, knocking away like a carpenter. Here was a problem—the kitchen was certainly not a no-noises-in-the-room room. Then I had an idea. When I reached the kitchen I got a chair and in the moonlight stood on it to get at the shell, hoping that one day I would be as tall as Hugh, able to look down on high shelves like a giraffe.

With the shell I barefooted quickly across the cool tiles into the front room. In there, with the photographs of the dead and the sleeping, it was totally silent, as the only clock was one in a black marble case that didn't go.

I took my place by the blacked-out piano, its glimmering keyboard floating in space, and stood ready to raise the shell to my ear. I hoped that in some way the sea, the cold, sunlit, restless, restful sea, the sea with its ships, the sea with its islands, the enormous sea—I hoped that in some mysterious way the whole sea was a prisoner in my shell. Please God, I begged, make me hear the sea. Make Uncle Hobart prove right, please God. Please God, make Rae an idiot. I lifted the shell, its toothy underside, where the opening was, icy and rough to my ear. At first there was no sound, but as I listened intently I could hear coming from far away the rolling of breakers upon a wild shore and the song of the wind in an enchanted land.

13

Hugh

THE COUSIN with whom I became friendliest was Hugh. Though he coughed and tired easily we often went walks together. With him I explored the far ends of the dirt lane that ran past the back gardens of the houses on Caerleon Road and discovered that they led to the Tip and the Reccy.

The Tip was the place where the Corporation dust carts deposited the town's refuse, a grey level plain broken by a few mounds of rubbish and littered with cans and bottles and old prams and wire. It looked like a battlefield and when the wind blew hard across it grit was hurled at you like machine-gun fire. Hugh and I often strolled there. It wasn't exactly a country walker's paradise—'Ach y fi!' Auntie Matti said when I mentioned it to her—but I enjoyed going there, probably because it was different from anything I had seen before. Hugh and I weren't the only people who liked it. There were always boys and girls playing on its breezy wastes. They storked along on stilts or larked up and down on pogo sticks.

The Reccy was also Corporation territory, a recreation ground equipped with seesaws and swings and goal-posts. The Great Western line ran alongside and I often went there to watch the trains.

One day I was looking at a book that Grandfather had lent me —*Common Objects of the Country* by the Rev. W. E. John: it contained many beautiful coloured pictures of butterflies and birds—when Hugh asked me to go with him for a walk. He was wearing his respectable brown suit, but the cap he had on and the art-silk white muffler round his neck made him look like a man from the hills.

It was a wonderfully sunny day, the sky as blue as a grocer's sugar-bag and the clouds as white as the sugar inside it. Daffodils

and crocuses were out in the gardens along Caerleon Road and
here and there a hyacinth stood between the looped-back curtains
of a front window like an actress on a stage.

We had been walking for a few minutes when a pretty girl
passed and Hugh turned round to stare at her. A little later we
met another girl who smiled at Hugh charmingly. He raised the
peak of his cap to her.

'There's a nice young lady,' he said, his eyes shining and his
cheeks flushing.

'Is that your sweetheart, Hugh?'

'No, mun.'

'Have you got a sweetheart?'

Hugh was silent.

'Well, you're old enough,' I said encouragingly when he
didn't answer.

He gave me a quick, sad smile.

'You're older than Olwen. She's got a sweetheart.'

'Yes, a good chap he is, Ivor. You'll like him, Cliff.'

'Is Olwen going to marry Ivor?'

Again there was no answer.

'That's what sweethearts usually do, isn't it?'

'Yes, they usually do.'

Hugh walked on with me in silence, as though deep in thought.
We came to a railway bridge, and there he cheered up. He pointed
to a spreading sprawl of tracks and trucks and some smoky
buildings in the distance.

'That's Mannesman's,' he said.

'What do you mean—Mannesman's?'

'A steel tube works that is. Where I had my job.'

'Did you have a good job?'

'Hard it was. Loading scrap into tubs. But, mun, what wouldn't
I give to be able to clock in there again tomorrow!'

'You must have liked it, then.'

Hugh considered a while. Then he said:

'Well, mun, you see I was strong then.'

'Was that a long time ago?'

'No, Cliff, not a long time ago.'

'Uncle Hobart works in a steel works, doesn't he?'

'Yes. At Lysaght's he is. Went there after his accident. At Cammell Laird's he was before that.'

Hugh gazed wistfully at the iron chimneys blowing out cinder-black and coke-grey smoke to drift about the sky among the white clouds. Then we walked on.

We looked into some shop windows. We stopped awhile, at Hugh's wish, to watch some girls playing tennis. We saw some men and a policeman helping a fallen dray horse to get up. We talked. Hugh told me that Ivor was a fireman. Funny, I thought. Mr Belton, Uncle G.B., Uncle Glyn—and now Ivor. Almost every man in my life worked on the railway. Funny.

There were a lot of men about the streets wearing blue uniforms and peaked caps with white round tops. I was delighted. At last I was seeing what Newport Mon was famous for—sailors!

'Are we near the docks?' I asked Hugh hopefully.

'We're a long way from the docks, mun.'

'Then where do all those sailors come from?'

'Sailors?'

I pointed.

'There. There. There.'

Hugh placed his hand on my cap and wobbled my head from side to side playfully. He laughed.

'They aren't sailors, mun. They're bus men. Near the Corporation Depot we are, see?'

I think Hugh was beginning to feel tired now, because when we saw a bench he suggested that we sit down and have a chat. He seemed anxious to speak to me about something, and I wondered what it was.

'What's that book, Cliff?' he asked when we were seated.

I showed him Grandfather's book, which I was still carrying. He took it from me and turned over the pages cursorily.

'Fond of reading you are, Cliff?'

'Yes. But I don't like books with all reading and no pictures.'

'Do you like poetry?'

The sudden question surprised me, because poetry was something I'd never given a thought to. I'd seen verses occasionally

in books and magazines, but I didn't think anybody was shame-
less enough to *read* them—except girls, perhaps. But as I'd been
asked the question by a grown-up, and by Hugh whom I liked, I
thought I'd better answer politely. So I said:

'Well, it's not so dusty.'

'Glad you like it. I write it sometimes.'

'Do you really, Hugh? Honest?'

'Yes, I do, honest.'

'Do you really make it up yourself?'

'Yes, mun,' Hugh said, shyly, but with a touch of pride.

'Can you recite me one?'

'Yes,' he responded quite eagerly.

He gave a quick glance around, as though he didn't want to be
overheard, and then recited in a low voice:

> What I relate did happen once
> In Belle Vue, I'd have you know:
> This is a pleasant public park
> Where Newport people go.
>
> I took my way to Belle Vue then,
> The flowers and trees to see,
> For I was sad, and strolling there
> I hoped would gladden me.
>
> Sudden across my vista's gaze
> A thing of beauty went:
> It was a maiden young and fair—
> I stopped in wonderment.
>
> With golden hair and gay blue eye
> She was a wondrous sight:
> The prettiest flower in the park,
> She made my dark world light.

'Hugh.'

'Yes, Cliff?'

'What does "vista's gaze" mean?'

Hugh stared at me in surprise, as though I had asked the
meaning of words that every child in the infants' class knew.

'"Vista's gaze"? Well, it's—it's'—for several seconds he
searched in his mind for the best way to make it clear to me—

'it's what you look at in the park or the country, see. It's scenery —like the Vale of Neath or Tym Barlym. That's "vista's gaze".'

'I see,' I said.

But I didn't.

Yes, I had many walks with Hugh. The most interesting one wasn't in Newport Mon at all, but in Pontypool. I had another aunt and uncle there—and more cousins, four girls. These cousins were called Myfanwy, Olwen, Dilys, and Matti, like my cousins and aunts in Newport Mon. The effect was confusing, especially as I didn't stay long enough in Pontypool—a day and a half—to be able to tell one new cousin from another.

Pontypool was an exciting place to me because just as Newport Mon was utterly different from West Bridgford, so Pontypool was utterly different from Newport Mon. It was up and down, for one thing. You were continually sweating in a climb or slithering in a descent. It was small, for another. In Pontypool a very large population was packed into a limited space, so that every day felt like a market day. Six men and women and two sheep were a seething mass, and two people on a pavement jostled each other. And another thing that made it different was that all the shops looked like booths, because instead of keeping their wares on shelves and in boxes they sensibly hung them out in the daylight where everybody could see them.

These shops sold cloth caps or boots and shoes. The caps were all flat as though they'd been sat on and were as round as wheels: they were arranged in a slightly overlapping formation around three sides of the plate-glass windows, making a drab border. The boots and shoes were tied like bunches of bananas to poles, which were hooked on to the shop fronts wherever there was foothold —children's sand-shoes and sandals, fireside slippers and cloth button boots, ladies' strap shoes and gentlemen's Sunday boots, and—most fascinating of all—clogs and boots like steam hammers, ruthless, oily, gigantic, ribbed with rivets and massed with thick steel plating.

What was most wonderful about Pontypool, though, was that the crammed streets, as narrow as laces, skipped and twisted busily up the mountain's face until, worn out, they gave up all of a sudden, and there, before you and all around you, was nothing but curving earth and sky.

They were startling, the abrupt silence and the solitude. But it only seemed to be silent there, for when your ears had got used to not hearing Welsh voices, Italian cafés, and tradesmen's Tin Lizzies, you could hear birds singing and grasshoppers whirring; and it only seemed to be solitary, for soon you noticed butterflies flickering in the grasses and bees nuzzling the clovers and cowslips. You remembered that coming here in the train you had gazed at a scenery of spoil banks, cinders, and slag ash, of smelting works and collieries, of houses like lines of discarded railway coaches on which jackdaws rested as though come up out of the anthracite workings for a smoke—you remembered, and these lean airy hills were all the more lovely and lovable.

On the morning of our second day—very early, before breakfast—I went out with Hugh. We puffed steam into the frosty air and the blades of grass on which we walked were sheathed in liquid silver. Soon our boots were dark with wet, a cold douche to our feet. We stamped, and walked fast. As we walked along Hugh kept his eyes on the ground and before long found what he was looking for—a snail. It was proceeding sedately up the stem of a plant, its mailed body glistening in the grey mist-filtered light. The instant Hugh touched it it contracted like a telescope, the horns retreating into themselves and then the body retreating into the shell. Hugh popped it into a brown-paper bag which he produced from his pocket.

'What are you going to do with it, Hugh?' I asked with surprise, but the only answer I got from Hugh was an enigmatic smile.

Hugh continued his search, popping the snails when he found them into the paper bag. When he had collected four he closed the bag up.

'Please, Hugh—what are they for?' I asked again, and again Hugh gave me his enigmatic smile.

Just then, however, my mind was diverted from the subject of snails by Hugh saying we were near the Roman road. The Roman road!—the wide straight highway with the war chariots flashing along and the cohorts marching!

* E

'There it is!' Hugh exclaimed.

'What—that little stone?'

'Yes. That's it.'

'Just that little stone?'

'Look.'

Hugh pointed forward and I saw that the grass ahead of us was slightly different from the grass on either side—darker, as though the shadow of a tree was falling across it. We walked along this shadow and found more stones—remains of the once great Roman way almost buried in grass and soil.

'Just think,' Hugh mused. 'As busy as Caerleon Road it was once.'

Soon the shadow of the Roman road faded.

'Now something else I've got to show you!' Hugh announced, and after a climbing walk we came to it—a white battlemented tower that stood on the summit of a hill as isolated as a lighthouse on a rock.

We stopped to look, a swift, cold wind banging at our ears.

'The Folly, that is,' said Hugh.

'Does somebody live in it?'

'No, mun.'

'What's it for, then, Hugh?'

'It isn't for anything. That's why they call it the Folly, see.'

'Can we go inside?'

'It isn't nice inside. A smelly old place it is. People go there to do their duty.'

'Their duty?'

'You know, mun.'

'Number two?'

Hugh nodded assent, colouring with embarrassment.

'Now I've got something *else* to show you!' he said. 'It's cold up here. Come on.'

We descended the hill quickly, our hands in our pockets, and presently came to a beech copse.

'In here,' Hugh said. Then: 'See?'

In front of us was something I'd never expected to find in the middle of a wood, miles from anywhere.

'A house!'

'What do you make of that now, mun?'

'It's round.'

'See the chimney?'

'Yes.'

'And the nice little porch?'

'Can we go inside this one, Hugh?'

'Yes, all right it is to go in here.'

I went to try the door handle, but paused.

'Do you think there's somebody in there, Hugh?'

'I don't know, Cliff.'

I peered through the window.

'You won't be able to see anything,' Hugh said. 'Like church windows they are. Stained glass.'

'I wish we could go in. I tell you what—let's knock.'

Hugh knocked. No answer. He knocked again. No answer.

'Turn the handle, Hugh.'

Hugh turned the handle, and when the door didn't open he pressed against it with his shoulder.

'It's a shame,' he said. 'There's looking forward I was to showing you the inside.'

'What's the inside like, Hugh?'

'A proper wizard's den, mun. All of shells the roof is——'

'Like the one Uncle Hobart gave me?'

'Yes, there's some like that. And lots of others, too—pink and white and blue ones, some like turbans and some like dunce's hats, some as big as a basin and some smaller than a threepenny bit—all kinds of shells from all over the world. The floor's made of bones——'

'Human bones?'

'Some are human bones. The others are animal bones.'

'Who do you think the human bones belonged to, Hugh?'

'I've no idea, mun.'

'Was he really a wizard—the chap who built this house? If he was, he could have turned people into skeletons, couldn't he, and then used their bones?'

'He was a hermit.'

'Well, that's a kind of wizard. He could have prowled about at night, conjuring dead people up out of their graves.'

'You're giving me the creeps, mun!' Hugh laughed.

'What else is there in the house?'

'A house.'

'You mean, inside this house there's another house?'

'I do, mun. And all over the walls, floor, and ceiling there are stars, flowers, circles, squares, hearts, and diamonds.'

'All done by hand?'

'Yes. And what do you think keeps the roof up?'

'Walls?'

I threw this out as a wild improbable guess, and wasn't surprised when Hugh shook his head.

'What, then?'

'Trees.'

'What, *real* trees?'

'Yes, leaves and all.'

'Do you think we could have another try to get in?'

'But we've tried already, mun,' Hugh protested.

'I know—but I'd like to see what's in there. It sounds marvellous!'

Our second attempt was no more successful than the first, so, greatly disappointed, I walked away with Hugh.

'It's a shame we couldn't see inside,' I said. 'Perhaps we can come here again?'

'Yes, Cliff. On your next visit. Better luck next time, eh?'

We came to a low stone wall under some trees and Hugh said he'd like to sit down. Over our heads the beech leaves, with the sun behind them, glowed like green lanterns. The same lanterns, with their candles blown out, silhouetted the grass. We were sitting quietly, enjoying the warmth now that the sun was up, when Hugh opened his paper bag and taking out a snail crushed it between his hands. Too astonished to speak, I saw him pick the ball of snail from the ruined shell and put it in his mouth. Ach y fi, I said to myself. I felt faint and sick.

Hugh tried to grin at me as he swallowed, and I tried to grin back.

'A cure for consumption it is, see,' he murmured. 'A chap I
know swears by it.'

He groped again in the bag. I turned my head away: if I'd
already had my breakfast I would have vomited it up. I heard the
splintering of a second shell and waited for the third. But there
wasn't a third. I turned to look at Hugh and saw him very still,
very pale, and very miserable. The bag was on his lap. Suddenly
he picked it up, screwed it savagely into a tight wad, and hurled
it away.

Poor Hugh! He so wanted to be a normal young man—to be
healthy and strong, able to work, to go courting, to get married,
have a family. But I never went with him again to the house in
the trees, because the next time we visited Newport Mon he was
dead.

14

Grandfather

AS WELL as Hugh, I saw a good deal of Grandfather, going often to Bank Street to borrow a book or to take one back—I'd quite got over my dislike of their brown antiquity. If Dilys was in I often got involved in some game or other with her—'Oh will you wash my father's shirt, Oh will you wash it clean' on the piano, or tip-cat in the street, or knuckle-bones on the doorstep. Rae sometimes condescended to join us in this game because he had become an expert at it by making a scientific study of its technicalities. He had worked out an enormous number of variations and permutations and had discovered the secret of successful play. This was, he said, to keep your eyes on the stones you were picking up and not on the one in the air. I tried this and found that it needed great strength of will to concentrate your mind on the stones on the ground and not to get panicky at the thought of the seconds fleeting and the catch hurtling downwards.

If Dilys wasn't in I went into the kitchen. Sometimes Grandfather would be sitting in his chair, but if he wasn't I soon learned to tell whether he was about the house or not. If his chair was quite empty I knew that he had gone into town, but if his white collar and scarlet tie were dangling from the chair back—this was like a ship's wheel, spoked, and with bosses protruding from its rim—I knew he was in the garden.

Grandfather was immensely strong and did a great amount of digging, planting, chopping, lifting, carrying, sawing, hammering, building. He had quite a menagerie in his garden—rabbits, hares, goats, and chickens. The rabbits and hares were of many colours—black, white, black-and-white, blue, grey, fawn—and some had pelts like fur-backed gloves and some like Persian carpets. They lived in wooden cages piled up on top of each other like modern flats, hunched on straw and dung pellets, for ever nibbling the air, darting away to a far corner when you put a finger through the wire netting but coming forward again when you coaxed them a bit. Their cages had a distinctive pungent odour compounded of skin, hair, tea leaves, mash, sawdust, and cabbage stalks. All the time you were looking at them hens walked about with lady-like steps pecking discriminatingly at the foodless ground about your feet and sometimes, experimentally, at your shoes, squawking away hysterically when you moved. The tethered goats, grinding their jaws and staring into space, had a self-sufficient introspective air and I left them alone.

Grandfather was great on goats. He milked them and got meat from them and cured the skins off them. There was a skin nailed outstretched on a board in the sun all the time of my visits to him. Goat-skins were all over the house in Bank Street—on the back of the horse-hair sofa like antimacassars, on chairs instead of cushions, on floors in place of tiger-skins.

Grandfather was nearly eighty years of age. When he was a baby a railway journey was a novelty, Bendigo was Champion of England, the cockpit and the ratpit were patronized by the fancy. But as he grew, modern England grew. Farms were obliterated by factories and smocks were thrown off for overalls. The working people sought power and knowledge. There were Factory Acts and Reform Bills, Trade Unions and Co-operative Societies, Mechanics' Institutes and Working Men's Colleges, Cassell's *Popular Educator* and the *Penny Cyclopaedia*. My grandfather was stirred by these developments: he joined the Amalgamated Society of Carpenters, studied economics and science, bought books to learn about the exciting world in which he lived. In the eighties, when there was a great surge of socialistic activity, he became a member of the I.L.P. and read the *Labour Standard* and the *Clarion*. Apart from politics, his favourite subjects were astronomy, zoology, and botany. He was informed in all three, especially botany. Once, when he was unemployed, he maintained his family by becoming a professional herb-gatherer, making profitable use of his familiarity with almost every lane, meadow, and copse in Monmouthshire. He always avoided doctors, preferring simples, tisanes, and tinctures.

There was a nobility and a dignity about my grandfather that made him look unlike what he really was—an ex-ship's carpenter and an ex-Royal Marine bandsman. With his mass of white hair, his deep worrying forehead, his blue eyes trained on the distant future, his kind, firm mouth and obstinate chin he had the appearance of a nineteenth-century prophet or social reformer—a William Morris or John Burns. In his middle age he had been known in Newport as 'the Father of the Socialists' and if he had been ambitious he could probably have gained a national and not merely a local reputation. But that was the trouble—he had no ambition. Even prophets have to have that if they are to become practical men, politicians and organizers. My grandfather didn't wish to become either a politician or an organizer: for him socialism was a faith, not an economic tool or a political weapon. It was a way of living, a way of being, which he thought every intelligent person should see the rightness of without having to be harangued into adopting it or enticed into it with the bribe of material benefits. His hero was Keir Hardie and his *bête noire* James Ramsay Macdonald, whom he nicknamed the Runaway Ram because, for all his pugnacious exterior, he was a sheep who would one day reveal his timidity. The quality my grandfather most admired was genuineness, for that comprised all the other human qualities he thought valuable—independence, sincerity, lack of affectation. He had no wish to rise in the social scale, because a man can only be on top by having a lot of other men under him and that, to a believer in equality, was abhorrent. He believed that it's what a man *is* that matters, not where he was born or educated, not what he wears or possesses. Holding these views it isn't surprising that he remained a workman all his life—unlike his brother, whose moral, social, and religious standards were the exact opposite of my grandfather's and who, by doing always the expedient or conventional thing, had the satisfaction of numbering titled people among his acquaintances and of seeing his son become a master in a public school. My grandfather used to make good-natured jokes about his brother. Every night, he said, his brother prayed—

God bless me and my wife
My son and his wife
Us four
No more
Amen.

Although my grandfather wished well for all people, all people didn't wish well for him. In the eighteen-eighties a socialist wasn't a popular figure in Newport, perhaps because the memory of the Chartist Rising there still lingered on. My grandfather was regarded by all law-abiding citizens as an enemy of what was decent and good. He was called a bolshevik and an anarchist. He was thought of as little better than a criminal. Hooligans jeered at his red tie, respectable neighbours crossed to the other side of the street when they sighted him, children looked on him as a bogy man and were forbidden by their parents to speak to his children. Grandfather didn't care one little bit about this, but his children, my mother, Auntie Matti, and Uncle Glyn, lacking his philosophy and experience, suffered deep humiliation and anger.

However, on the whole, Grandfather's children didn't do so badly. There were occasions when food was plain, but they were never hungry, and when times were good—when, for example, he'd been paid off after helping to fit out a vessel newly launched from one of the Clyde shipyards—there was so much on the shelves that they felt like children living in a warehouse. Whereas other fathers bought a pound of cherries, my grandfather bought a hamper, and whereas others ordered a sirloin of beef he came home with half a bullock on his shoulder. He loathed balancing budgets and anticipating rainy days. What the American show-man said of himself could easily be said of my grandfather: he was often broke, but he was never poor.

One day when I went to see Grandfather I found him wearing his collar and tie and cleaning his boots. He asked me if I would like to go into town with him and I said, gladly, that I would. With a velvet pad and a lot of breath he worked up a celluloid shininess on the front of his boots and then put them on. I pointed out to him, cheekily, that he hadn't polished them behind. He laughed.

'That's how I like my boots to be, son,' he said. 'Old soldiers never look behind.'

We walked the long Commercial Road to the docks. But instead of the giant *Mauretania* and *Majestic* I had hoped to see I saw ships that weren't much bigger than tugs, grimy, rusty, streaked, and stained. Instead of the exotic cargoes I had seen in vision—mangoes and pawpaws, native drums and boomerangs, parrots and monkeys—I saw slack coal and iron ore and stacks of deal boxes. Instead of the officers who had paced saltily about the deck of the steamer that had taken us to Colwick, I saw a few little brown men in jerseys and knitted hats.

'They're called lascars,' Grandfather said, 'and a lot of them live near here in a club for coloured men.'

Later on we walked past this club and I kept a sharp look-out for the coloured men Grandfather had mentioned. But I didn't see any. Not one of the men who came out or went into the building was green, or red, or blue. They were all just brown or black.

After we'd had our dinners in a pub—I standing outside and having bread and cheese and ginger beer—Grandfather showed me some of the other fine sights of Newport Mon: the Transporter Bridge, the Castle, the Olympia and Tredegar Hall picture palaces, the Theatre Royal.

'This is where your mam used to come before she was married,' he informed me as we examined the playbills outside the theatre. 'She used to sit in the gods. She never missed a play or a musical comedy if she could help it. She used to collect picture postcards of the actresses, but she was just as beautiful as an actress herself —you could tell that by the number of young men she had. Of all nationalities they were, come on the ships.'

Of all the things I saw that day what interested me most were the bullet holes in the doorway of the Westgate Hotel. I stared. Bullet holes in an hotel! There was a startling morbid glamour about them. Grandfather told me how they had got there. On the night of 3rd November 1839 a great rising of the workers was to take place in South Wales and the organizers hoped that it would be the beginning of a revolt of the poor all over England. Three bands of men from Blackwood, Ebbw Vale, and Pontypool, armed with old pikes and muskets, were to meet at Risca and march in a body on Newport. The night—it was a Sunday—turned out to be very dark and wet and the men from Pontypool didn't arrive at Risca until too late. The force that marched on Newport was therefore only two-thirds of the strength that had been planned. When the men arrived at Newport they found that the Mayor, who had been forewarned, had turned the Westgate Hotel into a fortress and they were fired on by soldiers as they approached. Many were killed and wounded. The leaders, John Frost, Zephaniah Williams, and William Jones, were arrested and sentenced to death for high treason, but the sentence was commuted to transportation for life and they were sent to Van Diemen's Land. So ended the glorious Chartist Rising of South Wales and all England.

Grandfather told me the story simply and seriously and afterwards took me into St Woolos's churchyard on Stow Hill to see the graves of the shot-down rebels. I was more than a little vague about the People's Charter and its Six Points and I was too inexperienced to appreciate fully the feelings of passion and despair that had made those men risk their lives and the livelihoods of their families in order to resist exploitation and oppression, but I was moved by my grandfather's account of their forlorn bravery, and their graves had for me that day a tragic splendour that I have never forgotten.

15

The Trombone

ON MY VISITS to Bank Street to get books I always hoped that one day I should find Grandfather sitting in his chair blowing his trombone. But I never did, so at last I had to ask him to play it for me.

He laughed.

'You'll have to ask your Auntie Myfanwy,' he said. 'She always says that when I make a bit of a tune all the neighbours think there's somebody playing in the street for pennies. You go and ask her—but that's what she'll tell you, see if she doesn't.'

Auntie Myfanwy was in the scullery, washing up dishes.

'Grandfather wants to know if he can play his trombone, please, Auntie Myfanwy,' I said.

'Whatever for?' she asked sharply. 'It's somebody playing in the street for pennies the neighbours will all think. And when they come to their doors nobody will be there. They will know it is Grandfather, then. Summonsed we'll all be for causing a nuisance.'

'Please, Auntie,' I pleaded. 'I've never heard anybody play on the trombone.'

Auntie Myfanwy beamed.

'So it's you who want it, is it? Different that is. But tell Grandfather to play something nice and soft, mind—no noisy music by Handel.'

I skipped back to Grandfather. He had already taken the instrument down from its brackets and was bicycle-pumping the slide to see that it performed smoothly.

'What would you like me to play?' he inquired.

'"That coal-black mammy o' mine", please.'

'That isn't an old tune, is it?'

'No. It's brand new,' I answered proudly.

'How would it go now?'

I started to sing it for him. When I reached the chorus Auntie Myfanwy came in from the scullery, drying her hands on her hessian apron.

'There's a voice you have!' she exclaimed. 'Another Charlie Appin he is, eh, Grandad?'

'A big instrument in a little case,' Grandfather said, patting me on the back. 'I don't know that black mammy tune. You'll have to let me play one of mine.'

'All right, then,' I consented generously.

Grandfather made a spitting motion with his mouth, though nothing came out of it, wet his lips, put the tip of his tongue between them, lifted the trombone and pressed his twinkling lips firmly against its mouthpiece. Then he played.

What a lovely sound came out of those lissom, slithering brass rods! A strong clean line of a sound that drew the tune in the air without any smudges or blurs or wobbles or erasures. I saw the song's shape, simple and fluent, and loved it. But I understood why Auntie Myfanwy objected: although Grandfather kept the sound low, there was a blaring swagger in it, a clamorous, gaudy egotism, that headed high the ceiling and elbowed wide the walls of the poky kitchen. If Grandfather let it rip the house would be a wreck!

But in spite of herself Auntie Myfanwy nodded with pleasure as she listened to the melody.

'Beautiful it was, Grandpa,' she sighed when the playing was over. 'But no more, mind.' She hurried back to her dishes.

'I wish I knew that song, Grandfather,' I said. 'What's it called?'

'"Watching the Wheat",' he answered, removing the mouthpiece of his trombone and shaking the condensed breath out of it. 'An old Welsh song—one of my real favourites. Now, do you want a book?'

'Yes, please.'

The book I chose was called *The Rambles of a Rat*. On the cover there was a black-and-gilt picture of rats and a sailing ship —the rats were disembarking like first-class passengers by walking along a hawser running from the ship to an iron ring on the jetty. The book turned out to be one that interested me very much indeed—it was the life-story of a rat, written by himself. The rat's name was Ratto. He was a black rat, proud that his family had come to England with William the Conqueror and gratified that so many of his race were of importance in the world—were auto*crats*, aristo*crats*, and demo*crats*. With his friend Whiskerandos he had numerous adventures and travelled as far afield as Kronstadt and St Petersburg. From him I learned that rats are intelligent, kind, and clever; and whenever I hear people speaking of rats with horror, or see films advocating rat persecution, or read advertisements for rat poison, I can't help thinking affectionately of the thoughtful Ratto, the daring Whiskerandos, the well-informed Dwishtswatshiksky (helpfully shortened to Wisky), the modest Oddity, the merry Bright Eyes, the tragic Brisk. They are mixed up in my mind with a trombone and a Monmouthshire kitchen, for the trombone looked golden and there was gold on Ratto's book and the sun that blazed through the window joined them with a golden link.

16

Ivor

WHEN I GOT back to Caerleon Road I found everybody having tea. And there was a visitor—Ivor, whom I met for the first time. He was a pleasant young man who wore on his lapel a badge in red-and-blue enamel lettered in gold around its oval border *Newport Rugby Club Supporters' Association*. Instead of putting sugar into his tea he helped himself lavishly to the tin of Nestlé's milk. This made his tea look beige. Susie and I, as well as having the Nestlé's in our tea, spread it on slices of bread and it was lovely.

I now thought I had a wonderful opportunity for a talk with Ivor about railways, so I went upstairs to get my book of notes and queries. I'd always been hoping to question Uncle Glyn about the G.W.R., but I had never seemed to be at Bank Street at the right time—Uncle Glyn was either on duty or he was asleep. But here, at my mercy, was Ivor, and I was eager to put Mr Belton's pro-L.N.W.R. views to him and hear what he would say.

He must have cursed me—he, Olwen's young man, longing to be islanded with her. But he was patient with me, who insisted on setting up a ferry service between them and the mainland. Taking my book, I followed Ivor and Olwen into the front room and rattled off my L.N.W.R. propaganda.

'The L.N.W.R. used water troughs in 1860—the G.W. didn't use them until 1896. The L.N.W.R. was the first main line to reach London. In 1861 an L.N.W.R. engine achieved a speed of eighty miles per hour. The L.N.W.R. was the first railway to heat its carriages . . .'

'Steady, mun, steady,' Ivor laughed, putting up defensive hands and backing away. 'Nothing nasty have I said to you, have I, mun?'

133

I shook my head. He took my book from me.

'So it's a railway man you are,' he nodded. 'So am I.'

'I know,' I said, and I told him about Mr Belton and his engines and how he and I were building a scale-model railway that was going to be the finest in the whole world and how Mr Belton thought the G.W.R. wasn't a patch on the L.N.W.R.

'It's only a footplate man I am,' said Ivor, 'and not a scholar like your Mr Belton. But know this I do, though—some of the compounds on your old railway were the devil for the crews on them.'

'Why?' I asked defiantly.

'They had two high-pressure cylinders, see, which didn't work properly with the low-pressure one. Bumpity-bump, bumpity-bump they made the engines go. And difficult to start they were, too, because the valve gear made the wheels spin round in opposite directions.'

'But they didn't need as much coal and water as other engines.'

'Perhaps. But given up they were as soon as the man who built them left your old railway.'

'Webb,' I informed him. 'He was an absolutely topping engineer.'

'Webb, so it was. An absolutely topping engineer the G.W. had, too—Brunel his name was.'

'He wasn't any good,' I protested.

'Oh, oh! Listen to that now! Who is it says Brunel was no good?'

'Mr Belton says so.'

'Well, it's rubbish Mr Belton is talking'—I felt my indignation rising, to hear such blasphemy—'a knowledgeable man though he might be. Just look at the bridges Brunel made. Beautiful they are!'

'Bridges?'

'Bridges, yes. The suspension bridge at Clifton, in Bristol. The bridge at Saltash. And wooden bridges as good as steel ones.'

'I don't think bridges are very interesting.'

'Very well, then. What do you say to a tunnel under the River Thames in London, made when he was a lad of nineteen only?'

I shrugged my shoulders. I was being ungracious, and I knew it. But I was obviously getting the worst of this argument and I felt resentful—not so much for my own sake as for Mr Belton's.

'Not satisfied you are?'

'Tunnels are pretty dull,' I said.

'All right. Then what about the ships Brunel built—the first steamship for regular service on the Atlantic ocean, for instance?'

'What—the first in the whole world?' I inquired incautiously.

'Yes, indeed—the first in the whole world!'

Ivor grinned, happy at having made me waver in my opposition. But I clapped my guard on again.

'You didn't say a ship,' I mumbled grudgingly, 'you said ships.'

'Ships I said, yes. What about the first ocean-going steamship with a screw propeller?'

'Not so dusty,' I conceded.

'And the largest ship in the world?'

'What!' I shouted, again taken off my guard. 'The largest ship in the *whole* world?'

'The largest ship in the whole world I did say! All built of iron it was.'

Ivor looked at me with the gleam of assured victory in his eye. I was indeed impressed. But—

'He was silly to try and make trains go without any engines,' I countered faint-heartedly.

'He tried to do that?' Ivor asked with delight, as though I'd mentioned a triumph instead of a failure. 'There's a daring man for you! Clever, too! A little man with a big brain, he was!'

'Anyway, he made a bloomer with Broad Gauge,' I threw in as a last hopeless, ineffectual blow.

'A bloomer you call it!' Ivor was gay. 'The very best thing for all railways it would have been—if they'd had the sense to see it. Quite right Brunel was about Broad Gauge—all the other people it was who were wrong!'

Defeated, I retired from the contest, and went away to brood in solitude over my humbled railway notebook.

I saw Ivor many times after that. He was very friendly. He

and I went several walks, sometimes with Olwen, sometimes with Hugh, sometimes with Mother and Susie, and sometimes just the two of us together. We went to Llantarnum, where my mother was born, roamed St Julian's hedgy lanes where I remembered gathering hazel-nuts as a baby, and went to Henlys to see the hermit's cairn on the summit of Tyn Barlym. We went to Caerleon, where I saw the tree where the grass snake had hung, the white gate through which the cows had gone when I watched them passing our cottage five years before, King Arthur's Round Table down which Susie and I had loved to roll like logs, the well that probably gave its name to Ashwell Terrace—a ray of water dazzling the eyes in the darkness of a wood. We saw the Bull Inn, where Tennyson had stayed while writing *The Idylls of the King*, went into the Museum to see the Roman relics, walked up the steep hill from Caerleon to Christchurch to see my father's name on the War Memorial there. One day we travelled into Wales to see my father's birthplace in Cowbridge, Glamorgan.

On these strolls and journeys Ivor talked a lot to me about railways, for since our meeting at Caerleon Road he had read all about the Great Western so that he could continue the teasing he had given me on our first encounter. He swung and uppercut at me with many telling facts, and though it was only sparring the blows hurt. The first underground railway in the whole world—the Metropolitan; the first Pacific type locomotive in Great Britain—the Great Bear; the longest tunnel in England—the Severn; the fastest train in the whole world—the Flying Dutchman; the longest non-stop run in the whole world—the Cornish Riviera Limited; the most powerful express engine in Britain—the Caerphilly Castle. These were all Great Western glories. When Ivor realized that I was taking his ragging seriously—and I was, for Mr Belton believed loyally in London and North Western supremacy and I believed loyally in Mr Belton—he tried to console me.

'This you can tell your friend Mr Belton when you get back to West Bridgford,' he told me kindly. 'Before Amalgamation the Great Western had the longest mileage in England. No more it has that now. The London, Midland, and Scottish Railway has it—

and that includes the London and North Western. So your Mr Belton can lift up his head a proud man!'

'Yes, I'll tell him,' I assured Ivor gladly.

A few days later Ivor cheered me even more by saying:

'A present I have for you, mun. Here.'

'A mouth-organ! Oh, thank you, Ivor.'

'A magic mouth-organ it is, like your shell. Double-sided. Two tunes it will play—"Ours is a Nice House, ours is" and "D'ye Ken John Peel".'

Olwen was with us that day.

'Pulling your leg he is, Cliff,' she laughed. 'It's Ivor and not the mouth-organ can only play two tunes.'

'Don't you take any notice of Olwen, mun,' Ivor said. 'Give it here a minute.'

I handed the mouth-organ to him.

'This is the side that plays "Our is a Nice House, ours is",' he said, pointing. 'Listen.'

He clasped the instrument between the thumb and outstretched fingers of his left hand and with his right hand made a vibrating sound chamber. Then he played the tune faultlessly, with a lot of wonderful vamping and wailing.

'Now let it play "D'ye Ken John Peel" on its other side,' I requested.

And Ivor played that melody, too, every note perfect.

'Now you have a go, Cliff,' he said.

I blew and sucked one side, over and over again, but all I could produce were chords and unconnected single notes. I tried the opposite side, but the results were equally unmusical.

'It's strangers you both are yet,' Ivor said. 'A little suspicious of you the mouth-organ is. Let you take time to get used to each other.'

The train on which Ivor was fireman passed along the line near the Reccy at eleven o'clock each morning, and it became a daily appointment for me to be there to see him go by. Sometimes I was with Dilys and other children, and they would be liberally supplied with confectionery that I never tasted anywhere but in Newport Mon—Lovell's Toffee Rex, Reeves' Cho-Hone, and

Lovell's Milky Lunches. For me, that corner-shop merchandise was honey dew and the milk of paradise, for it wasn't only sugar and fruit flavours that I licked and swallowed—it was sugar and the wide Severn waters, it was raspberry flavour and the Great Western Railway, it was orange flavour and Welsh accents, it was lemon flavour and the switchback streets of Pontypool, it was mint flavour and Caerleon, it was strawberry flavour and the trombone, it was lime flavour and the bare distant hills. Sometimes we chewed locust beans—very exotic—and Dilys's favourite sweet was nougat, which—like everybody else—she called nugg-utt.

Dilys was an expert on the swings at the Reccy. Standing on the narrow board that served as a seat, and holding on to the chains, she was able to rise high above the cross-bar at the top by driving the seat forward with powerful lunges of her flexed knees. There were two winds on the Reccy—a wanton wind and a prudish wind: when Dilys rushed forward and up the wanton wind blew her skirt inside out to her waist and showed the whole Reccy her brown thighs; when she swung down and back the prudish wind hastily pulled her skirt low and made the Reccy respectable.

At a few minutes to eleven I watched for Ivor's black engine to appear and when it came I waved deliriously and shouted and Ivor waved deliriously and shouted back. Sometimes he opened the firebox door and I saw an orange of heat and the front of his dungarees stained red. Sometimes Ivor wasn't in the cab but was rock-climbing on the tender: he would stand up on top of the coal and call to me through a hand-made megaphone.

When Ivor's engine had grunted by I still stood watching, counting the wagons until the brake-van appeared and the guard, leaning over his rail, waved farewell to me while being hauled slowly backwards into the future.

Ivor didn't mislead me about the mouth-organ. I blew and drew persistently and profitlessly hour after hour until one day, in Belle Vue Park, it played 'D'ye Ken John Peel' to me, suddenly, perfectly.

17

The Sing Song

ON OUR last evening in Newport Mon we had a party. All our Bank Street and Caerleon Road relations were crowded into Uncle Hobart's and Auntie Matti's front parlour—and in addition there was a Mr Honeyman, whom Uncle Glyn had brought along. Mr Honeyman had just started work in Uncle Glyn's signal-box and was new to the district. Uncle Glyn had thought a bit of company would be welcome to him. Mr Honeyman was ill at ease among so many strangers and said little, only smiled anxiously.

There was beer for the gentlemen, port for the ladies, and stone-jar ginger beer for the children. There was deliciously cool and smooth home-made, creamy-crumbly, blotchy-with-sultanas slab cake; and also jam tarts, currant buns, Banbury cakes. There were biscuits of all kinds; and, on a separate plate, stacks of Cho-Hones and Milky Lunches.

Everybody was rather constrained at first because it was to be a musical evening and we were all expected To Do Something. Grandfather had brought his trombone and it stood vertically beside his chair like a piece of burnished plumbing; Uncle Hobart had on his knee a small hexagonal instrument which he said was a melodeon but which I was used to calling a concertina; David had a kazoo, a sort of tin submarine with a disk of tissue-paper in the conning tower—when you hummed into it it made a bumble-bee noise; and Olwen had put aside two or three sheets of special Pieces that she intended to sing. Susie carried, shyly, a Swannee Whistle and I had my mouth-organ. So every artist was suffering from before-the-performance tension.

All except Dilys, who opened the concert by playing 'In a Monastery Garden' on the piano. She showed none of the deep respect for her instrument which most performers have when they take their place on the piano stool; the piano wasn't one of her betters, to which she must drop a curtsy; it was a pal, to have fun with, and she ran off the tune casually and carelessly, with lots of confident wrong notes.

Everybody applauded and Dilys prepared immediately to give an encore.

'"The Teddy Bears' Picnic" now,' David requested.

So Dilys played 'The Teddy Bears' Picnic', which was more suited to her style than the religiosity of the Alfred W. Ketelby work, though the grown-ups listened more attentively to the first piece than to the second because it was good music and the other wasn't. When she had concluded her performance Dilys raced her forefinger up the treble part of the keyboard with a joyous, abandoned swi-i-i-i-ish.

Olwen followed. As she came and stood by the piano there was a clearing of throats as people got their necessary coughs over well in advance; then there was a scraping and squeaking of chairs on floorboards and lino as they disposed themselves to listen with the required concentration. Olwen, in her formal dark velvet, her hair flowing over her white collar, pale in the soft evening light that came through the lace curtains—Olwen looked tranquil, gentle, and touching. She sang three of the most successful items in her repertoire—'On Wings of Song', by Mendelssohn, 'I Know That My Redeemer Liveth', from *Messiah*, and Gounod's 'Ave Maria'. She sang very correctly in the style of the concert platform, bent forward slightly, with her hands clasped in front of her breast. She received a colossal ovation from aunts, uncles, and parents, but for us children—except Rae, who efficiently accompanied her—her recital was boring.

'Something instrumental we should have now,' Auntie Myfanwy said.

'Where's that old gramophone to?' Uncle Glyn asked, and everybody laughed, glad to climb down from the high-class pedestal to which Olwen's songs had raised them.

'The gramophone, indeed!' Auntie Myfanwy admonished, smiling.

'Well, something instrumental you clearly said,' Uncle Glyn

retorted. 'An honour wouldn't it be, now, to have Charlie Appin here to sing for us?'

On hearing this name Mr Honeyman cocked his ear: he opened his mouth to say something, but Auntie Myfanwy spoke before him.

'You, Grandad,' she said. 'Your turn it is,' evidently not objecting to the trombone a bit if it was played in somebody else's house.

Grandfather lifted his trombone and began his imposing prelude of dry-spitting and lip-priming. Then he announced:

'I have two favourite songs—"Watching the Wheat" and "Bonnie Mary of Argyle". Cliff's heard me play "Watching the Wheat", so I'm going to play "Bonnie Mary" to let him hear that, too.'

Everybody looked at me kindly. I felt very awkward, and was relieved when the beginning of the song quivered violently from the horn and people concentrated their attentions on Grandfather. He played rapt, by ear and touch like a blind man, groping in the air for the notes and, finding them, listening that they were true. They always were.

'Play "Watching the Wheat" again, Grandfather, please,' I urged after the music had ended on a high, fervent, lingering declaration.

'So I will, Cliff,' answered Grandfather, pleased, 'but first the old machine needs a bit of lubrication.'

Auntie Matti immediately got up and started handing round the drinks. After two glasses Grandfather hemmed and hawed and everybody knew that he was going to tell one of his funny stories; and as they had heard Grandfather's funny stories dozens and dozens of times they prepared to listen and laugh politely, because he was a fine figure of a man and nearing his eighties.

'Most of you know my brother,' Grandfather said, swallowing from his third beer. 'When we were young men we had to go to Scotland together. We were travelling all day, and so as the train drew into the station at Edinburgh I remarked, just for the sake of something to say—as you do, you know, at such times—"Well, it's been a long journey, hasn't it?" My brother glared at me. "And quite rightly, too!" he snapped. "It cost a lot of money!"'

Ivor said: 'Did you know that the Wrexham, Mold, and Connah's Quay Railway never went to Mold? Get out and wait at a station called Hope the Mold passengers had to.'

Uncle Glyn had to tell a railway story, also.

'It happened when we'd been on an outing with the choir,' he said, 'out Merthyr way. In the train coming home there were some Salvation Army lasses selling the *War Cry* and all a bit merry we boys were. A Salvation Army lass pointed at one of our chaps—swaying from side to side he was—and said, "Young man, you're going straight to hell!" Our chap blinked at her. "Damn!" he mumbled. "In the wrong train I am then!"'

'My story about the Salvation Army lass and the Welshman— did I ever tell that to you?' Ivor inquired.

'No,' we all assured him.

'In the public bar Taffy was,' Ivor said, 'putting back a pint. In came a Salvation Army lassie and she went straight up to Taffy. "Oh, Taffy," she said, "I'm sorry to see you here again"— because, you see, it was a week ago only that he'd promised her that he'd go teetotal. "Why did you let me down, Taffy?" she asked him sadly. "Resist Satan I could not," Taffy answered. "Did you do what I told you, Taffy?" she asked him. "When you felt the urge to enter a public house coming over you did you stand on the pavement and say in a firm voice: 'Get behind me, Satan'?" "Yes, miss," Taffy said. "And right into here he pushed me!"'

We all laughed a great deal at that story and even Uncle Hobart Harry chuckled. He held up his hand and the company fell silent.

'A true story I'm going to tell you,' he informed us. 'In Cardiff once I ran into an old shipmate. Dressed up he was and looking so grand I hardly recognized him. "Well," I said, "you do look smart, mun." "Yes," he said, "I've left the sea and set up a factory." "Set up a factory, have you?" I said. "What do you make?" "Ten thousand a year," he said.'

We all thought that this was the funniest joke of the evening and so everybody was very good-humoured when Grandfather picked up his trombone to play 'Watching the Wheat' by public request. But soon everybody was serious, listening.

When Grandfather reached the second verse Olwen began to sing the words very softly in Welsh and after a moment Uncle Glyn joined her. They sang in harmony, the soprano and the bass, and the sound of their blended voices was beautiful.

After 'Watching the Wheat' Auntie Myfanwy, in her charity concert contralto, favoured us with 'O Rest in the Lord' from *Elijah* and 'God Shall Wipe Away All Tears', my mouth-organ performed 'D'ye Ken John Peel', Auntie Matti sang 'All Through the Night', Mother begged to be excused, and Uncle Hobart gave us a gasping rendering of 'Oh, Susannah!' on his melodeon.

The time had now arrived for Uncle Glyn's heavyweight exhibition. He chose 'The Cobbler's Song' from *Chu Chin Chow* and 'Im Tiefen Keller', which he sang in English. He had a remarkable voice that combined the oaken sturdiness of the *basso profundo* with the willowy nimbleness of the lyric tenor. It was thrilling to hear him toss his voice up from note to note with the ease of a juggler and then bring it down, lower and lower, and even lower, still vibrant and mighty even in bottom C.

> 'I boldly say the finest way
> To keep the heart from sinking,
> Care drive away, it cannot stay,
> Is drinking, drinking, drinking,
> Is dr . . . ink . . . ing
>   dr . . . ink . . . ing
>   dr . . .
>   ink . . .
>   ing.'

'There!' Auntie Myfanwy exclaimed triumphantly. 'You heard his voice in the cellar, didn't you, walking about as I said it would? That Charlie Appin can't walk about in our cellar with his voice, can he now?'

'Glyn,' Mr Honeyman said.

'Yes, Bill?' Uncle Glyn questioned, resuming his seat, his face pink with exertion.

F

'This Charlie Appin you go on about. At work and everywhere. Is he a Monmouthshire man?'

Uncle Glyn roared with laughter. We all laughed. Mr Honeyman looked at us in dismay. Then he realized that he had cracked a joke and joined insecurely in the merriment.

When the humour had died down to a gurgle from David and a splutter of giggles from Dilys Auntie Myfanwy said:

'Very quiet you've been all evening, Mr Honeyman. Do something for us, will you?'

Mr Honeyman replied with a self-deprecatory shrug.

'Do you sing, Mr Honeyman?'

'I'm afraid not.'

'Play, then?'

'Well ...'

'Rae!' Auntie Myfanwy commanded. 'Away from the piano now so Mr Honeyman can come there!'

'Oh—not the piano,' Mr Honeyman apologized.

'Not the piano? What a pity you didn't bring your instrument then.'

'Oh—but I have.'

'Where is it to then, mun?' Uncle Glyn inquired. 'I haven't seen it.'

'Here.'

Mr Honeyman opened his mouth.

'*Where*, mun?'

'Here, in my mouth.'

'In your mouth?' Uncle Glyn repeated incredulously.

'Yes—my teeth.'

'Your teeth?' Auntie Myfanwy said.

'Yes. I can play on my teeth.'

We all shouted in astonished wonder:

'Your teeth. Your teeth? Your teeth!'

'Yes. I'll show you.'

With a delicate gesture Mr Honeyman folded back the cuff of his right sleeve and, taking a pencil from his breast pocket, started to tap his teeth with it. We watched and listened, entranced.

'That's the Overture to *William Tell*!' Rae called out excitedly.

Mr Honeyman, without pausing in his performance, nodded agreement. He was giving a spectacular display of acrobatics. His head changed angle constantly, his mouth altered its shape every second, and the hand wielding the pencil did a jig of twinkling agility. The sounds produced by his novel and extremely portable xylophone were a little toneless, but they had a crisp percussive chime and a racy rhythm.

'There's *really* tickling the ivories!' Uncle Glyn burst out admiringly.

'Isn't that clever now?' Auntie Myfanwy exclaimed.

'Indeed it is,' nodded Grandfather.

Mr Honeyman grew taller and broader with pride. His manner developed a touch of pomposity.

'The Overture to *Orpheus in the Underworld*, by J. L. Offenbach,' he announced, and to the delight of us all struck out again with his pencil.

But he resisted our entreaties to play a third time.

'My wrist feels the strain,' he explained with the air of a fatigued virtuoso.

He was the hit of the evening. Susie, Dilys, and I discussed his art for hours afterwards and David turned against his kazoo. As Mr Honeyman sat carefully wiping his brow Grandmother offered him the last Cho-Hone, and Uncle Glyn filled his glass, right up to the brim, expertly, frothless, so that it was all good drink.

'Now to finish with something really nice,' Auntie Myfanwy said. Then she added, blushing: 'Oh, goodness gracious! No offence to you I didn't mean, Mr Honeyman!'

Mr Honeyman, contentedly chewing Cho-Hone, graciously inclined his head.

'Now, Hugh,' Auntie Myfanwy said. 'Very retiring you are. Recite us one of your poems, Hugh.'

Hugh shook his head.

'Go on, Hugh,' I urged.

Everybody, except Uncle Hobart, smiled encouragement.

Uncle Hobart stared at his son with insolent coolness. Perhaps it was his father's contempt that stirred Hugh's defiance, for he stared steadily at his father and said:

'All right, I will, then.'

Everyone assumed the pious expression considered suitable for recitations and made ready to listen with proper gravity, some cupping their chins in their hands, some looking at the floor, some looking at the ceiling, some looking merely profound.

'Now,' Hugh said. 'This one I've just finished.

> 'One day in downcast mood I walked
>   Along the busy street,
> Sick of my useless self—and then
>   A child's voice did me greet.
>
> "Please, sir, I want to cross the road,"
>   The child to me did say;
> "Please will you take me over, sir?"
>   I could not answer nay
>
> Because the child looked up at me
>   Without a doubt that I
> Was fit and fearless, being a man
>   Standing six feet high.
>
> So through the traffic I set out,
>   Small hand in large hand thrust—
> A hopeless life in which a child
>   Had placed a perfect trust.
>
> My eyes were wet with tears, though they
>   Weren't tears of grief, but glee—
> For I felt strong because a child
>   Felt strong through being with me!'

The poem was followed by silence. I was sitting near Hugh and I could see that the knuckles of his hands were white as they gripped the edge of his chair. He looked at his father, burly and impassive, and then quickly turned his face into the darkness that was now filling the room. We could hear him quietly sobbing.

18

Intimations of Immorality

MOTHER had sent our belongings back to Nottingham 'luggage in advance'—one shilling, 'including collection, conveyance, and delivery', as the railway company announced with justifiable pride—and so we didn't have to take a taxi from the station to Carlyle Road. We went by tram to Trent Bridge, and then walked home with our paper carrier-bags and folded macs.

I was looking forward to seeing Mr Belton again. I hoped he hadn't got worse while we had been away.

'Mother.'

'Yes, dear?'

'Will Mr Belton be better now, do you think?'

'He *could* be,' Mother answered. 'But he's been very poorly, you know, so it will take him quite a long time to get *completely* well.'

'He'll be pleased to see I've filled up the book he bought me, won't he?'

'Yes, he will be.'

'I've put down a lot of interesting things about the Great Western. Do you think that will upset him?'

'Why should it upset him, when you've been such a good boy and written everything down as he asked you to?'

'Because he *hates* the Great Western, Mother.'

'I see.'

'Ivor told me all about Isambard Kingdom Brunel. He was a great man, Ivor said. Mr Belton said he wasn't. I wonder what Mr Belton will say when he reads what I've written down about Brunel? Do you think he'll be ratty?'

'I shouldn't think so. He might learn something about that man you mentioned that he didn't know before and that will make him change his mind.'

'That will be ripping! Do you know another thing Ivor said?'
'No?'

'He said the L.M.S. is now the biggest railway in the whole of England. Mr Belton will be pleased to know that, won't he?'

'I'm sure he will, dear.'

'You see, Mother, the L.N.W.R. is now a part of the L.M.S.'

'That's very interesting. Look, dear—isn't that nice? New curtains to Mr Belton's windows! That probably means he's up and about again. Isn't that wonderful?'

'Rather! We can start on our working model railway!'

We went in the back way and found that Mrs Belton, who had been expecting us, was all smiles and had prepared a big tea in welcome. She had made herself smart for our reception, and was wearing one of her best frocks, and proper shoes instead of carpet slippers.

The kettle was simmering on the fire—there was always a fire in the kitchen range for cooking, even in heat waves—and Mrs Belton mashed the tea while Mother unpinned her hat and veil and took them off.

'Can I take a cup in to Mr Belton?' I asked when Mrs Belton was pouring out.

Mrs Belton didn't answer.

'Can I?' I asked again.

'I buried Mr Belton last week,' Mrs Belton said, not looking at me but at Mother.

'Oh, Mrs Belton!'

'Yes. The poor soul passed away just after you went to Wales. He went very peacefully, I'm glad to say.'

She handed a cup of tea to Mother, then sat down and took up a cup for herself.

'I've been dying for this!' she exclaimed, gulping with relish. 'Wasn't it a blessing?—there wasn't any pain or anything. Just said he'd like to close his eyes for a bit and off he went. He looked so beautiful in his coffin you'd have loved to have seen him, Mrs Dyment. As innocent as a lamb he looked, the dear.'

All through tea I sat numbed. Mother didn't eat, but drank a little. Mrs Belton, consuming bread and butter and potted meat and slab cake, explained that in her opinion it would now be a good idea if Mother, for a small extra rent, took on the front room as a sitting-room for the three of us.

'I've given it a thorough turning out,' she said, as she invited Mother in to look at it. 'You'll find it very pleasant in here now, I'm sure.'

Susie and I pressed into the room behind Mother and Mrs Belton.

'The engines are gone!' I exclaimed in horror.

There wasn't a single one of Mr Belton's scale models in sight. Not a single one. Most of the pedestals, brackets, and tables on which they had stood had gone, too. What was left of the furniture had been rearranged, new lino laid, new cushions scattered about, and the whole place swept and polished.

'Of course, a lad like you *would* notice that,' said Mrs Belton, giving me a hypocritically friendly pat. 'But they're best out of the way—we can start all over fresh, like.'

'Are *all* Mr Belton's engines gone?' I asked incredulously.

'You couldn't do anything with them, love. They were practically dropping to pieces. And the muck and dust on them —why, you'd hardly credit it! There, don't take on,' she said, as the tears started to my eyes. 'We can buy you a nice new train, can't we, Mrs Dyment?' And she added, like a dab of whipped cream: 'A clockwork one!'

I looked up through wet eyes at the faces—Mrs Belton's fleshy and self-satisfied, Mother's pale and sad. Mrs Belton's downward gaze at me was ingratiating, Mother's hopeful.

They didn't understand.

'That would be just a toy!' I cried indignantly.

The days immediately after our return went by slowly. I brooded on Mr Belton's death and came to the conclusion that I knew pretty well what had killed him. It was Railway Amalgamation. I knew this had depressed him, because it meant the extinction of the individual lines he had loved, especially the L.N.W.R., but I felt that if only he had hung on until we had got back from Newport Mon and I had been able to tell him that the L.M.S., which was simply the L.N.W.R. made bigger and given a new name, had a longer mileage than any other railway company in Great Britain he would have been cheered up so much that he would have soon got quite better.

It was almost impossible to believe that I would never see Mr Belton again, never see *Locomotion No. 1*, *The North Star*, *The Lord of the Isles*, or his Bloomers again. I spent every minute that I could out of doors, because I didn't think of him so much there. But as soon as I went inside I was reminded of him by the dumb wall between the front room and the kitchen. Now there issued from it no continual rasping and coughing, a sort of speech announcing Mr Belton's friendly proximity: now there was only emphasizing-his-absence silence.

Mother found it difficult to make up her mind about the front room. She didn't like the idea of walking into a dead man's home and taking possession. She said she needed time to think it over. I didn't encourage her. I couldn't bear the thought of going into the front parlour without seeing Mr Belton's gaunt, yellow, comradely face welcoming me from the bed, surrounded by his Lilliputian trains. I hated the room now, after its thorough 'turning out'.

But the problem was solved without Mother having to do anything about it. Sailor Sam moved in. He didn't do it formally— but the convenient arrangement he and Mrs Belton came to amounted to that. Three times a week, without fail, his Douglas motor-cycle broke down, and as Mrs Belton explained it was daft to walk all that way pushing the blooming thing when there was a bed in the house all made up and doing nothing. So nautical odds and ends became permanent additions to the kitchen furnishings, and a kitbag, lanyards, collars, blouses, boots, shirts, belts, and a trouser press gave the front room a residential function once more.

Sailor Sam often gave Susie and me pennies to buy sweets with, and in spite of our sensing that he was a shady character this made us like him. Hoping, I suppose, to compensate me somewhat for my lost friendship with Mr Belton he offered to make me a boat; he did so, using only a grocer's box and a jack-knife. But I hardly ever went near water suitable for yachting, and when I tried the boat in the local ditches it foundered on weeds and rubbish. Seeing that I didn't use the boat, and again using only his jack-knife, he made me a one-string fiddle out of a cigar-box. This, with its long handle, was rather like a warming-pan in appearance, except that it was made of wood instead of copper and the pan was oblong instead of round. I didn't use the one-string fiddle, either. So, no doubt in desperation, Sailor Sam asked me to name something that he could make for me which I would definitely like to have and I responded promptly with an order and a specification for a really practical present—a marble shy. This was a wooden board in which arches were cut in the lower edge with numbers painted above them: I set the board up, like a viaduct, on the pavement or school playground and boys aimed marbles at it, trying to shoot them through the arches. If they succeeded I had to pay out reluctantly the number of marbles indicated over the arch through which they had scored, but all marbles that failed I kept. The arches weren't imprudently wide. My mother had made me a shirt-flannel bag to keep my marbles in, and after a short period of operations with my shy the bag grew so bulgy that I found it difficult to close it with the draw string. I had become raffishly marble-rich.

But they were only clays, valued for quantity rather than quality. To add splendour to them, I owned a number of fine pieces that I held on to like guineas. Some of these were made of pottery and stone and were as blue as thrushes' eggs or as striped as footballers; others were of glass, with college-scarf colours spiralling up their centres; and one was a great steel ball-bearing, solid silver, a deadly cannonball among marbles, the Baron von Richthofen of ring taw.

Girls were still playing battledore and shuttlecock, which had begun around Pancake Day. And the top season was in full swing —mushrooms and parsnips flogged into still life with twopenny whips made of colourful sticks with leather thongs. Hoops, or bowels as we called them, rolled along the pavements, going for pedestrians' legs as savagely as bulldogs and sometimes running wild in the road like absconding cart-wheels. The upper-class bowels were large and made of laminated wood, the common ones were small and made of iron. The iron bowels weren't whacked along like the wooden ones, but were threaded through a ring on the end of a sort of metal meat skewer and with this implement were pushed along at a canter. Doing this was tricky, and only genuine urchins had the knack of it. You always knew when a wide boy was coming by the din his bowel made on the flagstones.

We were a very warlike lot in Carlyle Road, spending much of our time firing potato-pistols, water-pistols, pea-pistols, and cap-pistols at each other. A form of warfare that was against the Geneva Convention was to fill your water pistol from a dirty puddle or iridescent pool of horse's urine and squirt it down your luckless playmate's neck. One of the most exciting things you could spend a penny on was a box of caps, either singles—confetti with blobs of bang in the middle—or rolls, for Buffalo Bill six-shooters. We used the singles also in a rather frightening weapon called a bomb—a miniature hand-grenade consisting of two portions of grooved metal held together by a length of twine: you put a cap between the portions, tightened the twine, threw the bomb into the air, and it came down on the pavement with a cracking explosion.

All these things—whips, tops, guns, caps, marbles—you bought at the corner shop, where they also had gob-stoppers, Irish roll, Dolly Mixtures, Captain Webb matches, aniseed balls, Robin cigarettes, Easter eggs (reduced), Chinese puzzles (Hours of Fun), and terrifying masks (Surprise Your Chums).

They also had kali—pronounced kaylie. This was obtainable in various forms—as suckers, dabs-and-suckers, lucky bags. A sucker was a triangular paper packet with a tube of black liquorice projecting from one corner: through this you drew in the cool powder to fizz on your tongue; a dab-and-sucker was much the same, but it had an adhesive-ended stick for picking up the sherbet, as well as the tube of liquorice; a lucky bag often lacked both sucker and dab, but contained in their stead a present concealed in the kali. The present could be a whistle, or a wire ring, or a balloon with a squeaking mouthpiece. A balloon, all dusty like a baker, was what everybody wanted to get: when you blew it up, fresh from its packet, you tasted and sniffed a cocktail of confectionery and rubber. The appeal of lucky bags lay in this stimulating incongruity—in their daring concept of juxtaposing the edible and the inedible. It was thrilling to find hardware in your food. It was defiant, crazy, and wrong—like walking on cornflakes or filling a lady's hat with butter.

Another way of enjoying the sinister pleasure of heterodoxy was to save up for a smoking outfit. This consisted of a chocolate pipe with a silver-paper band on the stem, chocolate cigars, and very sweet cigarettes with ends already glowing in the packet. When you puffed at your solid pipe or blew smoke rings from your bending cigarette you were a vicious adult in little and experienced sin so powerfully you thought all the houses would fall down flat.

The infamous properties of lucky bags and sugary cigarettes were well within the range of my understanding, but there were other hellish things just beyond it. Only an inch or two beyond, however—near enough to make my curiosity stretch out to them until they almost brushed its finger tips. The brainy one in these matters was Pearl. She had enormous erudition. She seemed to know all that a human being could possibly know about the envelopes and booklets which were displayed by the corner shop at the rear of its window. These envelopes and booklets were sealed—that was their potent allure—and wrapped in unrevealing transparent paper of a reddish-mauve hue. Pearl willingly instructed Sid in their mysteries, but when I wanted to join in she drew him aside or playfully tossed stones and dust at me. NOT FOR SALE TO ANY PERSON UNDER THE AGE OF SIXTEEN said an adjacent notice in the shop window, and Pearl was continually daring Sid to go into the shop and ask for prices. At last Sid, wearing his eldest brother's trilby hat for the occasion, accepted the challenge and was told by the shopkeeper that unless he cleared out quickly he, the shopkeeper, would set the police on him for trying to buy intoxicating literature while under age.

Nevertheless, Sid got hold of one of these prohibited publications from some illicit source and brought it to Carlyle Road hidden under his jersey. Furtively, he revealed an inch or two of it to Pearl. Pearl tried to snatch. Sid jumped away.

'You bally blighter!' Pearl shouted.

'You can't catch me!' Sid shouted back, putting his fingers to his nose and wagging them derisively. Pearl darted at him, and Sid sped off along Carlyle Road in the quick way he could. Pearl ran after him, also moving fast on her long, bare, scratched legs. In the distance, I saw them dash into a jitty.

When I neared the alley I heard Pearl's giggles.

'You buzz off!' she commanded when she caught sight of me approaching.

'I'm not going!'

'Vamoose!'

'I want a dekko at that,' I said, pointing.

'It's not for children like you,' she said tauntingly.

'Go on, please,' I coaxed.

'No.'

'Tell me what it is, then.'

'You'll find out when you grow up.'

'It's pictures of Mrs Belton and Sailor Sam,' Sid informed me.

'Go on—it isn't!'

'Yes, it is. It shows what they do when they're together.'

'And if you want to know what *that* is,' added Pearl, 'ask Mrs Belton.'

Mrs Belton won't tell me, I said to myself. No, whatever I do, I mustn't ask Mrs Belton.

Abruptly, Sid suggested:

'Let's go and look for nests.'

He put the papers he and Pearl had been looking at into their envelope and stuffed it back under his jersey.

'Yes let's!' I agreed, pleased.

'Coming, Pearl?'

Pearl nodded. We wandered off. I felt proud to be with Pearl and Sid, both so old, so wise. But I felt jealous of them too— jealous that they were tall and could peer over the wall that hid from me the secrets of the grown-up world.

I spent many hours of the summer days with Pearl and Sid in

the fields. When I was with Pearl the time was passed in mooch-
ing about, in climbing fences, gathering watercress, angling for
frog spawn, eating bread and cheese off the hawthorn hedges,
digging up pignuts.

With Sid, however, being in the fields was systematic hard
work. He was an indefatigable explorer of trees and hedgerows.
Not that he was interested in nature study—he just wanted to find
birds' nests in order to remove the eggs from them. And with
practice he had acquired quite a considerable amount of skill in
the pursuit. He didn't care a gob-stopper for ornithology—but
he knew that you should look in holes for the nests of robins, blue
tits, starlings, grey wagtails, wrens; on the ground for yellow wagtails, lapwings, and larks; in trees for woodpeckers, owls, willow
warblers, and goldfinches; in shrubs and bushes and hedges for
linnets, blackbirds, corn buntings, and hedge sparrows. He knew
that the yellowhammer builds low and the wood pigeon high;
that the lesser whitethroat nests well inside foliage and the common whitethroat towards the inside; that you ought to look for
the song thrush's nest in hedges and for the mistle thrush's in
trees; that magpies build in isolated trees and jays in spinneys.
His nest-finding technique was based on what is known as hot
searching—that is, selecting a likely tree or bush and giving its
trunk a biff with your boot or a stick: if a bird flies off you know
there's a nest there and locating it is pretty simple. One of his best
tips for spotting a nest hidden amongst leaves was to look for it
with the foliage between you and the sun or from below with the
foliage against the sky: the nest showed up in silhouette. Sid's
field lore was highly successful: we collected scores of eggs to be
pierced and blown and carried weightlessly home to a shoe box
packed with cotton wool.

19

The Legacy

THE DAYS by which we measured the year—Pancake Day, April Fool's Day, Palm Sunday, St George's Day, Empire Day, Oak-Apple Day—had all come and gone. The August holidays passed. School began again.

I can't remember much of what we did at school in the way of lessons except the White Cliffs of Dover and the Poetry Recital. We manufactured the White Cliffs of Dover out of thick bundles of newspaper and countless pails of water—the messiest, wettest, pleasantest geography I have ever known. For the Poetry Recital we were told to learn a poem by heart. A lot of the scholars, particularly if they were girls, were very diligent about this, keen to show off to the rest of the standard and to demonstrate to the teacher how good they were. Accordingly, many long poems were committed to memory. When the day of the Recital arrived the teacher called out names, apparently at random, and the boy or girl concerned had to walk out and face the class. At a signal from the teacher the scholar received permission to begin reciting, and when the poem came to its end another signal from the teacher gave the scholar permission to return to his or her desk. Among the poems we heard were 'The Village Blacksmith', 'November', 'The Spider and the Fly', 'The Charge of the Light Brigade', 'The Falls of Lodore'. Then came the turn of F. W. Early.

F. W. Early's name wasn't Early, but Orme: he'd been nick-named Early because he wrote his name on his books and papers like this—'F. W.ORME'. He was a short portly boy with an oatmeal-coloured forelock and a pugnacious expression. He marched to the front of the class and there stood rigid, his hands pressed firmly against the seams of his shorts. The teacher gave her signal and F. W. Early recited at sixty miles an hour:

LittleTommyTittlemouse
Livedinalittlehouse
Hecaughtfishes
Inothermen'sditches.

There was a pause. The teacher smiled encouragement.

'Go on,' she said.

'That's all,' F. W. Early said.

'Well, that *was* a short poem, wasn't it?'

F. W. Early nodded complacently, accepting the teacher's surprise as a compliment. When he received the signal of dismissal he walked back to his desk beaming with satisfaction.

The poem I had got off by heart to recite was

Oh, dear, what can the matter be?
Oh, dear, what can the matter be?
Oh, dear, what can the matter be?
    Johnnie's so long at the fair.
He promised to buy me a bowler, a snorter,
A very small seven or six-and-three-quarter,
Oh, why don't he come and do as he oughter,
    To cover my lousy brown hair?

that Pearl had taught me. Perhaps it's just as well that my name wasn't among those that the teacher called out.

The school playground was a great grey expanse shut off from the street by a high wall topped with spikes. There were two gates in it, one marked 'BOYS' and the other 'GIRLS'—for though male and female were mixed in the building they were unaccountably segregated out of it. The girls' part of the playground was separated from the boys' part by another spiked wall, but there was a section of this which was low enough for us to be able to look over it and see the girls playing hide and seek or high jumping over skipping ropes. Sometimes the girls and boys had unlawful intercourse by throwing a Sorbo ball to and fro over the wall.

Some of the boys were extremely rough. These were the boys who had convicts' haircuts because of nits and ringworms and had snot rags pinned to their jerseys. They never used the snot rags, with the result that many of them had twin rivers of greenish-yellow slime flowing permanently down their upper lips. Occasionally the rivers were removed on a sleeve or a tongue's tip. The favourite recreation of these boys was to cause you physical injury by tripping you up, hitting you on the head with clenched fist, throwing sharp stones at you, hacking your shins, or stamping on your feet. A favourite method of aggression was to charge you with their shoulders in order to knock you down, running at you from a distance with a thunder and lightning of hobnailed boots on asphalt. Often several collaborated in an assault, and then you hardly ever got off without broken teeth, a black eye, sprained wrist, or grazed and bleeding legs. These bully boys frightened me to death, and I tried to buy off the worst of them by swopping my lunch bananas and apples for their slices of bread and lard.

When I wasn't a victim of violence I did well in the playground. My marble shy continued to make my fortune. Another lucky accessory was *Chatterbox* annual. The edges of the volume were stained sulphur-yellow and boys and girls deduced from this curious fact that the book was actually printed on sulphur-yellow paper. The possession of such a supposedly freak volume gave me enormous prestige—the only snag was that while I was on or near the school premises *Chatterbox* had to remain truly a closed book to me, for if it were opened I would have been instantly exposed as a fraud. Its pages were as white as *The Water Babies*.

What else did we do in the playground? Roller-skating, which I rather liked but of which my mother gently disapproved—because in order to walk on roller skates (you have to walk on them sometimes, in between skating proper) you have to plant your feet at right angles to your line of progress and when your skates are off this tends to make you walk like Charlie Chaplin. Then there were Felix the Cat transfers, which you wet with spit and slid on to the back of your hand, making you tattooed.

> Felix keeps on walking,
> Keeps on walking still,
> With his hands behind him
> You will always find him . . .

we sang, imitating his gait across the playground. Then there were fag cards. As bookies flaunt their bundles of pound notes, so we wagged our rubber-belted wads of cigarette cards. They were grimy and dog-eared—but that didn't matter to us, for the only use we had for them was to clip a card by a corner between the first and second fingers and with a wrist-flick send it spinning through the air like a sycamore seed. If it overlapped a card lying on the ground the covered card was yours. This explains why large packs were grubby.

For a short time an exotic touch was given to our standard by the presence of a boy from America. His cap was eight-sided and quite unlike our boys' caps, which were similar to men cricketers'. He wore baggy knickerbockers and a jacket with pleats at the back. His name was Waugh. As I had learned from *The Rainbow* that redskins always said waugh! waugh! to palefaces I was satisfied that his was a typically American name.

One afternoon when I came home from school I was surprised to see that Mrs Belton was laying a Sunday tea in the kitchen. The cloth was a starched linen one, with holes called embroidery in it, never used on a weekday; Mrs Belton's E.P.N.S. Apostle spoons graced the best cups and saucers; and as I entered Mrs Belton was removing her special tea knives from their rexine case. I hated these tea knives because they were so blunt: they were like reduced-size fish knives with imitation jasper handles.

'What's up, Mrs Belton?' I asked.

'Your auntie and uncle are coming,' she answered curtly.

'What for?'

'You'll find out soon enough.'

Susie and I waited expectantly while Mrs Belton went into the front room to tidy away Sailor Sam's possessions. When Mother came home from the Record Office she was as surprised as I had been to see the gala appearance of the table. To her Mrs Belton was more communicative.

'Your sister-in-law sent her maid Tishy over', she said, 'to ask if she and her husband could come and call on you this evening about something important. I sent a message that it would be all right. I trust I did the correct thing, Mrs Dyment?'

'Of course,' Mother answered, looking abstracted and anxious. She was always worried by a disturbance in the normal routine, fearing it to be a portent of disaster.

But the arrival of Auntie George and Uncle G.B. was reassuring. They looked amazingly well turned out and affluent, Auntie in her long blue coat and straw hat, with matching handbag, gloves, and shoes; Uncle in his pearl-grey suit, Panama hat, and white buckskin shoes with nigger-brown leather trimmings. They were the sort of uncles and aunts who die suddenly in the Argentine and leave you a bonanza in longhorns.

'Howdy!' Uncle G.B. greeted us. Then he turned to me. 'And how's this young hombre making out?'

'I'm very well, Uncle, thank you,' I answered politely.

'Got some good news fer yuh, son,' Uncle G.B. said.

'It can wait until after tea,' Auntie George interposed.

'Shore, shore,' Uncle G.B. agreed. 'Reckon it won't harm none if it's kept in the corral fer a while.'

There were tinned peaches on the table, and a carton of cream to eat them with.

'Peaches!' Auntie George exclaimed with appreciation. 'Your dear late husband', she said to Mother, 'and your dear late father', she said to Susie and me, 'was very fond of tinned peaches. He said they smelled like sweaty feet.'

Mother smiled. Mrs Belton glowered.

'They're the very best,' she asserted in an offended tone of voice. 'From the Maypole.'

'Shore, shore,' Uncle G.B. said. 'Maypole's a purty good brand.'

When we had all had tea—polony, haslett, thin bread and butter, and Madeira cake, as well as the peaches and cream—four of us went into the front room, leaving Mrs Belton to clear away and wash up.

In the front room Uncle said to me:

'Son, jest make shore thet door's properly closed, will yuh?'

I went to the door as he told me, wondering at his secrecy.

'Yes, it's properly closed, Uncle G.B.' I assured him.

'Thet's mighty fine,' he responded. Then he looked at us

solemnly. 'Now listen you-all,' he ordered, and we all listened earnestly. 'The late Albert Belton, in whose bunkhouse we're a-sett'n right now, wuz a pardner uv mine. He was a mighty fine feller, but fate shore dealt him out a pore hand uv cards. Yeah, he had a heap uv misfortune, pore feller. Afore I met up with him he was on the L.N.W.R. and rose to be a ticket examiner on the West Coast expresses. That was a powerful achievement. But then fate had to go fer him like a low-down two-gun killer and blast him with lead while his back wuz turned. That wuz doggone mean. But Al wornt yeller. Nope. He wornt no quitter. He fought right back. And thet's when Al and yours truly got acquainted— when he wuz a sick man and had tuh give up riding the range, as yuh might say, and joined the Midland outfit heah in Nottingham. He worked alongside me in the District Goods Manager's Office. He was a reel nice feller. And now he's crossed the Great Divide.'

Uncle G.B. lowered his voice and looked grave.

'But there's one thing I'm shore uv,' he went on, 'and thet's thet Al, right now, is enjoying hisself in the Happy Hunting Grounds, as the Injuns call it. We kin stake high on thet, fer it's what Al deserved. As I've said, he was a real nice feller.'

Uncle G.B. now raised his voice and smiled.

'Waal now,' he said, 'reckon I'd better start talking business. Not tuh make a tarnation long trail uv it I'm going tuh give it yuh straight. It's this: when the late Albert Belton was a-lying sick on his bunk in this same room where we're a-setting right now he made a will and appointed yours truly to be his executor. Yuh might think thet's queer, seeing as how'—he glanced uneasily at the closed door, through which came the sounds of Mrs Belton clinking crockery—'seeing as how . . . waal, I reckon he did it because him and me wuz old-time pardners. But'—he again glanced at the door—'there's somebody going to feel mighty riled when the news gits out. But thet's how Al wanted it. Now, I ain't going to waste time on details what don't concern us heah and, come tuh thet, there's nary a one heah what it does concern except thet little steer over there.'

Unle G.B. smilingly pointed at me. I stared at him in surprise, while Mother, Auntie George, and Susie stared in surprise at me.

'Yep,' Uncle G.B. resumed, 'as a mark of his undying affection and esteem and as a small recompense for many services willingly rendered—those are the late Mr Belton's words—he has left young Cliff heah an inheritance. He has bequeathed to him the sum of twenty-five pounds, with instructions tuh me tuh use it fer the purpose of opening on his behalf an account in the Post Office Savings Bank.'

'What's a ticket examiner, Uncle?' I asked.

There was silence for a moment. Then Auntie George inquired.

'Is that all you've got to say about your legacy?'

'I think it was very kind of Mr Belton to leave me all that money,' I said. 'But I always thought he was an engine driver. What's a ticket examiner, Uncle?'

'A ticket examiner is a purty important official,' Uncle G.B. replied. 'He goes through the train making shore passengers' tickets is correct and seeing there ain't no rustlers aboard stealing a ride what ain't theirs. Reckon he earns the railways a heap uv extry cash. Yep, he's a purty important hombre and yuh can feel powerful proud uv your old pardner, Albert Belton.'

But I was bitterly disappointed. A ticket examiner, however much he recovered for the railways, seemed to me a poor thing for Mr Belton to have been. I had all along been convinced that in his days of glory with the L.N.W.R. Mr Belton had been a driver on the crack expresses to the north, and I felt sure, looking back, that in our conversations together he had led me to believe this. Had he deliberately deceived me? Was he a liar? Or had he really believed it all himself? The questions harassed me for long afterwards—every time I, as a Depositor, slid my book and my sixpences under the grille of the local sub-Post Office.

20

Cold

MRS BELTON hated me because of the legacy. When she spoke to me and I said 'Baking powder?'—which I had heard well-behaved adults murmur instead of 'Eh?' or 'What say?'—she growled at me: 'Wash your ear-lugs out.' She cuffed me for the most venial crimes. She gave me the minimum to eat. And as soon as the meal was over she would say: 'Get outside where you belong, you little tyke'—and out I had to go.

In the worst of the winter, when in the house the handles of doors, the chair backs, and your morning clothes gave out cold like a fire giving out heat, this was an unpleasant thing to do. Outside, you moved in a twilit box because a lid of cloud shut out the light: when the sun showed through the sky's thick padding it looked like a snowball. The pavements were skinned with ice and you walked on splintering windows. The trees stood stiffly in a living death. Nothing was relaxed and generous, as in summer: every pore of macadam, stone, and brick was shut and bolted to keep out the hostile air.

There was often fog—and I remember well the feeling of inhaling fog: it was like breathing feathers sprinkled with pepper. There was often snow—snow like a storm in a flour-bag, flakes descending, flakes ascending, flakes engaged in private cyclonic frenzies, or snow falling through a grey-and-yellow gloaming, no bird flying, no bough stirring, everything but vertically moving snow as still as in a picture.

The chilled air in my lungs gave me a constant nausea. The flesh of my fingers was senseless and the bones inside the flesh ached. Frost grasped my cheeks like rubber suction caps, plucking the skin into scores of little cones of pain.

Sailor Sam wouldn't have allowed Mrs Belton to put me out in the really hard weather. But now, unfortunately, Sailor Sam's

Douglas didn't break down so often as it did. Mrs Belton took to wearing smarter dresses, curling her hair with tongs which she heated on the gas ring, using lip salve liberally, and polishing her nails with powder and chamois leather and then pushing whitening under their rims. But Sailor Sam came to the house more and more rarely and Mrs Belton became more and more vicious.

Sometimes, when my teeth were chattering and I looked starved, as she described it, Mrs Grudgings invited me into her house to sit by the fire. Another neighbour occasionally gave me a cup of cocoa.

I thought of complaining to Mother, but I knew it would be useless. Mrs Belton would only say that I'd always shown a liking for being out of doors and that if I made a fuss now it was because I was mardy. So I stuck it out, glad when each day was over. But the trouble was, frozen by day I found it impossible to go to sleep in a freezing bed at night. The sheets were thieves, taking from me every pennyworth of heat I possessed. I tried bringing my knees up to my chin, but that gave me cramp. I tried pulling my pyjama legs down to cover my feet, but that made my chilblains itch. What could I do to get comfort? I remembered a way. I was on the footplate of the latest and fastest express loco-motive in the whole world. We were flashing across the Siberian Plateau at five hundred miles an hour. I shifted the regulator a notch and we increased speed to a thousand miles an hour. My non-stop train skimmed the Ionian Sea, leaped the Altai Moun-tains, flashed over the Skagerrak and the Lofoten Islands, pounded the Great Plains, followed the Yukon, the Amazon, and the Orinoco, crossed Lake Chad, crossed the Libyan Desert, streaked through Calgary, Las Palmas, Amritsar, Cadiz, Naples, Bulawayo, and in Constantinople I greeted my relief driver and said good night to him and stumbled through a swaying narrow corridor to my bed in the leading coach, and we soared, soared, high, higher, as I got drowsy and drowsier and the rocking and roaring train bulleted on, accelerating, climbing, higher, highest, until it was impossible to tell whether the enormous flashes in the night sky were sparks from our chimney or were the Pleiades.

21

The Hospital

MEN AND women in white clothes. Our Beltons' bedroom. Somebody laying a white cloth on a table. Auntie George. Mother.

Mother said: 'You're going to have a birthday party.'

'But it isn't my birthday,' I said.

Mother lowered her head to listen to me.

'No, it isn't your birthday,' she agreed, 'but we're giving you a party now because you didn't have one at the proper time.'

But it was a funny party. A woman put a layer of cotton wool on my face. Was it a game? I was told to breathe deeply. A man poured drops on to the cotton wool from a bottle. I saw moving and mixing colours and whirling worlds.

I woke up to find myself in a cage.

But it turned out that it wasn't a cage, but a cot with high black railings on all four sides. And I wasn't in the Beltons' bedroom any more, but in a sort of hall called the Duchess of Portland ward.

I was in the Children's Hospital, Nottingham.

What had happened was this: I had fallen ill, the local G.P. had diagnosed pneumonia, then meningitis, and then had discovered that I had mastoiditis. By this time I was very ill indeed and an emergency operation was necessary. But the surgeon who was called in, on being told that my mother was a war widow, refused to operate unless paid in advance. It was only after his fee had been guaranteed in writing by Uncle G.B. that he agreed to operate—where I was, in the Beltons' bedroom, because I was too ill to be moved.

The genial specialist, announcing that I wouldn't recover, departed, leaving me to die. Auntie George, who was subject to fits of religious hysteria, went out in the middle of the night, roused the vicar from his bed, and brought him to the bedroom to pray for me. By morning I had rallied. Whether my recovery was a coincidence, or whether it was a proof of the power of prayer, I don't know.

In the hospital I was operated on a second time. Then, slowly, I began to get better. When I was well enough to walk I was dressed in a purple dressing-gown and put to work. Perhaps the matron thought that manual labour would build me up—but I hated it. I still dislike the sight of purple.

One of my jobs was dusting chairs, and I never managed to do this without painfully banging my knuckles on the staves and rungs. Another was feeding the babies. There were about a dozen babies and I was given about a dozen mugs, each mug containing a measured quantity of milky baby food. I had to spoon the liquid into each sucking red orifice while its owner belched and made rude noises. It was a tricky operation, because if I didn't push the spoon in far enough the food was spilled and if I pushed it in too far the baby choked. The secret was to feed in a series of tiny helpings. Each tiny helping was a link in what seemed to me an interminable chain of boredom. Enormous patience was necessary. I didn't have the patience, and often poured the contents of my mugs down the sink. The hungry babies howled. If there are today about a dozen people in Nottinghamshire whose lives have been blighted by early malnutrition I sadly confess that I am doubtless responsible.

But the job I disliked most was washing up. The hospital kitchen was a bleak place and in its icy air hot water was converted instantaneously to steam. When I bent over the bowl of crockery and cutlery balloons of vapour rose and, colliding with my head, burst their envelopes, spraying my face with a warm poison gas of animal fat. Every hole in my skin was charged to capacity with grease. Grease entubed every hair of my head and was rank in my nose.

After the washing, the drying. This was slightly less disagreeable than washing up, but only slightly. In a short time the teacloths became soggy and useless, and the hollow handles of saucepans and the concavities of spoons were cold-water traps which sent a deluge trickling down my sleeve whenever I unwarily lifted one of these utensils above shoulder level. The damp adhesive state of my sleeve made it feel horrible.

After a session in the kitchen I wanted a bath to wash away the stink and slime. The bathroom was as large as a living-room, with walls painted in two colours—faded brown and yellowing white. The lighter surface was a large temptation to anyone with a pencil —and many had succumbed to it. The bath itself was a piece of mid-Victorian ironmongery, all bones with not a voluptuous curve anywhere, and when you touched any part of it it broadcast pulsating rings of sound like a bell. When I got in and lowered myself its sides slid upwards past my ears to the ceiling and made me think I was in a lift. This was a sensation that I enjoyed. Another enjoyment was to gaze for ages and ages (until a nurse came to see if I was all right) at the black patches where the enamel had been chipped off, seeing them as faces, animals, and islands. Yet another enjoyment was to pull out the plug when I'd had my bath and stare at the thick blue water rushing past as I sat in it until I had the illusion it was carrying me with it to the waste pipe: it was reassuring to feel stationary metal under my bottom. As the water ran through the pipes under the floorboards it set up an appalling clanking and I thought that at any moment there'd be an explosion. I hopped out quickly, and drying was always an exciting race against an imminent catastrophe.

I wasn't a domestic worker for long. I got ill again and had to have a third operation. And after that a fourth. I was then pronounced as well as could be expected. When I was thought to be sufficiently recovered to be permitted to hobble about it was found that I couldn't because I'd lost the use of my legs. The nurses were sorry for me, but I was glad: if I couldn't walk I couldn't work!

I now began to enjoy hospital life. The nurses were kind and gave me presents. One, knowing my taste, gave me a Railway Guard's outfit with blue peaked cap, green flag, and whistle. Twice a week the porter collected our pennies and returned with bags of sweets for us—triangular bags with saw-toothed top edges and a bit missing off the corner where the hanging string had been, the emeralds, rubies, and ambers of the wine gums and mixed fruits inside giving enticing hints of their charms through the veiled transparency of the paper.

I don't know if it was because the Duchess of Portland was poor, but we didn't have any egg-cups in her ward. We cupped our breakfast eggs in our hands, and for that reason the eggs were supplied tepid and hard boiled. Our dinner of minced meat, vegetables, and gravy came in a mug and we ate it with a teaspoon.

The only unpleasant happening during these days of convalescence was the periodic dressing of my ear and replacement of rubber drainage tubes. When the steel-and-glass trolley approached and the side of my cot was lowered I lay despondently on my stomach; out of the corner of my eye I saw the forceps taken off the tray; I felt the shock of cool metal on my flesh; there was a sore pulling sensation; then a hissing pop as the rubber tube came out of the hole behind my ear; then a continuous unrelenting sore pressure as the new tube was pressed in. While this was going on I gripped the sheet hard.

Then came the day when the stitches were taken out—it sounded in my ears like fetters being struck off—and soon after that Mother and Auntie George came and I was wrapped in a blanket and carried through the sunny hospital grounds, where I'd often sat in my guard's outfit eating mashed strawberries and cream, to a hired car waiting outside the hospital gates.

As the car drove away from the hospital I turned to gaze at its outside, which I'd never seen before. It looked strange—but everything else looked strange, too. I'd been confined to the same scene for so long that I looked now at a foreign land. Through the great empty market-place we went, a Gobi of hot, shimmering cobbles where a few stalls covered with tarpaulin drooped like abandoned tents; then along the narrow pass of Lister Gate into the wide plain of Corrington Street.

We approached, on our left, an elaborate long building set back from the carriage way and Auntie George pointed it out to me with pride.

'That's the Midland Station,' she informed me. 'It's where

your Uncle G.B. works. Perhaps one day, if you're a good boy, you'll work there, too.'

Along Arkwright Street—would we ever get to the end?—we sped in the fine, soft car; then over Trent Bridge and its broad placid river into West Bridgford.

'Turn left at the telephone box,' Auntie George told the driver, and he did, and we rolled down the gentle slope of Rectory Road.

'Stop just before the railway bridge,' Auntie George instructed.

The car drew up outside the home of Auntie George and Uncle G.B. It was my home, too, now, for I'd done with Carlyle Road for ever.

22

A Visit from Pearl

IN RECTORY ROAD I lived in the best bedroom, reserved for guests. I lay in the enormous mahogany double bed, under a counterpane of comics and annuals—*Chicks' Own, Puck, The Rainbow, Tiger Tim's Weekly, The Magnet, Adventure, The Wizard, The Rover, Mrs Hippo's Annual, Blackie's Boys' Annual, Partridge's Children's Annual, Young England*. I also had two real books—a 'reward' bound in synthetic vellum called *That Little French Baby* by John Strange Winter (who was a lady) and a volume of a very different character, Peck's *A Bad Boy's Diary*. Some of these publications, supplied by Susie, I considered below my intellectual level; others, provided by Auntie and Uncle or brought back from hospital, were above it—but that made no difference: I read omnivorously.

I still have vivid memories of some of the stories: there was one about a family who woke up one morning to find that everybody in London except themselves had vanished, being replaced by malevolent people made of wood; there was 'Bushranger's Gold', 'For the White Rose of York', 'On the Wings of the Morning' (about aviators), and 'The Island' (about a miser); there was a story in which the characters were prehistoric reptiles with unpronounceable names like Archaeopteryx, Stegosaurus, Triceratops, and another in which a missionary quelled a native uprising by projecting a magic lantern slide of Queen Victoria on to a screen of cloud. Why is it that I remember these, whereas many masterpieces of literature, read later, have been forgotten?

My favourite weekly papers, I think, were *Kinema Komic* and *Film Fun*. These consisted almost entirely of black-and-white strip cartoons illustrating the activities of current screen personalities—Louise Fazenda, Polly Moran, Ford Sterling, Chester Conklin, Ben Turpin, Larry Semon, Jackie Coogan. A large number of drawings depicted alleys and courts furnished with dustbins and bent iron posts and inhabited exclusively by wide-shouldered gentry in striped jerseys, tilted bowler hats, and thick boots with up-curling toes, who carried ferocious crowbars and sacks honestly labelled 'SWAG'—they reflected the influence, I suppose, of Charlie Chaplin's *Easy Street*. In *Film Fun* or *Kinema Komic*—I can't remember which—there were some special characters whose adventures I followed eagerly week after week: the two swells, Roland Butta and Hammond Deggs, and, in democratic contrast, the two tramps, Weary Willie and Tired Tim.

Most of the comics occasionally gave away free gifts—bumper joke books, cut-out models, motor-car badges—and getting your copy with 'FREE INSIDE!' on the cover and the stiff feel which had to be cherished in order to avoid injury to the windfall within was terrifically exciting. One paper, *The Jester*, even included complimentary confectionery—a strip of liquorice inserted between the pages like a black book-marker.

Apart from having my ear syringed daily (horrid) and suffering hot fomentations (worse) and eating Brand's Essence of Chicken, Calves'-Foot Jelly, and Parrish's Food (all of which Tishy brought up regularly on a tray) I had nothing to do all day except sit up in bed and read or lie back on my pillow and daydream. And reading and day-dreaming led to my making up stories of my own.

'I'm going to read you a story I've written,' I said to Sid Byron, who had come to visit me with a supply of *Boys' Magazines*, *Union Jacks*, and *Nelson Lee Librarys*.

Sid nodded deferentially. He was very respectful to me now that I was a distinguished convalescent and no longer living in Carlyle Road.

'"The Rustlers of Bar-20",' I began. '"Chapter One. One evening, as the sun was going down behind the snow-capped peaks of the Rocky Mountains, a lone rider could be seen galloping over the mesquite towards Arizona . . ." do you think that's all right?'

'Sounds spiffing!'

Encouraged, I searched among the papers on my bed.

'I've written a thriller as well,' I said. 'It's called "The Clue of the Twisted Fork".'

'Ripping title,' Sid complimented.

'"Chapter One. One evening, as the sun was going down behind the pine-clad hills of Norfolk, a lone roadster could be seen speeding towards Scotland Yard . . ."'

Sid looked puzzled.

'How's it go on?' he asked.

'I don't know. I gave it up and started a tale of the olden days. Shall I read it?'

'All right.'

'"For the Red Rose of Lancaster. Chapter One. One evening, as the sun was going down behind the rugged mountains of Lancashire, a lone stage coach could be seen travelling towards London . . ."'

Sid now looked very puzzled indeed—even doubtful—and I couldn't understand why: I thought all these beginnings were absolutely first rate, for they were all based on one which I had seen in *The Rover* and liked very much—and if *The Rover* approved, why didn't Sid?

Next day I had another visitor. Tishy opened my door and announced: 'A lady to see you, sir.'

A lady! Who could it be? A nurse from the hospital? At first I thought I was right in my guess about the nurse—for the person who walked in was tall and dignified and fashionably dressed. Then I saw it was Pearl. How she had grown up while I was in hospital! I felt awed by her.

She took off her pull-on hat and shook her yellow bobbed hair. Without her hat she was less scaring—more like the Pearl I used to know, freckled, pretty, venturesome, cheeky.

'I put my new costume on to come here,' she said. 'What a swanky house! A maid and all!'

'It's my auntie and uncle's. I live here now.'

'I know.'

'Who told you?'

'Sid.'

She had placed her hat, her handbag, and a Home and Colonial carrier on the bed and now she began unpacking the carrier. She handed me bananas, oranges, sweets. Then:

'Here are two presents,' she said. 'This one's from Sailor Sam.'

It was a wooden biplane, complete with a pilot in the cockpit. I was touched to think that Sailor Sam had remembered me.

'It was nice of Sailor Sam to make this for me, wasn't it?' I said.

'Umm-umm. This is from me.'

It was a book. I looked with interest at the coloured jacket, which showed men in pigtails staring at a red motor-boat in the sky.

'It's called *The Flying Boat by Herbert Strang*,' explained Pearl. 'It's the one I've told you about. It's good—all about the Yangtze.'

I put it among the other books and periodicals on my bed.

'Crikey!' Pearl exclaimed. 'What a lot of comics you've got. Is that what you do all day—just read?'

'I write stories as well,' I answered with pride. 'Shall I read you one?'

'Yes—if you like,' Pearl directed, without much enthusiasm, sitting on the edge of the bed.

I began quickly, in case she should change her mind.

'"The Clue of the Twisted Fork. Chapter One. One evening, as the sun was going down behind the pine-clad hills of Norfolk——"'

Pearl interrupted.

'There aren't any hills in Norfolk.'

'Aren't there?'

'No. Norfolk's flat.'

'How do you know?'

'Geography.'

'It doesn't make any difference. It can be anywhere.'

'What about Rutland?'

'Are there pine-clad hills in Rutland?'

'Don't know. But it's the smallest county in England.'

'All right, then. Rutland.' I began again. Pearl listened, as before, with ill-concealed patience. '"The Clue of the Twisted

Fork. Chapter One. One evening, as the sun was going down behind the pine-clad hills of Rutland, a lone roadster could be seen speeding towards Scotland Yard——"'

'Scotland Yard isn't in Rutland.'

'I know. But that's where the lone roadster was going.'

'Why don't you say it was going to London, then?'

'But it wasn't just going to *London*,' I explained as patiently as I could to my carping public. 'It was going to *Scotland Yard* in London. That's where the detectives come from.'

'I know that, you chump. If I was you I would say a lone roadster could be seen speeding towards London. Then when it got to London I'd say the lone roadster weaved and twisted its way through the dense traffic of the great metropolis until it drew up with a screeching of tyres on gravel outside the imposing portals of Scotland Yard. A lithe, military-looking man leaped out. Tall, handsome, bronzed, a pipe between his teeth, his square-cut jaw set firmly—that's how I'd do it'.

'That's a rattling good beginning!' I said. 'You ought to be a writer, too.'

'I am.'

'Go on!'

'You know I am. I write poems.'

Of course. Pearl's funny verses.

'Have you written any more?'

'Heaps.'

'Can you recite some?'

Pearl furrowed her brow and stared up at the ceiling, thinking deeply. Then her face cleared and she said:

> 'I've a nice little house in the country,
>   And all that I've wanted I've got:
> I sit on my porch when I'm lazy,
>   And I sit on my porch when I'm not.

'Here's another.

> 'The boy stood on the burning deck,
>   His breeches needed mending:
> "You naughty boy!" the captain said,
>   "Don't let me catch you bending!"'

I shrugged my shoulders.

'Don't you think they're funny?' Pearl asked.

'No, not very.'

'All right!' she responded in a fighting tone. 'Listen:

> 'Oh look at my Uncle Jim!
>   He's diving in the chamber-pot
>   And learning how to swim.

Like that better?'

I didn't know what to say. It was vulgar, and I'd been taught not to repeat vulgar stories and poems or to listen to them.

'Can you make up a sentence with the word Income Tax in it?' I asked Pearl.

Pearl thought. Then she said:

'No. You tell me.'

'All right,' I grinned, delighted to have defeated her. 'I heard a dog barking outside my house and when I opened the door Income Tax.'

Pearl made a rude face.

'My dog was called Tax,' I pointed out. 'When I opened the door in come Tax. See?'

'Can you make up a sentence with the word Defender in it?' Pearl retaliated.

I thought, but without success.

'I give up. Tell me.'

It was now Pearl's turn to look triumphant.

'De boss was out, de pot was full, so I peed in de fender,' she declaimed.

This also was vulgar, and I was silent.

'It's supposed to be a black boy saying it,' Pearl elucidated. 'See?'

I was feeling thirsty. It wouldn't be long now before somebody brought us up some tea.

'Have an orange, Pearl,' I invited, handing one of her gift oranges to her. I took one for myself. It was a Jaffa, thickly upholstered, and when I dug my thumb-nail into it my face was sprayed by a pungently scented mist.

G

'I'm getting juice all over my new costume,' Pearl objected. 'It's crumpled already from sitting on the bed.' She stood up. 'Oh, golly! Just look.'

It was true that her clothes were a bit wrinkled, but I didn't think it was anything to worry about.

'It isn't *very* crumpled,' I assured her.

'I know what. I'll take it off.'

'Take your costume off?'

'Yes.'

'But, Pearl . . .'

'It's all right, mardy. I've got a petticoat on.' She started to unbutton her jacket. 'And, anyway, you don't have to look. Shut your eyes.'

Closing my eyes as ordered I turned over on my stomach and buried my face in the pillow. Uneasily, I listened to Pearl's jerky breathing, the soft rustling of materials, the snap of elastic. As Pearl stepped off one foot on to the other the floorboards creaked. At length I felt the bed give under her weight as she sat down on it.

'Can I open them now?'

There was a short silence.

'You can now.'

Pearl's reply was spoken softly and from somewhere very close. When I opened my eyes I saw her lying beside me in the bed.

'Why not?' she demanded, though I'd said nothing, being too surprised. 'It's big enough for two.'

'Yes,' I mumbled.

'It's jolly comfy. Must be a feather bed.'

'I think so.'

'It's top hole.'

She bounced herself on the resilient mattress and then, after lying still for a moment, inched towards me until I could feel the full length of her warm body pressing against mine. Her bare toes stroked my instep.

'I've never been in a feather bed before,' she said in a low voice.

Her body was keeping up a persistent pressure against my

body and the aggressive stranger's warmth made me fearfully excited.

'I know a poem I bet you don't know. Shall I tell it you?'

'Yes.'

'Listen then.

> 'When I was young and had no sense
> A boy took me behind a fence.
>
> He felt in his pocket and gave me a shilling;
> I gave him a kiss to show I was willing—

have you got a shilling?'

'Baking powder?'

'You *are* a fathead. I said, have you got a shilling?'

'No.'

'It doesn't matter. You can give me a kiss instead.'

I hesitated.

'Come on. I won't bite you.'

Ashamed of my backwardness I leaned over and kissed her on the forehead.

'Can you smell my perfume?'

'Yes,' I murmured.

'It's Phūl Nānā. This is the first time I've put it on. Now I've got to kiss you.'

She kissed me on the mouth. Until then the only kisses I'd had were overpowering wet welcomes from aunts or polite dry farewells from cousins. Pearl's kiss was a totally new experience. It gave me goose flesh.

'That shows I'm willing,' Pearl said.

Together, we pushed back the bedclothes. I slipped off my pyjama trousers. Pearl pulled up her petticoat. We were in the middle of our fascinated mutual examination when the door opened and Auntie George entered with the tea tray.

23

Tishy

'I *was* going to buy you a novelty,' Auntie George said.

In the short time I'd been at Rectory Road I'd already learned that this was Auntie George's favourite method of inflicting punishment. Whenever I displeased her she said: 'I *was* going to buy you a novelty—but now you've been such a bad boy I've changed my mind.' On the other hand, if I managed to remain good the presentation of a reward was a topic on which my aunt was disappointingly silent. Because of this I began to wonder if trying to be good was worth while—it was, after all, quite hard and it had apparently the same negative result as being bad. Why this should be so was a mystery; and as I lay in bed I speculated for hours on the complicated subject of morality and reached no conclusion except that the world I was growing up in was one in which logic seemed to have no place.

Sometimes, when she considered me deserving of especially severe punishment, my aunt would chastise me with descriptions of the novelties she *was* intending to bring home for me until I proved to be so naughty—an optical instrument that enabled you to observe what was happening behind your back, an electric pencil for writing in the dark, a pair of geometrical compasses with a retractable point, a pocket microscope. I never received a single one of these ingenious objects—grammatically speaking, my future was always in the past. For parsimonious aunts, uncles, mothers, and fathers, who wish to have the advantages of generosity without any of the disadvantages, my Auntie George's formula is one to be unreservedly recommended.

'I *was* going to buy you a novelty,' Auntie George repeated, 'but now you've been such a bad boy I've changed my mind. Your father who is in heaven must be turning in his grave (how could he be in heaven and turning in his grave at the same time?

I wondered) at the nasty, dirty, horrible thing you've done. That brazen hussy Pearl, who looks as though she'll grow up to be worse than her mother—if she ever comes to this house again or tries to see you I'll hand her over to the magistrates. And if you ever try to see her——'

Auntie George paused, leaving the rest of her sentence to be finished by my fertile imagination. She glared at me in frightening disapproval.

'Do you know what happens to wicked little boys like you?' she resumed. 'They go blind, their noses drop off, they become deaf . . .'

Here I felt it necessary, in honesty, to remind Auntie that I was deaf already—at least in one ear, my mastoid one.

'Then you'll go deaf in the other one!' she snapped. 'If you weren't ill I'd get your uncle to thrash you!'

After Auntie had gone I lay for a long time in remorse and shame. What I had done was very awful, I knew. I had known it all the time I was doing it. I touched my nose—would it really drop off? Yes, I thought it probably would, for Auntie George, being old and experienced, knew a lot about life and she wouldn't lie to me. I stared at the dressing-table, with its porcelain pot-pourri bowl and balloon hair tidy made out of an inverted electric light bulb with a little basket underneath—would I really go blind? It seemed a high price to pay for half an hour's pleasure. I closed my eyes and lived in darkness. It was terrible. I opened my eyes and felt how wonderful it was to see the pot-pourri bowl and balloon hair tidy again. All I had done was to take an interest in Pearl because she was different from me. It was God who had made her different. If He hadn't meant me to take any notice of her why had He made us so unlike each other? It seemed very unfair of God to put boys and girls in the world and then to blame them for enjoying being boys and girls.

I was in the middle of these profound thoughts when I heard a little tap on the door. I waited, wondering. Then the door handle turned and the door was moved open slowly. Tishy came in on tiptoe.

'I came in quietly because I thought you might be asleep, pet,' she said. 'I've brought you some mashed bananas and cream and some lemonade. And some *Sketches.*'

Tishy knew that I was fond of the *Daily Sketch* because it had Uncle Oojah and Jerrywangle and Pop in it. I liked Uncle Oojah and Jerrywangle because they were elephants and I liked Pop because he looked like Uncle G.B. Susie had recently joined the Oojah Club and had been issued with a badge and a certificate on which she pasted a silver star every time she recruited a new member. She was pressing me to join, but I hadn't made my decision yet—I felt I was a bit too old for it, though I had to admit I greatly coveted the round enamelled badge. Tishy carefully preserved each *Daily Sketch* from the kitchen flames and brought it up to my bedroom with the Parrish's Food.

'I hear you've been a terribly bad boy,' Tishy said.

I looked at her pale face, shingled black hair with a curl on the forehead, her forget-me-not blue eyes, and I felt so overwhelmed by love and misery that I threw my arms around her and burst into tears.

'There, there, my pet,' Tishy comforted. 'Don't give on. It's all over now.'

'But I've been very bad,' I sobbed. 'You said so yourself just now.'

'Yes, you have been. But it's all over now.'

'Will my nose drop off?'

'Of course it won't, you silly.'

'Will I go blind?'

'Good gracious! What bally idiot's been telling you that?'

'Auntie did.'

Tishy bit her lip.

'Of course you won't go blind,' she said.

'Auntie said I would.'

'Well, aunties aren't always right—though some of them think they are.'

'How do you know my nose won't drop off and I won't go blind?'

'Never you mind. I know.'

'How?'

'Well!' Tishy's pale face flushed. She was lost in reflection for a while. 'If you really want to know I'll tell you. When I was your age I knew several boys and girls who did what you did this afternoon and *I know for a fact* that they aren't blind and their noses are exactly where they ought to be.'

She caught hold of her nose and waggled it, laughing. Then she dabbed my eyes on her frilly maid's apron.

'Now drink up your lemonade,' she said.

'Is it crystals?'

'No. It's real lemons. Drink it up like a good boy.'

'But I'm not a good boy,' I objected artfully.

'You're a little rascal, I know that much!' Tishy scolded affectionately. 'Drink it up—it will make your hair grow curly.'

'It's crusts that make your hair curl.'

I was disappointed that it wasn't lemonade crystals. They were just like sweets.

'Tishy.'

'Yes, pet?'

'Did you do it, too?'

'Do what?' Tishy asked innocently.

'You know.'

'I was a good little girl. I went to Sunday School and I knew that God was watching everything I did.'

'God made us, didn't He?'

'Yes, pet.'

'Then why did He make boys and girls if it's wrong?'

'It isn't boys and girls that's wrong. It's boys and girls *doing* wrong.' She caressed my hair. 'Eat the banana and cream I've brought you.'

'Tishy,' I said through pulp and cream.

'Yes, pet?'

'Sid Byron said Mrs Belton and Sailor Sam did what me and Pearl did this afternoon. Is it all right when grown-ups do it— but wrong when it's boys and girls?'

'You do ask tricky questions.'

'But is it?'

'You know what killed the cat, don't you?'

'Curiosity.'

'That's right. You're too nosy by half. What you've got to do, pet, is forget what doesn't concern you and concentrate on getting well. Then when you're a big strong boy you can come out with me and have an ice-cream at Ballingall's. I bet you've never had an ice-cream at Ballingall's, have you?'

'No.'

'Then you just wait—they're marvellous.'

They were. Ballingall's was a confectionery shop in Arkwright Street, and after a few months I was strong enough to be able to hobble in there and have a famous ice—not a cornet, but a white shining buoy on a glass plate, floating in cream and carrying a wafer like a sail. It was an interesting experience to have a sit-down ice in a café, instead of licking one standing up. I took saltspoon helpings to make the delicious sensation a long-drawn-out one.

I was taken out by Tishy in a push-chair, for I still wasn't able to walk. Every time we went along Rectory Road we passed a pillar-box which had G R painted in black letters on its fat, red stomach. Sitting in the push-chair I was on the same level as these letters and as we drew near them the pillar-box went GRRrrrrrrr at me. We passed many other pillar-boxes in our journeys about West Bridgford and they all went GRrrrrrrrr at me. I was amused by this, knowing they couldn't leap at me and bite, in spite of their growl and gaping, hungry mouths. Sometimes Tishy and I went along residential Musters Road, passing the Modern School, until we came to the strip of commercialized pavement on which stood Mona Spencer's, the milliner's, and Prince's, the chemists. Sometimes we went along residential Melton Road and glimpsed Wilford Suspension Bridge: it looked frail, as though made of grey hair, and it was impossible to believe that people were at that very moment treading on it safely. As we traversed the broad suburban pavements traffic passed us on its way into or out of Nottingham: Urban District Council buses, large open touring cars, high-roofed saloons, two-seaters with dickies. Sometimes we tarried outside a building where men in hospital blue leaned out of windows and talked to

Tishy for minutes lasting hours. She was very happy after these conversations and always bought me something on the way home.

Gradually my legs gained in strength. As time passed I was able to walk about the house, following Tishy while she worked.

'What thin white legs you've got!' she teased. 'They're like two sticks of celery.'

And to give them further exercise she taught me the Charleston.

'Wish we had some dance records,' she said, 'but your auntie'd have a fit if I suggested buying some.'

She rolled back the kitchen mats and rugs and danced on the red-and-blue brick floor, her legs scissoring out and in so rapidly that I blinked trying to follow them.

'Now you do it,' she said.

I made a few feeble steps.

'You *are* a duffer! Watch me.'

Again she danced, giggling, enjoying herself, *spiritoso, accelerando, presto*.

'Now you try again,' she panted.

'You go too fast,' I protested.

'All right. Watch.'

And she danced *rallentando*, a clockwork ballerina running down. It was fascinating, seeing the intricate movements becoming gracefully slow, slower, slowest.

'Your turn, pet.'

'Please do that again.'

'What's the good of *me* dancing all the time? *My* legs are all right.' She glanced at them appreciatively. 'It's your legs we're trying to improve.'

'You're so good at it.'

'I'll tell you what, then. We'll dance together. I'll go slow and you copy me.'

And so we danced the Charleston together, then and often afterwards, until I became quite an adept—but never a wiz like Tishy. When she was dancing Tishy would often forget about her work until she would stop and cry suddenly:

'Crikey! I've still got my bedrooms to do' or 'I'd better go

*G

and get on with swilling the backyard' or 'It's raining and I must put the aspidistra out for a drink.'

'Can't we practise a bit longer?'

'No we can't. You don't want your Auntie George to come after me, do you?'

'No.'

'Well, she will if I don't make haste with my work. Your auntie's a bit of a Tartar, you know.'

'Is she? What is a Tartar?'

'A Tartar's somebody like your Auntie George.'

My happiest hours at Rectory Road were spent with Tishy, talking to her while she scrubbed the chequered tiles of the passage that led from the front door to the kitchen, or while she bathed the leaves of the aspidistras in milk (they took a lot of looking after, the aspidistras), or rubbed Ronuk on the furniture, or cleaned knives with powder and a wheel, or scraped carrots and shelled peas.

The job I liked doing with her most of all was polishing the brass. She spread newspapers on the kitchen table and put all the portable tea-coloured brassware on it—the teetotum, the Three Wise Monkeys, the toasting fork (decorative only), the caddy spoon (ditto), the big ladle (ditto), the Lincoln Imp, the Isle of Man Legs. Then, ready to begin, she collected her old Brasso gloves: these had become very worn at the ends, so that when she put them on the tips of her fingers and thumbs were visible and she appeared to be wearing five pink thimbles on each hand. I loved the acrid chemical fume of the Brasso because it meant that Tishy was immobilized and we could gabble as much as we liked; and I found it interesting to see the tarnished metal grow a skin of grime which was later rubbed away to expose a clean, shining face. It was like watching a chimney-sweep having a bath.

One day I said to Tishy:

'Don't you think it's funny—me living here?'

'What's so funny about it?'

'Well, I ought to be living with my mother.'

'Should you?'

'Of course. All boys with mothers do.'

'I know why you don't.'

'Why?'

'You're living with your Auntie George because she is a trained nurse and can take care of you while you're an invalid.'

'That's right.'

'Your Auntie George is a very kind lady.'

'Is she?'

'Is she, indeed! Of course she is!'

'Well, I haven't known her very long, really. Not as long as you have.'

'Well, she's a very nice auntie and you're a lucky boy. Aren't you glad to be able to live in this nice house and have lots of nice food to eat?'

I thought about this question for a while and then decided not to answer it.

'Tishy.'

'Yes, pet?'

'You said Auntie George was a bit of a Tartar.'

'Did I?'

'Yes, you did.'

'All right. Suppose I did. She *is* a bit of a Tartar. She gave me a dickens of a time until I had it out with her.'

'Did she?'

'Yes, she did. When I was new here I almost left before my first week was out.'

'Why did you almost leave?'

'Because I'd never known such a mistress for fault-finding. She was always on at me. She didn't like the way I had my hair cut, my dresses were too short, it was wrong to put powder on my face. And she told me I mustn't go dancing. Really! You know how much I like dancing, don't you?'

'Yes, I do, Tishy.'

'She used to read my private letters when I was out—to see if I'd got a sweetheart. And because she saw pretty underclothes in my chest of drawers she used to make nasty remarks about me. Really scandalized me, she did. You know, with her nose all wrinkled up.'

'Yes!' I laughed in recognition. 'With her nose all wrinkled up. I know!'

'But it's all right now. We're a proper pair of love birds now.'

'Did you have it out with her?'

'Yes, I did. The fact is, your auntie *is* a nice kind lady if you keep on the right side of her. And the way to do that is not to give in to her. You mustn't cheek her, mind—just show her you can stand up for yourself.'

'Is that what you did, Tishy?'

'Yes.'

'How? Did you have a row?'

'Oh, no. I'll tell you. She used to lay traps for me all over the house, to catch me out not doing my work properly. She put threepenny bits under dressing-table runners and vases, and hair-pins and needles under floor mats. Then at the end of the week she'd go all over the house, upstairs and down, and if she found any of the things she'd hidden still where she'd put them she'd play Hamlet with me for neglecting my housework. But I found a way of putting a stop to that.'

'Do you mean you had it out with her?'

'Mmmm. One day I polished and dusted under my vases and mats very carefully and then put the threepenny bits and hair-pins back underneath. I can remember it now—I almost had a fit of the giggles when your auntie came home! Her ladyship lifted up the biscuit barrel in the dining-room and then said to me, all very innocent, but with her nose wrinkled up: "Look, Tishy, I've just found a threepenny bit that I'd lost. It was under this biscuit barrel. Just fancy, it must have been there for a week at least. I wonder when this sideboard was last dusted?" I didn't say a word. "There are some houses I go into where you can write your name on the furniture," she said, running her finger along the top of the sideboard. When she lifted up her finger it was as clean as a new pin. She *was* surprised. She had another go—there still wasn't any dust on her finger. Then she tried the table and then the mantelpiece. Still nothing doing. Then she gave up. She was beaten and she knew it. She just glared at me and left the room.'

'What did she do after that?'

'Nothing. She was as nice as anything to me.'

'I'm glad she wasn't ratty.'

'Well, as I told you, you've got to stand up to your auntie. She's a funniosity in a way, but she's all right really. And it suits me being here, because with your uncle on the railway and your auntie out all day sick visiting I've got the place to myself.'

When she wasn't doing a sedentary job like brass cleaning, which gave us an opportunity to talk, Tishy moved about the house singing. She sang all the popular numbers of the day, but she had two favourites which she performed over and over again. In one of these there occurred the refrain:

Smile a while and kiss me S'Ad 'Adu

and I wondered who S'Ad 'Adu was. What kind of man was he that Tishy should be so fascinated by him? Eventually I decided that he was an Eastern prince, a Saracen, handsome, dark, armed with a scimitar and wearing a turban ablaze with jewels. Tishy's other favourite asked a question:

Where do the flies go in the winter time?
Do they go to Gayparee?

and this refrain puzzled me, too.

'Where's Gayparee?' I asked Tishy.

'Gayparee?' Tishy said, surprised. 'Why, it's in France, of course. Everybody knows that.'

But when I tried to find Gayparee on my tin globe I couldn't see it anywhere.

Now that I could walk about I often went with Tishy to the cinema. There was one called the Globe Picture Palace that we sometimes went to, and another right in the town called the Élite, but the one I enjoyed going to most was The Pavilion on Trent Bridge. This was a thrilling place, because it was white and made of wood and it was an adventure to sit in a picture palace that was almost swimming in a river. Outside the building there was usually a plywood cut-out of Charlie Chaplin—floppy floor-walker's trousers, shrunk jacket, frizzy hair, pimple bowler, barley-sugar cane. When you passed through the outer doors into the inner vestibule you heard the loud continuous clicking of the projector. This magical whirring noise was a powerful part of the cinema's spell: it preceded your entrance into the dark cave like an initiatory processional hymn, titillating your fancies and luring you on into the blindfolded, stumbling future.

The screen was a dirty creased sketching-block and the figures that zigzagged across it were drawn in charcoal and chalk. The romantic figures were Tishy's idols, while the comics and cow-boys were mine—Mary Pickford, Hoot Gibson, Tom Mix, Alice Terry, Rudolph Valentino, Harold Lloyd, Buster Keaton, Buck Jones. They lived, loved, loathed, and looneyed, these gesticulating players, in a world as strange and silent as the moon.

But though their world was soundless, ours wasn't. Somewhere in the cinema there was an invisible musician who accompanied the pictures on a banjo-like piano and in an interval between films provided the music for community singing. The verses of a song flickered on to the screen and a little ball bounced above the words to show us the right way to sing them.

'Oh, what a pal was Mary,'

we sang in bashful discord,

'Oh, what a pal was she;
An angel was born
One Sunday morn
And God sent her down to me . . .'

After this, if we were lucky, we saw Rin-Tin-Tin pencilling a swift dark line across the Alaskan snow.

Tishy's efforts to turn me into a strong boy were slow in show-ing results, and she made two suggestions to Auntie and Uncle that she thought would hasten the process. One of these was that I should be given a scooter. I would have preferred her to recommend a Fairycycle, a really classy vehicle, but it was considered better for me to stand and push than to sit and pedal. Accordingly, a scooter was purchased for me by my mother. It was a Tan-Sad, sturdy, graceful, fast. Auntie George approved of it because it was a novelty—it could be folded up for storing away. Laced to the handlebars was a label informing me that the scooter was manufactured from Mild Steel and this testimony to a good character made me take to the Tan-Sad at once: I felt that it was going to be a true, tolerant, and trustworthy companion —and time proved me right.

Tishy's second suggestion was that I should join the Wolf Cubs. Everybody agreed to this, also, and I was taken by Tishy to Redmayne and Todd's to be fitted out with my uniform. I acquired a green jersey, a green cap decorated with yellow braid and a wolf's head as saucy as a fox's, a yellow and green necker-chief, a white lanyard, a leather belt with *Ich Dien* and the Prince of Wales's feathers stamped on the buckle, a jack-knife, and a whistle.

Our H.Q. was an old army hut in a field, and going there was adventurous. Immense looming adults of twelve or fourteen reared out of the dusk, muttering in gruff voices as they plodded along the lanes with poles as tall as themselves. When you got inside the paraffin-lit hut you saw that these intimidating beings were Boy Scouts in North-west Mounted Police hats and khaki shirts with cloth badges sewn along their sleeves like patches. Colourful ribbons fluttered from shoulders and stockings, turning each Boy Scout into a perambulating garden fête. Not content with probing their immediate environment with poles, the scouts used to lug out an ex-service searchlight and prod the night with its long blue ruler. In fact, the scouts seemed to make a fetish of illumination, for every one of them flaunted a flash lamp of some sort—either a signalling lamp with adjustable red, green, and clear lenses or one of a variety of instruments fitted with great bulging bull's eyes that when you switched on washed the black countryside white in an instant.

My happiest moments in the Cubs were when we went on Church Parade. How gleefully we marched, with pendulum legs and arms, between the lines of staring windows, proud to be making such a din in the quiet Sunday air! The bump, bump, bump of our big bass drum and the gravelly rattle of our side-drums beat time to our stamping feet; and the shrill, primitive, challeng-ing, rallying cry of our copper bugles pierced the fences, privet hedges, and the walls of the houses as we passed them. As we banged and blasted along Rectory Road I smirked up at Number 7, because everybody—Auntie George, Uncle G.B., Tishy, and, I hoped, Mother and Susie—would be watching. And there they were! crowding the front bedroom window through which I had stared as a convalescent.

Two important events occurred while I was a Wolf Cub. The first of these was the visit to Nottingham of the Prince of Wales —the very person whose feathers I wore and whom I had asked God to save when I was at the Infants' School. I was one of the Cubs chosen to take part in crowd control. With brand-new lanyards and well-laundered neckerchiefs we stood in the gutter of Parliament street and linked hot hands to form a fence of eight-year-olds that prevented a mob of frenzied millions stampeding on to the roadway and blocking the Royal progress. I had an excellent view of the Prince as he went by in a car—this compensated for the injustice of having to work on a public holiday— and saw a pink-cheeked, blue-eyed, fair-haired young man in medal-heavy naval uniform, his officer's white-drill peaked cap exactly like the one Sid Byron used to wear in Carlyle Road.

The second important event was the Route March. This was supposed to be a disciplined trek through streets, through fields, and then through streets again. Somehow, in the middle stage of the March—that is, in the fields—I got separated from the rest of the Pack. I didn't know which way to go. I consulted my magnetic compass, but as I didn't know in what quarter our destination lay, whether north, south, east, or west, this wasn't of much avail. I ran rapidly through my esoteric Wolf Cub lore—the Cub Promise, the Cub Salute, clove hitch, bowline, sheepshank, eye splice, tenderpad, dixie, jamboree, totem pole—all to no purpose. I stood on the top rail of a five-barred gate, so as to be able to get a view above hedges, but I saw nothing but grass and cows. I climbed a tree as high as I dared go, but all I saw from there was a leaf-stippled version of the same grass and cows as before. Nowhere could I descry a welcome green-and-yellow cap. I was beginning to feel cold. Would I *ever* be able to find my way home? The fields looked like boundless prairies. Nevertheless, I started off. I crossed one field, two fields, three fields, crawling under gaps in hedges and through entanglements of barbed wire. To get from the third field into the fourth I had to climb a fence. It wasn't high. Once over the top I just had to let myself down gently. Just a little bit lower. Just another little bit. My feet ought to be touching the ground by now. Just a little lower. Just a little farther to go. To my alarm I suddenly felt my feet cold and wet. Startled, I let go of my hold and dropped up to my waist into a small river. I blew my whistle.

Now if you are a Wolf Cub, to blow your whistle is as grave an act as pulling the communication cord in a railway train. The emergency has to be a very dire emergency indeed. My whistle certainly brought help—the Cubmaster and some of his cubs, who dragged me to land and partially de-mudded, de-weeded, and de-hydrated me—but just as operating the communication cord disrupts all train services in the area, so my blast disorganized the whole Route March, which had to be abandoned. The Cubmaster, in addition to being humiliated before the whole of West Bridgford, had to suffer the ruin of a new pair of kid gloves, which he had used to rub some of the water and muck off me. It seemed a pity about the gloves, for the Cubmaster hadn't even done the job very well: when I got home I spent hours peeling scraps of weed off my person and discovering parched water beetles in my clothes. Even a month afterwards I was still coming across the corpses of little fishes in the linings of my pockets.

That was the end of my career as a Wolf Cub and the end of Tishy's adventitious aids to health and strength.

24

Visitors

MOST OF our living at Rectory Road was done in the kitchen, where, as you sat, you could hear Tishy in the adjoining scullery scraping burnt toast or sloshing crockery in the sink. The kitchen possessed a magnificent range which was black-leaded until it was as shiny as a piano, and in front of its hot coal brazier dozed the hearthrug, a shaggy beast made by Auntie George out of rags threaded through hessian and knotted on the underside.

Once a week we visited the front room for Sunday Dinner, Sunday Tea, and Sunday Supper. To reach the front room you had to penetrate the passage already mentioned, a long gloomy tunnel with a tiled floor that Auntie George insisted on being kept as bright as the squares of a draught-board. Opposite the door of the front room was a small oak table on which stood a lady in a crinoline of many layers of pink silk, and under her crinoline was a telephone. It was a distinction to have a telephone in West Bridgford in those days, but in spite of Uncle G.B. and Auntie George being early subscribers their telephone number looked to me as long as the mileage to Mars.

In the front room itself was Auntie George's finest furniture—a roll-top desk, a massive dining table, and a corpulent three-piece suite in uncut blue moquette accoutred with antimacassars on the backs and ash-trays on the arms. Kept in the front room, too—for it was an object of pride rather than of service—was the gramophone. This was very different from the old gramophone of my father's which I had heard in Newport Mon: this was a console model in lustrous figured veneer, elaborately equipped with brilliant metal needle-cups and volume and speed controls and an internal exponential horn. The records owned by Auntie and Uncle were not of a frivolous nature. The works favoured by them belonged to that category of popular respectable music in which the name of a composer is incorporated with his composition to form a title. Thus, on their records, Handel was as indissolubly wedded to his Largo and Schubert to his Serenade as Parkinson is to his Disease or Stephen to his Ink. It was impossible to have 'Song of Songs' without the attendant (Moya) immediately following, or 'Because' without (d'Hardelot), or 'Sylvia' without (Speaks). Darby and Joan were not more enduringly affianced than were the creators and their creations in that front room of Rectory Road.

The gramophone flanked one side of the mantelpiece, a marble structure on which stood a clock in the shape of a castle and a china Chinaman with a nodding head. Flanking the other side of the mantelpiece was the bookcase, made of carved oak and housing Uncle G.B.'s extensive library—his flat-backed Hodder and Stoughton Western novels, arranged tier above tier like rows of bright red bricks. Here were the works of Clarence E. Mulford, William MacLeod Raine, Jackson Gregory, Charles Alden Seltzer, James B. Hendryx, and, above all, of Zane Grey. Nearly all the Master's books were here, from early classics like *Riders of the Purple Sage* and *The Light of Western Stars*, to recent publications such as *The Call of the Canyon* and *To the Last Man*. A shelf beneath the Westerns was spared for Auntie George's books, a miscellaneous collection that included *In Kedar's Tents* by H. Seton Merriman, *The Infamous John Friend* by Mrs R. S. Garnett, Robert Keable's *Simon Called Peter* and *Lighten Our Darkness*, Sir Francis Younghusband's *Kashmir*, and *Notes on Lying-In Institutions* by Florence Nightingale.

Over the books there was suspended a text inscribed on wood with a red-hot needle: 'Lose An Hour In The Morning And You Will Be All Day Looking For It.' Over the mantelpiece hung another motto: 'Eat, Drink, And Be Merry—For Tomorrow We Diet'. In fact, these poker-work adages and aphorisms, suspended from coloured ribbons together with Mabel Lucie Atwell drawings and a dog called Bonzo, dotted the walls of the whole house—the stairway, the bedrooms, the scullery, the bathroom, the coal-house, the lavatory: 'Economy Is Pounds, Shillings, And Sense'; 'Many A False Step Is Made By Standing

Still'; 'An Auctioneer Is A Dangerous Man With Whom To Be On Nodding Acquaintance'; 'Many A Man Who Thinks He Is A Shining Light Is Only A Flash In The Pan.' There was a text in my room, too: 'It Is Only People With Push Who Have A Pull.'

The front room was where our visitors sat and talked—unless they were Mother and Susie, in which case they counted as family, and not guests, and sat in the kitchen like us. We had a lot of visitors at 7, Rectory Road. Auntie George loved visitors, who were essential to her religious life. For, although she rarely went to church, Auntie was extremely pious. Her religion was derived from the Calvinistic part of the Evangelicanism in which she was brought up. Like other Victorian Evangelicals she believed firmly in salvation through works, but simplified the doctrine by interpreting 'works' to mean *work*. To her, cleaning, polishing, ironing, baking, were acts of worship; the scrubbing-brush and the dolly-tub were sacred symbols; spring cleaning and autumn fruit bottling were important festivals in her spiritual calendar. If she sacrificed sleep it wasn't to attend compline, but to lay the foundations of next day's dishes; if she rose early it wasn't for mass, but to get her washing on the line before her neighbour. If her sheets were bounding in the breeze half an hour before any other woman's she felt she was half an hour ahead in the race for heaven; if she drudged while others played she felt that the angels were applauding.

It was here that the visitors came in. Without them she couldn't have practised her piety. Their function was fourfold: one, to act as an audience, for unless there were people to note her industry she felt cheated of the admiration which was her due; two, to provide a background of sloth and sin against which her own purity would appear as a white candle in the night; three, to act as the instigators of her envy, for she derived a perverted sort of pleasure from feeling jealous of people who were still free to enjoy the delights she had virtuously renounced; and, four, to minister further towards her happiness by enabling her to dwell on the contrast between her certainty of future bliss and their certainty of eternal damnation. To perform these offices, her guests had merely to loll about in easy chairs and sofas and be waited on hand and foot, their simple indolent presence stimulating Auntie to toil fantastically and so to rise to exhilarating heights of sanctity.

When she wasn't labouring in the house domestically Auntie George was labouring outside it professionally. Her nursing experience had secured her an important position with an insurance company, her job being to visit men and women drawing weekly sickness benefit under the panel system. In the course of her duties she travelled all over the Midlands, from Walsall, Tamworth, Stafford, and Stoke to Sheffield, Worksop, Doncaster, Rotherham, Scunthorpe, and Goole. For local work she used a green Raleigh bicycle, sometimes taking me with her through Robin Hood villages strapped to the rear carrier. When she entered cottages to conduct her interviews she left the bicycle leaning against a wall or fence, with me attached to it like a tradesman's delivery basket. Auntie's considerable secretarial and organizational work was done by Uncle G.B., who drew up intricate graphs and schedules and papered the kitchen walls with maps of England on which itineraries and territories were plotted in coloured inks like a general's battle plans.

The result of this ceaseless application indoors and out was, of course, that Auntie George and Uncle G.B. became modestly prosperous and were able to fill their house with many of the worldly baubles which Auntie George condemned. To Auntie George there was no paradox in this. Other people, she believed, acquired material goods in a spirit of wicked self-indulgence, whereas she did so sacramentally: her electric cooker and vacuum cleaner and the silk blouses which she kept pristine in tissue-paper were unmistakable outward and visible signs of her inward and invisible grace.

Visitors came in singles and couples on all days of the week, but the really big gatherings took place on Sundays. Midday Sunday dinners were talkative informal affairs because they were mostly attended by relations of Auntie's or Uncle's—Auntie's being short wobbling women from Somerset and Devon who all seemed to be nurses and Uncle's tall scrawny men from

Nottinghamshire and Derbyshire who all seemed to be railway officials. These midday dinners were often quite opulent, with Sandeman's port and Three Castles cigarettes afterwards and sometimes—if Uncle G.B.'s brother-in-law, a booking-office clerk from Pye Bridge, was present—even cigars. Gifts of six-pences and shillings were given to me as the guests sipped their wine—and if the dinner was a cigar occasion, half-crowns. I also received cigarette cards. Not fag cards—not the creased grimy oblongs with the corners turned up like Persian slippers which I had played with at school, but unfingered rectangles of paste-board as crisp as starched collars and still carrying the scent of fresh golden tobacco. Such immaculacy of picture and print was worth treasuring, and so I started a collection that became in time a miniature illustrated encyclopaedia and was my private school for years. Wills's *Arms of Oxford and Cambridge Colleges*, Player's *Natural History* and *Struggle for Existence*, Carreras' *Highwaymen*—I kept my library in a cardboard box as carefully as my birds' eggs.

Sunday Teas were as rich in their different way as Sunday Dinners. In winter the table was laden with hams and ox tongues and pork pies and with iced cakes decorated with hundreds of thousands and silver beads that glittered in the radiance of the chandelier. In summer we had yellow tomatoes—a rare delicacy— and Bartlett pears fished up from gallons of tinny juice. As we ate there came to us, like the sound of a basin being tapped with a pencil, the bell of the corrugated mission hall down the road, being rung by my friend Mr Beeston, the part-time verger who looked after Uncle G.B.'s garden.

But Sunday Teas were more formal than Sunday Dinners because the people who came to them were less intimate—weren't relations, but business colleagues. However, the words 'less intimate' are only true in an hereditary sense: in a physical sense some of the people who came to Sunday Tea were far more intimate with me than the Sunday Dinner guests. This intimacy was initiated and encouraged by my Auntie George. Ever since my birth she had been convinced that there was something seriously wrong with my genito-urinary apparatus and whenever a visitor came to Sunday Tea who had the slightest pretension to medical knowledge she commanded me to let down my shorts and lift my shirt and present myself for an opinion.

'But he's circumcised, Mrs Buller!' one of these visitors, a Nurse Lazenby, said in astonishment one afternoon as she fondled my private parts with one hand and held a cup of tea in the other.

'Of course he is,' said Auntie George.

'I understand. I didn't know you were a Jewish family, Mrs Buller.'

'We are not a Jewish family!' Auntie George declared.

'But I thought it was only Jewish boys who had to be circumcised.'

'Then you haven't read your Scriptures very carefully, Nurse Lazenby,' Auntie George answered, going to the roll-top desk and taking out a Bible bound in limp black leather. 'Listen.' Rapidly, she turned over the pages. '"And he that is eight days old shall be circumcised among you, every man child in your generations, he that is born in the house, or bought with money of any stranger, which is not of thy seed. He that is born in thy house, and he that is bought with thy money, must needs be circumcised: and my covenant shall be in your flesh for an everlasting covenant. And the uncircumcised man child whose flesh of his foreskin is not circumcised, that soul shall be cut off from his people; he hath broken my covenant." I brought Clifford into the world. He was born in my house. How could I break the covenant of the Lord?'

'But that's the Old Testament, Mrs Buller. Surely, in the New . . .'

Auntie George turned quickly to a new page.

'Luke One, verses fifty-nine and sixty,' she announced. '"And it came to pass, that on the eighth day they came to circumcise the child, and they called him Zacharias, after the name of his father. And his mother answered and said, Not so; but he shall be called John."' More pages were turned. 'Luke Two, verse twenty-one. "And when eight days were accomplished for the circumcising of the child, his name was called *Jesus*, which

was so named of the angel before he was conceived in the womb."
There you are,' she concluded with a ring of triumph in her
voice, 'Jesus and John the Baptist! They were Christians, weren't
they?'

'Of course they were, Mrs Buller. But they were circumcised
before St Paul began his ministry and I seem to remember'—
Nurse Lazenby's face shone with anticipated triumph and in her
excitement she absent-mindedly gave me several painful tugs—
'I seem to remember having it explained to me that St Paul made
it unnecessary for Christian boys to undergo *physical* circumcision because he put *spiritual* circumcision in its place.'

Auntie George was taken aback. She stared at Nurse Lazenby
in silence.

'May I have the Bible a moment, Mrs Buller?'

Nurse Lazenby released me and reached out for the book.
While she was looking for her place I, the passive but embar-
rassed cause of the dispute, pulled up my shorts and buttoned my
braces.

'St Paul's Epistle to the Romans,' Nurse Lazenby read.
'Chapter Two, verses twenty-five to twenty-nine. "For circumcision verily profiteth, if thou keep the law: but if thou be a
breaker of the law, thy circumcision is made uncircumcision.
Therefore if the uncircumcision keep the righteousness of the
law, shall not his uncircumcision be counted for circumcision?
And shall not uncircumcision which is by nature, if it fulfil the
law, judge thee, who by the letter and circumcision dost trans-
gress the law? For he is not a Jew, which is one outwardly;
neither is that circumcision, which is outward in the flesh: But he
is a Jew, which is one inwardly; and circumcision is that of the
heart, in the spirit, and not in the letter; whose praise is not of
men, but of God."'

Auntie George looked nonplussed. Then, with her nose
wrinkled up, she said with sour finality, glaring at me:

'Anyway, his foreskin's gone now. Reading texts from the
Bible won't bring it back.'

She took the fat black book from Nurse Lazenby and snapped
it shut.

25

Eating and Beating

THE EXPERIENCE I have described, though an indignity, was an irregular occurrence and therefore wasn't as disagreeable to me as something that recurred with truly sickening monotony. This was being over-fed.

It was one of Auntie George's pleasures to spend every moment that she could spare from her other occupations in shopping and cooking, and because of this she was implacably determined that everybody who ate in her house should show an outrageously enthusiastic appreciation of her every beloved dish. First helpings were dinosaurian—but you were supposed to ask for a second, and even a third, portion. Even if you didn't ask it made no difference: you got your second or third refill just the same. Grown-ups could refuse to eat them and if they were adamant Auntie had to accept their refusal. But I, a child—a delicate one, moreover, who needed building up—was unable to resist: I was forced to consume more—far, far more—nourishment than I needed. The result was that I grew to hate Auntie's food—even the superb lemon-curd tarts that were the flower of Auntie's culinary genius.

The only relief I got from this surfeit of good things was when Auntie George was away from home and I ate off a newspaper tablecloth in the kitchen with Tishy. Then, if Tishy had taken me out or I'd been riding my scooter on the lawn, I might have enough of an appetite to be interested in what she put before me. If it was a boiled egg I tried to slice off its top in the way I'd seen Uncle G.B. do it—with one swift cutlass-stroke he snicked its head right off—and if I succeeded I then enjoyed sniffing in the sudden new-laid-eggness that flew from the opened shell like a bird from a cage, leaving behind a tiny feather of steam that lay on a small white platter with a marigold centre. If it was curved sausages, fried by Tishy to a beautiful brownness that ranged from rich tan to biscuity fawn, I'd enjoy plunging my fork with a crackle into their crusty skins and then sawing off sappy rounds plump with pork and savoury with sage and laying them hot and succulent on my tongue. If it was a poached egg I'd enjoy making an incision in its filmy dome, seeing the yolk flood a savannah of buttery toast like the Yellow River, and then, when I'd finished my meal, impaling a swab of bread on my fork to polish off my plate as clean as a dog's lick.

Sometimes Tishy did without a midday meal—she was thinking of her boyish figure, popular then—and left me to eat alone. On these occasions I amused myself while masticating in solitude by reading the words printed on the labels of cartons and bottles, several of which I invariably saw on the table. I conned them over day after day, week after week, month after month until A. Bostock-Hill and William T. Rigby, Public Analysts, were personages as famous to me as King George and Queen Mary. Slogans became as familiar as nursery rhymes. 'Out of the strong came forth sweetness,' I recited; 'See how it runs'; 'Ready, aye, Ready'. I sang with gusto

'High o'er the fence leaps "Sunny Jim"
"Force" is the food that raises him'

and I pored long over the educated notice which said 'Cette sauce de première qualité digestive est appétissante et délicieuse avec viandes chaudes et froides, poisson, jambon . . .'

I absorbed compelling combinations of words not only at the table but also when nosing in cupboards or when gazing about in streets and shops during outings with Tishy. 'Won't Wash Clothes'; 'Worth a Guinea a Box'; 'Prevents that Sinking Feeling'; 'Born 1820, Still Going Strong'; 'He Won't be Happy till He Gets It'; 'His Master's Choice'; 'The Mighty Atom'; 'Queen of Watering Places'. I liked these words for their music and their mystery. I had no wish to understand them. I knew that there are some secrets that it's best not to want to understand. I knew that it was best not to ask why Watson's was the 'Matchless' Cleanser, Waterman's the 'Ideal' Fountain-pen, Rowntree's the 'Elect' Cocoa. There were some boxes which, if opened and looked into too closely, might reveal nothing, or something disappointing, or something terrifying, or something merely ordinary. I knew that some keys are best left unturned. So I was content that these visual and aural patterns should remain runes and spells, abracadabra.

I wasn't made uneasy by obscurity. My whole life was full of things inexplicable. I accepted them with only perfunctory questioning. I accepted them as I had accepted the fact that drawings on steel were drawings on paper, as I had accepted that people said baking powder by way of apology, as I accepted that pillar-boxes growled at me in the street, as I accepted the national petition to God about Victoria plums.

Oh, those Victoria plums! The skin cool as a spring in summer, the plump beauty yielding ripely to gentle pressure, the golden pulp pregnant with a Niagara of juice! 'So they ought to be,' Auntie George answered when I told her how wonderful they were. 'They're the best. They're Victorias.' And so I knew perfectly well why everybody sang:

> God save our gracious king,
> Long live our noble king,
> God save our king—
> Send him Victorias,
> Happy and glorious . . .

Of course the king wanted Victorias! I accepted the rightness of that without any doubts whatever. Victorias were enough to make anybody happy and glorious and if I were a king I'd live on nothing else!

Sometimes cartons and bottles boasted realistic facsimiles of gold, silver, and bronze medals that had been won for Superior Excellence and Consistent Quality at exhibitions and fairs in Paris and Brussels and other great cities of Europe. These exhibitions all appeared to have taken place a long time ago and I couldn't help wondering, as I ate and drank, why the manufacturers didn't refer to triumphs of a more recent date. Hadn't they bothered to enter any competitions? Had they tried to win prizes and failed? Was their reticence diplomatic, because excellence wasn't as Superior nor quality as Consistent in modern times as in days past?

Occasionally, when she was doing laundry, Tishy left a bottle of marking ink on the table. This was a marvellous object. The label was as closely printed as a railway ticket and cited scores and scores of medals, *all* gold. What's more, the glamorous titles Count, Prince, and Excellency were mentioned again and again. But the words that had a special fascination for me were: 'Prepared by the Daughter of the Late John Bond.' They had a fine, solemn rhythm, like a sequence of drum beats. And as I intoned them I thought of an old-fashioned photograph of a brown and faded man adorned with a great thick beard and wearing a jacket with great thick lapels, the late John Bond himself. He inhabited the walls of a cellar and underneath him was a little old lady in a black dress upon whom he would have smiled sternly if he could, for she was none other than the celebrated daughter of the late John Bond herself. She was labouring, poor woman, over a great vat into which she alternately poured black liquid from a pail and black powder from a sack, stirring, pouring in more liquid, more powder, stirring again, hour after hour in the dark damp cellar, for she had the whole of Great Britain, as well as the colonies, army, and admiralty, together with many crowned heads throughout the world, to supply with Crystal Palace marking ink prepared by her in solitude according to the secret recipe bequeathed to her and to her *only*—no one else must *ever* know it—by the late John Bond himself.

Unfortunately, it wasn't often that I could eat just with Tishy or by myself, for there were considerable periods when Auntie George was working in Nottingham and district and during these times she had her meals in the kitchen with us. These commonplace meals, prepared with great prodigality by Auntie, were just as revolting to me as her more ceremonial productions. Whenever I had an opportunity—if Auntie had gone to the pantry for more food, say—I threw what I was eating on the fire. One day I was found out doing this, because the food I had discarded— tapioca pudding—spluttered and exploded in the flames like an Australasian geyser.

'I *was* going to buy you a novelty,' Auntie George said, 'but you've been such a naughty little boy that when your uncle comes home I'm going to see that he gives you a thrashing.'

'Yuh're an ornery little cuss, ain't yuh?' Uncle G.B. growled at me later that evening. 'Waal, son, yuh've shore been caught with a pore hand. Unhitch yore pants and drop 'em some.'

As I undid my braces I wondered why it was that for one reason or another I had so often to unhitch my pants and drop 'em some while I was living at Rectory Road? I couldn't think of a really satisfactory answer.

'Bend over, yuh doggone maverick,' Uncle G.B. said sternly, sitting on the kitchen stool and pointing to his lap. 'I'm going tuh brand yuh. I gotten a hunch yuh ain't going tuh be able tuh sit in a saddle fer a week.'

I suffered this form of corporal punishment quite often—for being a bad boy (that is, not having an appetite or entering the house with muddy shoes if it had been raining) or for not knowing my Tables. Uncle G.B. and Auntie George both agreed on the importance of my mind being developed as well as my body and so for a progressively lengthening period each day I was shut in an attic or made to sit in the summer-house at the bottom of the garden in order to study my *Help to Scholars*. This was a little paper booklet 'published by the Proprietors of Beecham's Pills with the hope of rendering some assistance to the Youth of the Country'. I haven't any doubt that this little volume, crammed with vital statistics about figures called divisors, quotients, and factors was of indispensable assistance to many youths of the country, but to one particular youth living at 7, Rectory Road, West Bridgford, Nottingham, it was a source of misery. The trouble was that if I learned a table 'heart off by heart' as Auntie George called it, from the top to the bottom, Uncle G.B., when he put me through my arithmetical catechism at night, didn't let me go through it consecutively but picked out multipliers and multiplicands at random and expected me to state the product instantly.

'Thirteen times seven are . . . ?' he demanded, sitting in his big new Windsor chair, and when I hesitated he barked, glaring at me impatiently, 'C'm on!' or 'Shoot!' or 'Pronto! Pronto!' and made me so mixed up that I couldn't think or speak. He often— unfairly I thought—turned multiplication into division, asking me:

'Thirteen into a hundred and seventeen is . . .?' and took me unawares with tables that I hadn't been learning that day at all. The sequel invariably was:

'Unhitch yore pants, son, and drop 'em some.'

He beat me with one of the black cylindrical rulers they used in his office for drawing straight lines in ink. It didn't sting, but fell on my behind with a merciless bruising weight, again and again and again, crushing my flesh and producing an enduring dull ache.

Life was awful. I thought I'd been unhappy at Carlyle Road, but in some ways Rectory Road was even worse. Yet I didn't rebel. As was my stoic way, I accepted—accepted unreason and injustice as the way of the world. Yet, though it was the way of the world, I didn't have to remain in the world all the time. I could open a door. I could play the Railway Game. Whenever I felt that conditions were intolerable I could step on to the footplate of the newest and fastest express locomotive in the whole world. Inch by inch I could open the regulator and in a flash be away from West Bridgford, zooming above Asia, the Pacific, America, the South China Sea. The beauty of the arrangement was that just as I could step on to the footplate whenever I wished I could also step off it whenever I wished. The train was always at hand to take me away and was always able to look after itself when I had no need of it. I saw a good deal of the world in this way: New Guinea, Greenland, Samoa, Morocco, the Sandwich Islands, Tenerife, Salonica, Cochin China, Guadeloupe, Mozambique, the Aegean Islands, Tristan da Cunha, Juan Fernandez, the Bermudas, the Moluccas, the Seychelles, the Celebes, Sarawak, Zanzibar. And at any time I wished I could steam away from the world and cruise among the planets.

26

Going to Town

IT WAS Saturday morning and I was sitting on the top step of the stairs, looking through the banisters and the half-open door of the bathroom at Uncle shaving. It was wonderful to watch. First, with brush and lather, Uncle put on an octogenarian's beard and became unrecognizable. Then, with strokes of his cut-throat razor, he mowed the white beard off and his own familiar face emerged swathe by swathe. It was quite magical, the way an old man was transformed into a younger man before your eyes. The fingers played a great part. The finger tips of the right hand lightly held the razor, the finger tips of the left hand stretched the skin, lifted a nostril, positioned a lip.

'Clifford, dear!'

It was Auntie, calling to me from the bedroom. Reluctantly, I got up from my seat at Uncle's conjuring show and went to see what Auntie George wanted. She was sitting at her dressing-table, pinning on her hat.

'I'm going to take you up to town with me this morning, dear,' she informed me, twisting round and beaming at me as I walked into her room.

This was really unusual news for me. I'd never been to town with Auntie. With Tishy, yes, often—but with Auntie I'd only gone shopping in West Bridgford.

'Are you, Auntie?'

'Yes. Now you've become a strong boy again I'm going to take you out shopping with me every Saturday morning.'

She scrutinized me, and frowned.

'But I must buy you some new clothes. Those things you're wearing aren't fit to be seen.'

I looked down at my clothes in wonderment. Mother had bought them for me. It was the first time that anybody had said there was anything wrong with them—my blue jersey, my green-and-red narrow boy's tie, my grey flannel shorts. Yes, they looked all right to me.

'I want you to be dressed like a little gentleman. Wouldn't you like that?'

I didn't say anything. I was afraid.

'Don't you want to look like a little gentleman?'

'Yes, Auntie,' I lied.

'Have you washed your face?'

'Yes, Auntie.'

'Come here.' She turned my face to the window. 'It looks so brown and dirty.'

'It's sunburn, Auntie.'

'Gentlemen are pale. Only common people who work in the fields have brown faces. Let's see if this will make you any better.'

She dipped a puff into a cardboard box of Swandown powder and dabbed my face with it.

'There! See yourself in the mirror. That's how a well-bred little boy should look.'

She took up a small phial of Ashes of Roses and scented my forehead and the backs of my ears with it. Then she gave me a heart-shaped scented cachou to sweeten my breath.

'Isn't that nice?' she smiled. 'Now you're almost as refined as I want you to be. A new suit of clothes and Auntie'll be proud of you.'

Outside it was very hot. The asphalt pavement of Rectory Road had been softened by the sun and it was like walking on yielding rubber. We caught a bus at the telephone box, a brownish, flat-tyred vehicle lettered all over with advertisements for Borwick's Baking Powder and New Pin Soap. Auntie George didn't take me on to the open upper deck, as Tishy did, into the breezy zone of male smokers, but hurried me below to sit in a calm atmosphere of proper ladies and gentlemen. At Trent Bridge we changed into a tram. This change, I always thought, really was a change. For if the bus was a friendly lumbering outhouse, the tram, by contrast, was an elegant travelling conservatory. Its maroon and yellow paintwork was always beautifully bright, and the glass in its sides gleamed with spotlessness and gave you a magnifying-lens proximity to Arkwright Street as you dipped and swayed along it, so that you could almost count the polished ebony lumps in the model railway wagons standing so hygienically on display in the windows of the coal merchants' offices. The seats of the tram were the colour of bananas, but they were as smooth as almond shells and similarly pricked with dots. I liked to sit near the front of the tram and watch the driver madly twirling his brass handle. What was such fun about trams was that you could sometimes get off at the front as well as the rear and if you felt daring enough you could stamp on the steel stud that protruded from the floor and make a sonorous clang. But today I was too subdued for such larks.

We went straight to Dixon and Parker's, the outfitters. When we emerged three-quarters of an hour later I was a little gentleman. On my head was a white straw boater girdled by a black-and-blue ribbon: a black silk cord clipped to the boater's brim tethered it by means of another clip to my right lapel. In place of my jersey I wore a black-and-blue striped blazer. Instead of a flannel shirt I wore a cream honeycombed cricket shirt and a new tie. Instead of my grey shorts I had on a pair of cream ones. And instead of my comfortable scratched boots I wore patent leather black shoes: these were a size too small for me because Auntie George wanted me to grow up with dainty feet. Into my left eye there was screwed a monocle, attached by a further black cord to my left lapel, and under my right arm, tucked military fashion, I carried a short rattan cane.

I felt bitterly ashamed of my appearance. When we went into Parr's for sage sausages, into Salmon and Gluckstein's for Uncle G.B.'s round tin of Gold Flake, into Skinner and Rook's for groceries, and into Griffin & Spalding's for buttons Auntie George ordered me to turn round like a mannequin and show myself off to the assistants. I saw them wink and tap their foreheads behind her back. I felt sure that my shameful cheeks were visible through my face powder. I longed with all my heart to be wearing my old jersey again, to be inconspicuous so that people

H

wouldn't notice me. As we pushed our way through the crowded lanes of the market, where pigeons glided above the canvas booths like flying roof slates, as we traversed Clumber Street and Low Pavement on our errands, and later passed through St Peter's Gate and Carrington Street on our way home, I longed to be far away from the grinning faces and the curious stares. I longed to be in Colorado or Samarcand, but Auntie kept addressing remarks to me or taking my arm and dragging me along because I was absent-minded, and I could never forget that I was in a street, in a tram, in a bus; among people, shopping baskets, and week-end cut flowers.

As we walked along Rectory Road I saw Sid on the opposite pavement with some strange boys. The boys pointed at me and laughed. 'Left, right, left, right,' mocked one boy, keeping time to my footsteps, 'left, right, left, right, he had a good job and he left, right, left, right . . .' Sid pulled off the jeering boy's cap, there was a scuffle, Auntie and I walked aloofly on, I slipped through the front garden gate of Number 7.

What a relief it was to be on the lawn at the back of the house, where there were no people to look and laugh! It was a long lawn, as long as a street, and at the far end of it was the green summer-house. Uncle G.B.'s gardening tools were kept here, and nailed up inside was one of Auntie George's mottoes: 'Many A Wife Has Turned An Old Rake Into A Lawn Mower.'

Ever since my misbehaviour with Pearl, Auntie George had confined me to the house and its garden, forbidding me to go into the street except with her or Tishy. She didn't want me to mix with rough boys and girls, she said. The tall lattice door, which led from the back garden to the front garden and freedom, was kept permanently locked. As a result, the back lawn became my world, and I knew its every inch.

I enjoyed looking at the insects, birds, butterflies. There was always something interesting going on, even in one square foot of grass. I could listen to grasshoppers whirring like sewing-machines, I could scrape some of the cuckoo spit off the long grass behind the summer-house and watch the insects inside struggle to get under the bit of remaining froth like people with only one blanket, I could watch a beetle going a walk among Giant Sequoia stalks and Himalayan pebbles, I could throw fragments of rubbish into a spider's web and see him come lurching out thinking they were flies—though he quickly learned to know better.

One of the nurses at the hospital had given me a book on natural history. But I didn't like the book, because it wasn't about animals moving but about animals that were dead. To me, nature study meant life, but to the author of this book it meant collecting. He told you how to treacle trees to catch moths, how to make a killing bottle for your captured butterflies, how to examine the contents of shot birds' stomachs. There was one passage, about preserving caterpillars, that made me vomit whenever I read it. 'Lay a full-grown caterpillar on a sheet of blotting-paper,' the author instructed, 'and turn the blotting-paper around until the caterpillar is crawling away from you. Place a pencil on the caterpillar firmly, just behind the head, and roll it towards the tail. This kills the creature instantly, and presses its internal organs out through the anal orifice. Roll the pencil over once or twice again, to make sure that all the contents of the body are emptied out, then insert a blowpipe into the anal orifice, hold in a hot-air oven, and applying your mouth to the blowpipe inflate the caterpillar gently . . .' There were chapters on taxidermy, preserving specimens in spirit, making a skin. There was information on naturalists' enamel pins, scalpels, trepanning instruments. Was this *really* nature study? I wondered in distress, because if so nature study seemed to have more to do with the mortuary than with the open air.

A high railway embankment ran alongside the lawn, separated from it by a hawthorn hedge. The grass on the sloping sides of the embankment grew tall—but straight up, not leaning at an angle, as I would have thought—and every now and then a man with a scythe came to mow it down. He never had a collar on his shirt, but he always wore a belt as well as his braces. In his mouth, always, was a pitch-black pipe, which sent smoke bubbles continually ascending towards the sky. To begin, he made a few wide casual swings with his scythe, laying circles of grass, marguerites, and buttercups low. Soon he was standing like a tyrant at the centre of a widening domain of prostrate turf. At every dozen strokes he paused, deftly swung his weapon upside-down so that its blade made a silver arc across his chest, and sharpened its deadly edge with a white stone. Then he went on mowing, conquering legions with every effortless irresistible foray. Rank upon rank the tall uncut grasses and flowers surrounded him, and rank upon rank they fell, until he possessed a battlefield like a vast amphitheatre and stood in the middle of it alone and victorious and screened in smoke.

But on this particular Saturday morning there wasn't any mower to divert my thoughts from my misery. I sat in the summer-house, looking out through its open front at the shimmering lawn. Soon they would be calling me in for dinner. I hoped I wouldn't hear. Sometimes, because of my mastoid operations, I was deaf when people spoke to me—if the sound came from a direction unfavourable to my one good ear or if a breeze was blowing sound away from me instead of towards me. I hoped a strong breeze would spring up today.

I didn't want to go into Auntie George's house ever again.

A blackbird clawed the lawn with his foot and devoured the insects that flew up into the air. It was his dinner time. I was quite willing to miss my dinner. A butterfly was sunning itself on the summer-house window ledge, opening and closing its wings in luxurious languor: a flurry of air ruffled it slightly and it crouched low, holding on to its perch as dramatically as if a gale was blowing. On the geraniums that hung in wire baskets from the summer-house roof I saw a fly with a yellow-and-black banded body like a wasp's. I watched it stretch its wafery wings and snap them shut like a silent jack-knife. It did this several times. I saw a flash of sun as the wings opened again—then the fly took off vertically into the air, almost too quickly to see, looped the loop, and was half across the garden in one enormous aerial stride.

A train clanked along the top of the embankment. I looked up. It was a black goods engine, followed by a long line of wagons with the names of collieries, iron works, and railway companies

painted on their sides: Clay Cross, Langley Mill, Sherwood, they
filed past, Bolsover, Stanton, Bolsover, Stanton, Hucknall,
Hucknall, Hucknall, clattering, clinking empties travelling at
speed, Mapperley, Butterley, Staveley, M.R., M.R., M.R., Shire-
brook, Bulwell, Bulwell, and then the terminal brake van with
its porch and cosily smoking chimney. The guard was leaning
upon his rail, looking out at our lawn, but I didn't bother to
wave.

Could I get out of the garden somehow? If I could, perhaps I
could find Sid—he might still be somewhere near—and then,
together, we could go and look for Pearl. I'd never seen Pearl
since she was ejected from the house in ignominy. But I'd never
forgotten her. She had introduced me to delights that I wanted to
experience again.

Perhaps all three of us, Pearl, Sid, and me, could run away?
Perhaps I could go and live in Pearl's house? Or, if that wasn't
possible, in Sid's? I didn't care where I went, what I did, so long
as I didn't have to eat tomorrow's Sunday Dinner and Sunday
Tea, didn't have to learn multiplication tables, didn't have to be a
little gentleman again next Saturday.

But how was I to get away? It wasn't any good trying to
climb over the locked garden door because it was in sight of the
scullery and kitchen windows. My only chance was the railway
embankment. I had to find a way through the dense hawthorn
hedge that separated me from it like a wall.

I prepared to make my bid for freedom. I took off my white
straw boater and trampled on it until it looked as though it had
been chewed by a horse. I smashed my ridiculous monocle. I
snapped my rattan cane into many pieces. What about the patent
leather shoes? They were a problem. I would have liked to have
got rid of them because of their swanky appearance and because
they were painful to walk in—but I hadn't any other shoes to put
on and going barefoot would be even more unpleasant. So I
compromised by scraping them all over with grit and grinding
dusty soil well into their mirrory brilliance.

I found a way through the hedge, a spidery and earwiggy
valley smelling sweetly and pungently of decay. Somehow,

reckless of broken knees, I scrambled up the startlingly steep side of the embankment and crossed the forbidden rails on its summit. I slithered and tumbled down the embankment's far side, emerging near Bonser's the grocer's. For the first time in my life I stood *alone* in Rectory Road. I had escaped!

27

Escape

I WAS lying in grass, in the hot sun. The grass was coarse and dry, fragrant like hay. If you closed your eyes, shutting everything out, memories as well as scenes, and pressed your face deep into the grass, down until your forehead felt the warm cast-iron ground, you could hear an insect hum that was so loud it over-powered the clatter of the reaping machines in the next field. But the stiff grasses pricked your ears. I rolled on to my back.

I could feel my skin sucking in brownness. I opened my eyes, but shut them immediately because of the brightness of the sun. Then I opened them gradually, letting in the furnace light bit by bit. The sky glared so intensely—it wasn't blue, but almost white with heat—that I turned on my side and looked to where Pearl and Sid were lying. Sid was kissing Pearl.

I turned away, on to my back again, and closed my eyes. I had been happy, altogether forgetful, but the sight of Pearl and Sid brought back the memory of Pearl and me and that reminded me of Auntie George and her anger. I felt a blow on my knee. It was Pearl.

'Hey, you!' she said. 'Sid's caught a butterfly.'

'Did you catch it in your cap, Sid?' I asked.

'Yes,' Sid answered.

'What are you doing to it?'

'Hark at Nosy Parker!' Pearl jeered.

I crawled over to see what Sid was doing. He was trying to push a pin through the butterfly's wriggling body.

He gave a jubilant shout and held the insect up for me to inspect. The pin went right through it, protruding underneath. The butterfly was raising and lowering its wings, like the one I had watched in the morning. But this was agony, not pleasure.

'You shouldn't have done that!' I protested.

'Why shouldn't he?' Pearl asked.

'It's cruel.'

'It isn't. It's the right thing to do. You push the pin through and stick it in a piece of cork.'

'But you have to kill it first. With cyanide or crushed laurel leaves.'

'Hark at Mr Know-all!' Pearl mocked. 'Aren't we high and mighty now we live in a big house and dress up like a toff!'

'I didn't want to dress up like that,' I objected.

'You'll be too proud to speak to common folk like us before long, won't he, Sid?'

Sid grunted a reply. He was busy detaching the butterfly's wings. They fluttered to the earth like bits of tissue-paper. The butterfly's body squirmed up and down on the pin.

'It looks like a crow out of somebody's nose,' said Pearl. 'Chuck it away.'

Sid dropped his toy and put his foot on it.

One of the reaping machines drew near to the field in which we were idling and we could see the top of its rotating reel above the hedge.

'Do you know what they're doing in that field, Mr Know-all?' Pearl demanded.

'I'm not Mr Know-all.'

'They're cutting the corn,' Sid answered.

'I didn't ask you. I asked him.'

'They're cutting the corn,' I said.

'They aren't.'

'Don't be daft. Of course they are!'

'They aren't.'

'Of course they are!' Sid confirmed.

Pearl winked at Sid.

'What are they doing in that field?' she asked again.

'Don't know,' Sid said.

'Shall I tell you?'

'Fire away.'

'They're searching for Cliff.'

'Don't talk piffle!' I said contemptuously.

'All right. If you don't believe me, just climb up a tree and let one of those blokes see you. You'll soon find out.'

'What are they searching for me for?'

'Because you've run away from your auntie and uncle.'

I laughed.

'Go on! They're just cutting corn.'

'They aren't. They're searching every inch of that field with special machines. And then they're going to search this one.'

'And when they find you', Sid joined in, 'they'll slice you up like a tomato and eat you between two rounds of bread.'

'We'd better all keep down low,' Pearl suggested.

I knew that Sid and Pearl were talking tommy rot, but they both fell flat to the ground as though they believed what they were saying and so I followed their example. Through the drowsy air, as we lay, the rattle of the reaping machines came to us for, it seemed, hour after hour. My legs burned, the muscles of my neck ached. My knees and my palms seemed to be resting on nutmeg graters.

'I'm fed up,' I said.

'Let's scout a bit,' Sid suggested.

'I'm not coming,' I said. 'I'm going home.' Then I remembered. 'No. I'm not going home. I'll come.'

We moved across the field on all fours. You had to dodge the sharp stones, and progress was slow because even the baked crumbly soil could pierce your skin. When we reached the hedge that divided us from the wheatfield my hands and knees were bleeding.

We found a gap and peered through. We couldn't see much, because the tall toasted wheat blocked our view, but quite near to us, standing under a tree, we saw a man drinking out of a bottle, his head back and his Adam's apple going in and out. He put the bottle down, in the shade of the hedge, took a large red spotted handkerchief from his trousers pocket, and swabbed his sweating face. Then, loosening the brass buckle of his belt, he pulled off his shirt.

'Look at the knife in his belt!' Pearl whispered.

The man threw his shirt down and mopped his body with the

handkerchief. His chest was almost as dark as his face. After a few moments he walked away, still naked to the waist, glistening.

'Let's go,' I said.

'Shhhh,' warned Pearl. 'Let's wait till he's a bit farther away.'

Though the wheat was in our eyes we could just see him as he walked to his machine, climbed into its metal seat, flipped the reins on the horse's back, and drove away.

'Phew!' Pearl let her breath escape slowly. 'That was a close shave.'

With bowed backs we hurried along the hedge, reached a fence and climbed over it, ran across another field, climbed another fence, and got on to the road.

'You aren't half going to cop it when you get home,' Pearl said to me unkindly, looking at my torn clothes and bloody flesh.

I said nothing. As we walked along, towards houses, I wondered about my future. My hopes of going to live in Pearl's house were all gone now. Pearl wasn't interested in me any more. She was against me. And I couldn't go and live with Sid either, because he had sided with Pearl. I'd seen the wink that had passed between them. And I'd seen them spooning. Pearl was grown up. She had a real lady's wristlet watch on and her hair was marcel waved.

When we were near Pearl's house she said:

'Coming out tonight, Sid?'

'Yes.'

'Calling for me?'

'Yes.'

'Toodleoo, then.'

'Toodleoo.'

Without a word or a smile to me she left us.

'You know that chap we saw take his shirt off,' Sid said.

'Yes?'

'Well, he's my dad.'

'Your dad!' I said in surprise.

'Yes. That wasn't his proper job, driving a reaping-machine with a horse.'

'I know. He drives a traction-engine.'

'That's right. He's lending a hand now because they want to get the corn in. He gets paid overtime,' he added proudly. 'Next week they'll thresh the corn. Dad'll work his traction-engine then. You can come and watch if you like.'

'I shan't be here.'

'You going away, then?'

'Yes.'

'Where to?'

'Don't know yet.'

'We went to Mablethorpe this year. It was top-hole. Last year we went to Skeggy. You're going away late, aren't you?'

'Yes.'

'It doesn't matter for you, though. You don't have to go to school—lucky blighter! Isn't it funny, living with your auntie and uncle instead of with your mum?'

'It's all right.'

'Why don't you know where you're going?'

'I don't know.'

'Don't your auntie and uncle tell you?'

'Yes.'

'Well, why don't you know?'

I shrugged my shoulders. It was all too difficult to explain to Sid.

'You weren't scared in the field, were you?'

'Of course I wasn't!'

'I thought you weren't. It was Pearl's idea to have you on.'

'Why?'

'She's got it in for you.'

'Why?'

'Because your auntie gave her a talking to and said she was bad.'

'Well, she *is* bad.'

'Wouldn't you like to see my dad's traction-engine?'

'I've told you. I'm going away.'

'I know. But if you don't.'

'I am!'

'All right. Keep your hair on, grumpy.'

After leaving Sid I made my solitary way towards Rectory Road, limping because the patent leather shoes were drawing my feet in the hot weather. But it was becoming cooler. That meant it must be quite late. Auntie George and Uncle G.B. must have wondered where I'd got to. Perhaps they'd already sent search parties out? Or the police?

I was returning without my boater, without my cane, without my monocle. My face was sunburned again. I was dirty. I was bleeding with scratches and cuts. My shoes were ruined. 'I *was* going to buy you a novelty,' I could hear Auntie George saying, her nose wrinkled up in the worst bad temper she'd ever had. She would certainly ask Uncle to thrash me. 'Unhitch yore pants, son, and drop 'em some'—I could hear Uncle G.B.'s voice quiet with ferocity. Yes, I was in for an awful walloping. Not even Tishy could save me. And after the walloping, more Sunday Dinners, more Sunday Teas, more multiplication tables. And Auntie might buy me another boater, another rattan cane, another monocle! I daren't go on.

I was at the top of Rectory Road now. My footsteps became slow. Then slower. I was standing still, being carried forward on the footplate of the latest and fastest express locomotive in the whole world. We were flashing over Persia at five hundred miles an hour. I shifted the regulator handle several notches and we increased speed to ten thousand miles an hour. With maximum steam-pressure and minimum cut-off my non-stop train crossed the Coral Sea, sprang over the Great Barrier Reef, leaped the Dodecanese, pounded the Russian steppes, flew along the Susquehanna River, crossed the Bosporus, crossed Mesopotamia, streaked through Verona, Peking, Basra, Yokohama, La Paz, Papeete, Damascus, Rangoon, and here was Australia, where it was night, and we soared, soared, high, higher, and the rocking and roaring train bulleted on, accelerating, climbing, higher, highest, until it was impossible to tell whether the enormous flashes in the sky were sparks from our chimney or were the Pleiades.